The Busi
of Government

J. Denis Derbyshire

Chambers Commerce Series

Published by W & R Chambers Ltd Edinburgh, 1987

British Library Cataloguing in Publication Data

Derbyshire, J. Denis
    The Business of Government — (Chambers commerce series)
    1. Great Britain — Politics and Government — 1964-
    I. Title
    350'.000941   JN309
ISBN 0 550 20704 X

Typeset by Blackwood Pillans & Wilson Ltd. Edinburgh

Printed in Great Britain by
Richard Clay Ltd,
Bungay, Suffolk

Contents

Chapter 7   The Monarchy

Chapter 8   The Judicial Process

Chapter 9   Parliamentary Government

Chapter 10　The Prime Minister and the Cabinet

Chapter 11　The Central Departments

PART III　THE DECENTRALISED GOVERNMENT PROCESS

Chapter 12　Government Off Centre

Chapter 13　The Local Government System

Preface

This book has been written as an introduction to what I call the *Business of Government*. I have chosen this title because government today is so extensive and varied that it has virtually become a huge national business.

Because it is so extensive and varied, a study of modern government cannot confine itself to the constitutional and political aspects. The legal, social and economic features are just as, if not more, important, so they are covered as well. However, I have assumed no prior knowledge of politics, law or economics and, where necessary, have included a brief explanation of some commonly used terms.

We are all shareholders, as well as customers, of the business of government and, as such, should take an interest in how it operates. I hope this book will do something to stimulate that interest.

J.D.D.

Chapter 1

The Business of Government

Government is a device invented by human beings to help regulate their lives in harmony. If we did not have some form of government we would revert to the law of the jungle and the survival of the fittest.

Historically, government in Britain has developed from being just a passive regulator of social and economic affairs to actively intervening in day-to-day lives by managing the economy and providing communal services which many people would not have if they relied on their own resources.

There are similarities between government and a business, but in the case of government the ordinary people are the shareholders and it is they who elect their representatives and should make them account for their actions.

Regrettably, only a minority of the population play an active part in politics, many not even bothering to vote at national and local elections. It is hoped that this study of government will stimulate as well as inform and encourage a more active interest.

1.1   What is Government?

Government is one of mankind's most notable social inventions. It is a device for regulating human activities so that men and women can live together in reasonable harmony. In many ways it is a larger version of the family.

The average family has a head whose job should be to guide and lead the rest, and particularly the younger members, so that they can develop their natural abilities to the full. The head of the family has to try to avoid disputes between members and act as some kind of referee when they occur. The adult members of the family are expected to contribute part of their incomes to a common pool from which all can draw. One member of the family manages this common income, buying what is needed and paying the bills. This is called housekeeping. The head of the family is also expected to protect it from outside, unwanted interference.

Looked at in this way, the responsibilities of government are similar, but applied on a national scale. Government is expected to create an environment in which everyone can prosper. People are expected to contribute part of their incomes to a communal fund and this collective wealth is then spent on their behalf. It is the job of government to settle disputes between individuals and groups, and people look to it for protection from outsiders.

1.2   The Need for Government

The case for government is that we need it whether we like it or not. Without it, so the argument runs, only the strong would prosper and the weak would suffer.

Against this, the cynic would argue that all governments tend to favour the rich and the strong at the expense of the poor and the weak. What about the Jews in Germany in the 1930s or the Blacks in South Africa today? There is more than an element of truth in the cynic's view—but is the alternative any better?

The alternative to government is anarchy: everyone for himself and the survival of the fittest. The law of the jungle: and the evidence is that the human jungle can be much harsher than that of the animal kingdom. So the debate should not be about whether or not we need government but about its quality.

Does it do its job well? Does the political system which produces representatives to form a government operate successfully? Do we have the means for checking the effectiveness of a particular government and for changing it if we do not like what we get? Do we have enough opportunities ourselves for joining in the political process? These are some of the questions we shall be trying to answer as our study of government proceeds.

1.3   The Justification of Government

For centuries philosophers have sought to explain and justify the need for government. Some have said that, left to their own devices, men would, because of their selfish instincts and the will to survive, simply destroy each other. There is ample evidence of man's tendency towards self-destruction in the world today. So government can be justified if only on the basis of the need to preserve law and order.

Other philosophers have taken a broader, and more positive, view. They have spoken of a social contract, or agreement freely entered into between individuals and the state, whereby some personal freedoms are given up in return for the protection and assistance which governments can provide for the community at large. Arising from this idea of a social contract has been a series of philosophical debates about how much personal freedom should be surrendered and how individual rights and liberties can be protected.

While men have been devising and discussing these theories civilisation has continued to develop and attempts have been made to put some of the theories into practice.

In the early part of the 19th century Robert Owen, the shopkeeper's son who had become manager of a cotton mill in Manchester at the age of nineteen and then gone on to run highly successful factories in Scotland, felt so strongly about the need to achieve social harmony that he put all his wealth into an experiment, in Virginia in North America, which he called 'New Harmony.' His aim was to create an effective, self-governing co-operative to which all members would contribute and, in return, share the fruits of their labours. It unfortunately, but perhaps predictably, failed.

In 1917 Vladimir Ilyich Lenin successfully led a revolution against the Tzarist regime in Russia and set about putting into practice the philosophy developed in England by the German, Karl Marx, thus creating the first communist, or Marxist-Leninist, state. That experiment is continuing in Russia today and being copied in other parts of the world.

So the need for government can be argued on social and economic grounds without great difficulty. It is also possible to justify government, whatever its form, on moral, and even religious, grounds, but, in practical terms, what is government expected to do?

The best way of answering this question is to look briefly at how government has developed, particularly in Britain, over the past hundred years or so.

1.4 The Growth of Modern Government

Historically, the growth of government has been a staged process.

The first stage saw it in a mainly negative role, merely providing an environment in which individuals and groups could live and work together. The rule of the British Raj in India, sometimes described as **night watchman** government, was an example of this first stage. The emphasis was on the preservation of law and order and the minimum of interference in social affairs.

The second stage saw governments recognising the need to **regulate and control** social and economic affairs. In Britain the industrial revolution of the late 18th and early 19th centuries starkly threw up the need for government action.

We have already likened the role of government to that of the head of a family. This second stage saw it very much in a paternalistic stance, regulating the railway system, coal mines and factories, partly for reasons of safety and partly to prevent the abuse of monopoly power.

The third stage appeared in the 1930s when governments took upon themselves the job of trying to regulate, not just individual activities and industries, but the whole economy. The world economic crisis of 1931 showed how weak some of our major, long-established, industries really were and how mass unemployment could spread around the world. This alerted the Democratic administration of Franklin Roosevelt, in the United States, to formulate a 'New Deal' policy of economic expansion, and even a basically Conservative government in Britain, which called itself a National Government, to attempt some form of **economic management**. This was to be greatly extended by both Labour and Conservative governments between 1945 and 1979.

The fourth stage, which accompanied the third, has seen government in a more positive role, which is best illustrated by the growth of what we have come to describe as the **welfare state**, demonstrated by the provision of minimum standards of health care, housing, transport, social insurance and so on.

The business of government today in Britain embodies all four stages of development: providing a stable social and legal environment; regulating aspects of industry and commerce; attempting forms of national economic management; and providing communal, or social, services for people who might be unwilling or unable to provide them for themselves.

It is interesting to remember that this four stage development in Britain corresponds with a similar expansion of the democratic process. Until the 1830s representative government was based on a very narrow population, with the majority of people not having a vote. It is to the credit of an enlightened section of the ruling minority that, gradually, the voting base was broadened.

In 1832 middle class, male, property owners got the vote. In 1867 it was extended to working class men in the towns, and in 1884 to male rural workers. In 1918 all men of 21 or over were entitled to vote. It was not until 1928 that women were given the same electoral rights as men. Then, in 1948, the additional university and business votes were abolished and eventually, in 1970, everyone of the age of 18 or over was awarded voting rights.

So the struggle for democratic rights, led by groups such as the Chartists and Suffragettes, ran alongside the growth in government activity. This was no coincidence because, as Parliament came to reflect more accurately the social and economic structure of the nation, so it demanded greater economic and social equality, and this, inevitably, meant more government.

1.5   Paying for Government

The services and facilities provided by government all cost money, and, since it is no more than an organisation set up by the people of nation to do things on their behalf, the money must come from them.

A hundred years ago the amount needed to finance government in Britain, as a proportion of annual national wealth, was infinitesimal. Today it amounts to over 40%.

This need for money has created a complicated taxation system, at national and local levels, involving levies on income, wealth, property and spending, as well as specific charges for a wide range of publicly provided services.

1.6   The Business of Government

It seems sensible, therefore, to speak of government as a business: a very big business. Indeed, as we look at what government does, and can do, the similarities to a business become more obvious.

Like all businesses, government has to be managed. This is the job of the civil service nationally and the local government services, directed at the highest levels by ministers and councillors.

The shareholders of a business take an interest in how it is being run and, ultimately, can bring the board of directors of a company to account for what they have done. We are the 'shareholders' of the nation's business and we elect our representatives to run it for us or to keep an eye on how it is being done on our behalf. Like company shareholders, we ultimately have the right to call our representatives to account and to replace them if we think they have not performed satisfactorily.

A business can expand or contract. It can widen or reduce its scale of activities. So can a government.

A business usually has to function in competition with other businesses and it has to comply with the laws of the different countries in which it operates. A government, on the other hand, enjoys a monopoly position but the political party currently in power is constantly challenged and threatened by other parties anxious to take its place. It also has to operate in an international climate, with its own international laws.

There are, of course, real and important differences between a government and a business. A government, for example, cannot really go bankrupt, although if we look around the world today we can see examples of poor nations which, in international terms, have virtually reached the point of bankruptcy. Indeed, it was to help such countries that, after the Second World War, international agencies such as the **International Monetary Fund (IMF)** and the **World Bank (International Bank for Reconstruction and Development)** were set up.

There are enough points of similarity to entitle us to describe the study we are about to embark on as a study of the business of government, and there are good reasons for our doing so. It will help us to remember the **purpose** of government and will remind us that it is not just some abstract thing to look at from a distance. It has been set up to **serve** us, and this is something we should not forget.

1.7   The Study of Government

In our study of government we may expect to learn more about its structure, central and local; how it goes about its business; and how it is held accountable for its actions.

But we must remember that government operates within a political framework, the main job of which is to encourage and allow ordinary people to take part. You do not have to stand for election to Parliament or your local council to be active politically. You do not even have to join a political party. The opportunities for you to participate are there. It is a pity that so few people take advantage of them.

In certain countries, such as Australia, there is a legal obligation to vote. In this country it is not compulsory and not everyone exercises this right. In local elections as many as 50% of the electorate do not bother to vote, and even in national elections about a third do not mark a ballot paper.

Our most popular national papers give only a minority coverage to political events and often the reports are distorted. Fortunately, television and radio in this country have established a high reputation for their objective approach to politics, but the political programmes are seldom high in the ratings.

This examination of the business of government will, it is hoped, not only inform but stimulate. It will seek to remind you constantly that government and politics are real, and not abstract, things and that a study of them can be interesting as well as informative and, perhaps, even entertaining.

Questions and Assignments

1 Why do we need government?
2 Why has government been called a 'social contract'?
3 What were the four stages in the development of government in Britain?
4 How did the right to vote expand in Britain between 1832 and 1970?
5 In what ways is government like a business?
6 Why is a study of government useful?
7 Write, in not more than 500 words, *either*
   a letter justifying the need for government to a friend who claims to be an anarchist, *or*
   a letter to a friend who has strong political views arguing that all governments are corrupt and unnecessary.
8 Draw up a list of the Acts of Parliament extending the parliamentary franchise between 1832 and 1970, indicating briefly alongside each the degree of extension, in the form of:
   (i) a description of the new, additional voters, and
   (ii) the additional numbers on the electoral register.

PART I

THE POLITICAL SYSTEM

Chapter 2

Constitutional Government

Most governments today are based on the nation state, resulting from the coming together of people, often from different backgrounds, to form one single country. The structure and functions of government for such a state are usually set out in the form of a written constitution. Britain, unusually, does not have a written constitution of this kind.

Government can operate in many forms, ranging from rule by a single person or a few to rule by a majority, or what is termed democracy. But democracy is a word which is often misused and can disguise a system of government in which the majority of people do not have a real say.

Politics is the process which is supposed to create democratic government. It is a means of settling disputes by argument and discussion, rather than force. But politics is another frequently misused word. The British system of government is a representative democracy, or politics operating within a framework of law.

2.1 Some Important Definitions

Before we begin our study of government we should be clear about the meaning of certain words which we shall use from time to time.

Power is the ability to get things done. In political terms we talk about the power of the House of Commons or the House of Lords, or the Queen or the Prime Minister In all cases we are speaking about whether or not they are able to do things they set out to do.

Authority is the right to get things done. It is formal evidence of power. Often power and authority go hand in hand, but not always. For example, we will see later that the House of Lords has great authority but relatively little power. Its authority

11

comes from traditional respect shown to it and from the reputations of its active members, many of whom were national figures before they entered the Lords. A policeman has the authority of his office and power as well. A criminal, on the other hand, may have no authority but a lot of power. Some people exercise power in an authoritarian way, or, in everyday terms, tend to 'throw their weight about'. This does not prove they have the authority to do what they do. Indeed, some people with great authority and power use it in a very quiet and unobtrusive way.

A **nation** is simply a group of people, often from different backgrounds and sometimes from different races, who, over the years, have come to live together and have adopted a common identity. The usual symbols of a nation are a common ruler, such as a king, queen or president; a common flag; a common piece of music, called a national anthem; and usually, but not always, a common language.

A **state** is the name given to the whole apparatus of government which a nation sets up. In Britain, for example, the state includes Parliament, central and local government and the judicial system. The Queen is the formal head of the state and the Prime Minister the practical, political head. Because Britain is a monarchy, with the Queen as its traditional ruler, all state activities are carried out in the name of the Monarch, formally called the **Crown.** The Crown, therefore, represents the state in all its forms. For example, people are prosecuted in court by the Crown and many state institutions carry that name, such as the Crown Courts, the Crown Agents and so on.

These are not the only words whose meanings we will have to use with care. Others will come up as we continue our study.

2.2   The Nation State

Most communities have governments based on the nation state. If all, or most, of the people in a nation have shared a common culture and language for a long time they are more likely to be able to live together peacefully than if they have been suddenly thrown together from very different backgrounds and forced into an artificial nation state.

England, for example, has existed as a reasonably settled community for hundreds of years but has not always enjoyed internal peace. In the 17th century religious divisions resulted in a civil war. Scotland and Wales have had separate and different histories so that it has been more difficult to integrate them into the nation of Great Britain. Indeed, a minority of the Scots and Welsh still resent being part of a wider group than the one they see as their own nation. Maintaining the United Kingdom of Great Britain and Northern Ireland has proved to be even more difficult, the religious divide producing problems which have yet to be solved.

2.3   The Constitutional State

The greater the mix of cultures, races, religions and languages in a nation state, the greater is the need to have a clear and strong machinery of government to bind the inhabitants together. The United States of America is probably the clearest example of a nation which is the result of mixing together a wide variety of people. It is no wonder that it has been called the melting pot of the world. Its system of government is clearly set out in a written document, or **constitution**, which incorporates a **bill of rights**, guaranteeing individual freedoms.

When a community becomes established as a nation it will claim authority, through the government it sets up, over a clearly defined territory. It will exist as a state and will assert its authority as a fact of **sovereignty.** In other words, it will say to other nations that its laws apply throughout its territory and anyone who lives within the state must conform to them.

The dispute between Britain and Argentina in 1982, which resulted in Argentina's occupation of the Falkland Islands, hinged on the question of sovereignty, with each nation challenging the other's right of ownership.

The basic laws of a state are usually drawn up in a document called a constitution. Virtually every community which becomes a nation state draws up a written constitution setting out the machinery of government and how it should operate.

For example, the constitution of the new state of Zimbabwe was agreed at a conference in London convened by the British Foreign Secretary. There had been a long guerrilla war in Rhodesia and eventually a constitutional conference had been arranged to be attended by representatives of both the white minority settlers and the black majority tribes. The Lancaster House Agreement, as the final document was called, set out the rules and institutions of government in the form of a constitution to take effect from 1980.

There are, of course, many earlier examples of constitutions being drawn up for newly-established nations: the United States in 1787, Italy in 1861, Germany in 1871. Major wars tend to disrupt established distributions of power and result in newly-created, or redesigned nations, each needing a new constitution. The two world wars of this century had such effects. Some countries, such as Czechoslovakia, Hungary and Yugoslavia, were post-1918 creations. The post-1945 period saw the division of several nations, such as Korea, divided north and south, and Germany, divided east and west. Even a well established country such as France, after the overthrow of the monarchy in 1793, became a republic, then later an empire under Napoleon, reverted briefly to a monarchy, and finally became a republic again. The present constitution of France is that of the fifth republic. The constitution of the United States is the longest surviving written constitution in the world and has now been amended 26 times.

Constitutions will, of course, vary greatly in detail but most set out the powers and functions of government in broadly similar terms. Most have an opening paragraph, or preamble, which sets out briefly the constitution's aims.

The preamble to the United States constitution of 1787 reads:

'We, the people of the United States, in order to form a more perfect Union, establish justice, insure domestic tranquillity, provide for the common defense, promote the general welfare, and secure the blessings of liberty to ourselves and our posterity do ordain and establish this Constitution for the United States of America'.

America had just fought a war to rid itself of its British rulers so, understandably, the preamble to its constitution put emphasis on liberty. Its authors were also anxious to knit the original 13 colonies together into a single, new nation.

The preamble to the French Constitution of 1958 reads:

'The French people hereby solemnly proclaim their attachment to the Rights of Man and the principles of national sovereignty as defined by the Declaration of 1789, reaffirmed and completed by the Preamble to the Constitution of 1946'.

The 1958 French constitution refers to the first declaration of the republic when, in 1789, a bloody revolution rid the country of an oppressive monarchy. This was confirmed again, after the Second

World War, in 1946. It is understandable that the French would have emphasised their belief in what they called the rights of man.

The United States constitution has seven main Articles, or sections:

Article 1   defines the legislative, or law making, powers.
Article 2   deals with the office of President, as the nation's chief executive.
Article 3   sets out the powers of the courts, including the Supreme Court.
Article 4   deals with relations between the individual states.
Article 5   describes how the constitution can be amended.
Articles 6   deal mainly with arrangements for transforming
and 7   a loose federation of states into a full union.

The constitution of the fifth French republic has 14 main sections, which are called Titles:

Title 1   deals with the sovereignty of the Republic.
Title 2   sets out the powers and duties of the President.
Title 3   describes the role of the Prime Minister and the rest of the government.
Title 4   sets out the structure and functions of Parliament.
Title 5   deals with the relationship between Parliament and the government.
Title 7   sets out the composition and role of the Constitutional Council.
Title 8   describes judicial powers.
Title 10   sets out the composition and role of the Economic and Social Council.
Title 14   describes how the constitution can be amended.
          The other titles deal with detailed, specific matters.

Most countries have a **Bill of Rights**, guaranteeing certain basic individual rights, such as freedom of speech and freedom of assembly, either incorporated in or associated with a written constitution.

Britain has never had a written constitution in the sense of a single document, which is perhaps why a study of its political system is so interesting.

2.4   Forms of Government

Theorists have tried to define an ideal form of government but it is surely more sensible to judge a political system on its practical merits: that is whether or not the people who live under it find it acceptable.

For hundreds of years the people of England accepted one person rule, or an absolute monarchy. Then, as certain groups became unhappy with some of the decisions of the monarch, they demanded, and obtained, greater powers of decision making. The Magna Carta signed by King John at Runnymede in 1215, is often quoted as a landmark in the development of popular government. All it really did was to deny absolute power to the king and transfer some of it to a wealthy minority, the aristocracy.

The growth of popular government in this country has been a long and painful process, not really benefitting the ordinary man and woman until nearly the end of the 19th century. We now tend to pride ourselves on living in a **democracy** but we should not assume that our system, although widely copied, is necessarily the best.

We should, in any case, be wary of words such as democracy. The majority of countries in the world today claim to be democratic but their systems of government vary widely. Democracy is an idea rather than a fact. It is something which appeals to the imagination but is difficult to put into practice.

2.5   Democracy

Democracy began in the city states of Ancient Greece, and particularly Athens, in the 5th and 4th centuries BC. It was rule of the citizens, the demos, and gave everyone the right to take an active part in the process of government. In the city states of Greece, with populations no greater than that of a medium-sized town in Britain, it was possible for everyone, at some time in their lives, to hold political office. In fact, it was accepted as a normal part of life in the city. In modern states, with millions of people, government operates through representatives, although some examples of direct involvement, such as the jury system, have survived. The use of plebiscites and referenda are also present day examples of direct democracy.

A **plebiscite** is a direct vote by the electors in a state or region on some particularly important issue, such as union with another state or the acceptance of a government programme. The word has a Latin origin, meaning an appeal to the people. Nowadays a similar device, the **referendum**, is sometimes used to test popular opinion. It was used in this country in connection with membership of the

European Community, in 1975, and devolution for Scotland and Wales, in 1979.

Representative democracy means government through chosen representatives. The great American president, Abraham Lincoln, summed up its intentions as 'government of the people, by the people and for the people'. As an idea it has an obvious appeal and it is not surprising that most states claim to be democracies. If, however, democracy is based on a belief in the value of the individual human being, as most people would probably argue, it should be judged on the basis of how free we are to choose our representatives and how well they look after our interests.

States of the Eastern bloc describe themselves as democracies yet operate single party systems with no official opposition to the government in power. Single party systems are also growing in popularity in black Africa. Defenders of such systems say that the citizens' choice is within the party, rather than between parties, and that the party is the true representative of the people. They might also argue that our system of parliamentary democracy is far from perfect, because many people are not represented by someone who would be their first choice, and only a small minority is really politically active, the vast majority being passive onlookers.

2.6 Politics

Politics is another word which we should use cautiously. It too has an Ancient Greek origin, coming from the word polis, meaning the city. In his book 'In Defence of Politics', Professor Bernard Crick praises politics by saying 'The hall-mark of free government everywhere . . . is whether public criticism is allowed in a manner conceivably effective—in other words, whether opposition is tolerated . . . men cannot act freely without politics'.

Dr Salazar, the one time dictator of Portugal openly admitted that he detested politics from the bottom of his heart. He wanted something more clearcut than the 'messy manoeuvring' which political activity inevitably produces. But ask someone in a country ruled by a military dictatorship which he would prefer: strong, clearcut government or politics and you could predict what his answer would be.

Politics is a means of settling disputes with the minimum of violence. Instead of imposing a solution it operates on the basis of discussion, compromise and agreement. Winston Churchill is reported to have said that 'jaw jaw is better than war war.' Wars have never in themselves provided permanent settlements to disputes. They may have forced opposing parties to come together but eventual agreement has always been reached by discussion around a table. Even the end of the Second World War, with Germany and Japan accepting 'unconditional surrender', was, in effect, the prelude to a political settlement with representatives of two new systems of government.

Since 1945 this country has been involved in many conflicts in which opposing leaders have been described as 'terrorists', and often imprisoned as such, but each conflict has been eventually settled by political means and the former 'terrorist' has often become the respected statesman. Archbishop Makarios of Cyprus, Jomo Kenyatta of Kenya and Robert Mugabe of Zimbabwe are all examples of this. It is not unreasonable to guess that the problems in Northern Ireland and the Falklands will eventually be solved in this way.

Using this interpretation of politics as our guide, it makes sense to judge a democratic system of government on the basis of whether or not political activity is present. We might go on to argue that a genuinely democratic state is one which not only tolerates politics but positively encourages it.

2.7   Representative Democracy in Britain

As we have already seen, Britain has no written constitution nor is there a bill of rights. Democracy therefore rests on foundations which are less clear than in nations which have written constitutions.

This is not to say that the constitution is completely unwritten. Indeed, it would be possible to write one based almost entirely on existing Acts of Parliament. In countries with written constitutions, however, constitutional law is separate from ordinary law and usually protected in a particular way against change. An amendment of the United States Constitution, for example, requires either two thirds of the States to ask Congress for a change, or a two thirds vote of Congress itself. In Britain no Act of Parliament is considered to be superior to any other and Parliament itself has an absolute right to repeal or amend any laws which it or previous Parliaments have made. This is what is meant by the term **sovereignty of Parliament.**

In addition to Acts of Parliament which set out aspects of the constitution there are unwritten understandings called **constitutional conventions**. A convention is something which was originally done for convenience and, over a period of time, has become accepted as the normal thing to do.

If you go to an orchestral concert it is usual to applaud after each piece of music, except in the case of a symphony or concerto which contains a number of movements or parts. You are expected to wait until the end of the whole work before you show your appreciation. You will find nothing in the programme to tell you this, and occasionally a few people will clap between movements. The practice which most people follow, however, is to wait until the end. There are good, practical reasons for this. A symphony has been written to be played as a whole, with one movement linked to another, and applause in the middle not only distracts the musicians but also destroys the audience's concentration. It is a sensible and customary practice: in other words, a convention.

In politics a practice does not become a convention by someone formally declaring it one. It usually takes many years before something which is done because it is sensible and convenient becomes so generally accepted that politicians of all parties adopt it. Then some political historian tells us it is a constitutional convention. Occasionally, a practice which was generally regarded as a convention becomes unnecessary, or even harmful, and so goes out of use. The disappearance of a convention is likely to take as long as its introduction.

Political systems all over the world use conventions mainly because they add flexibility to the way government operates. In Britain some of the most important features of the constitution, such as the role of the Cabinet and Prime Minister, are based on convention and, as we continue our examination of the business of government, we will identify and comment on them.

We argued earlier that democracy is based on a belief in the value of the individual and we can apply three tests to see whether it exists. How much choice do we have in selecting our representatives? What opportunities are available for reviewing their work and for criticising it? To what extent are individual rights protected? As we continue our study we will keep these tests in mind and apply them where appropriate.

We will add two other factors to our judgement of whether or not the British system of representative democracy is living up to our expectations of it. The extent to which ordinary people are able, and indeed encouraged, to take part in politics, and the extent to which politicians, and particularly those in positions of power, are prepared to take the people into their confidence and to show that they have the public interest as their major priority.

Questions and Assignments

1   What is the main purpose of a constitution?
2   What is meant by a nation state?
3   Why is democracy such a popular word?
4   Why do dictators dislike politics?
5   What is the difference between direct and representative democracy?
6   What is a convention?
7   You have just received a letter from your imaginary uncle, Fred, who has a reputation as a great cynic, seeing the worst in everything and the best in nothing. In his letter he writes: 'Don't believe all that rubbish they teach you about politics. It's the dirtiest business I know and if I had my way I'd line all the politicians up against a wall and shoot the lot'.

Reply to his letter, in not more than 500 words, trying to convince him that he is wrong.
8   If you were given the job of writing the draft of a written constitution for the United Kingdom, what would you include in it?

Simply draw up a list of what you think would be the main ssential points e.g.

1 Voting rights
2 Freedom of Speech
. . . and so on

Chapter 3

Pressure Politics

Likeminded people often join together to pursue common aims and interests. The groups which are formed usually go on to represent and promote these interests and defend them from attack. They are often referred to as pressure groups to show that they try to achieve their aims by putting pressure on public opinion and government.

Although they form part of the democratic process, they are different from political parties in that they operate outside the parliamentary and government systems but they often have spokesmen in Parliament as well as direct contacts in Whitehall. Some of them constitute very powerful groupings or lobbies, such as the car lobby or the farming lobby.

Although pressure groups have been criticised as being undemocratic, because they tend to give power to minorities at the expense of the majority, they can be said to add to and improve the political system by allowing more people to take part in the democratic process.

3.1   Interest Groups

Everyone has an interest in something. It may be a very personal interest, perhaps connected with the family, or it may be wider and more social. You may wish to share your interest with others and so you decide to join a group.

An **interest group** is, therefore, an organisation set up to represent, promote and defend a particular interest or set of interests. There are numerous examples to choose from.

The Royal Society for the Prevention of Cruelty to Animals (**RSPCA**) is clearly interested in the protection of animals and the National Society for the Prevention of Cruelty to Children (**NSPCC**) in the protection of children. A trade union is another

21

form of interest group. The National Union of Mineworkers (**NUM**) is concerned with the interests of miners and the National Graphical Association (**NGA**) with the interests of print workers.

Most interest groups are permanent and have resulted from people coming together for a common purpose and feeling the need to have some sort of organisation behind them. Some groups are set up to deal with a single, immediate issue and when that issue is resolved the group is disbanded. For example, an interest group might be set up to fight a proposal to drive a new road through a town or village. Once a decision on the precise route has been taken and given legal approval there is nothing more for the group to do so it disappears.

3.2   Types of Interest Group

It has become fashionable to classify interest groups but it is difficult to separate them successfully into neat categories because few of them are concerned with only one aspect of an interest or with one activity.

Some groups are described as **promotional**, but most are anyway, at least for part of the time. Some are called **defensive**, but, again, when their interests seem to be threatened, most groups go on to the defensive.

Then there is a possible distinction between functional and preference groups.

A **functional** group can be said to be one which is the product of a country's economic structure. Such groups are, in fact, an essential part of that structure. Good examples of functional groups are the Confederation of British Industry (**CBI**), representing the owners of industry and business; the Trades Union Congress (**TUC**), representing organised workers; and the British Medical Association (**BMA**), representing the medical profession. There are, of course, many others also representing industry, working people or the professions.

A **preference** group is one which represents a number of likeminded people who share a common purpose or concern. The Campaign for Nuclear Disarmanent (**CND**) is a significant group in this category. Such a group does not confine its activities to a narrow sectional interest but campaigns for everyone, whether or not the average person wants it to. The RSPCA and the NSPCC, which we have already mentioned, can be said to be preference groups, even though they cater for only specific sections of society.

The **Howard League for Penal Reform**, which campaigns for better treatment of the criminal offender, is another example of a preference group with a specific section of the population in mind. Many preference groups are of a charitable nature, in that they collect money by appeals to the public and rely very much on the work of unpaid volunteers. They are the typical 'flag day collection' groups.

It is also possible to identify **cause groups**. They are the groups set up to fight for a particular cause, such as women's rights, or the plight of the homeless and so on. CND falls into this category as does **Greenpeace** and other groups concerned about the preservation of the environment.

But having attempted to classify them, it must be obvious that it is a very difficult operation because, as we have already said, they do not fit easily into a single category, or even two or three.

3.3 Pressure Groups

Some writers use the term pressure group to describe all groups of the kind we have been looking at, but this can, at times, be misleading.

A **pressure group** is a group representing an interest or cause which seeks to achieve its aims by putting pressure on government. It will use a wide range of means to change public opinion but it knows that ultimately the pressure must be on the government of the day.

All pressure groups represent some kind of interest but not all interest groups rely on pressure to secure their ends, although even the quietest and least demonstrative group may at times feel obliged to come out into the open and act as a pressure group.

In the next chapter we shall be looking at political parties and it will be useful at this stage to make a distinction between a party and a pressure group.

Sometimes the aims of a pressure group may be supported by a political party. For example, the **Hansard Society** has, among other things, argued for the reform of the voting system and this is very much in line with the thinking of Liberals and Social Democrats. But a political party tries to achieve its aims by actually getting its hands on the levers of powers, or, at the very least, getting its members elected to the House of Commons. A pressure group, on the other hand, does not seek direct parliamentary representation or a seat in government. It operates indirectly by putting pressure on politicians.

Occasionally, however, a pressure group can decide to pursue its aims directly in the political arena and actually become a party. An example of this is the **Green Party**, whose objectives are similar to those of Greenpeace.

3.4   Pressure Groups and Parliament

Many interest and pressure groups, however, have their spokesmen in Parliament.

Nearly half the Labour MPs are **sponsored** by trade unions. This means that the sponsoring union will pay up to 80% of the candidate's election campaign expenses (electoral law preventing it from contributing more) and, subsequently, probably contribute substantially to the constituency party's funds. This sort of sponsorship is not surprising since it was the trade unions who played a major part in creating the Labour Party at the beginning of this century. Then there are MPs in other parties who are also 'sponsored' in one way or another. For example, the Police Federation, representing the bulk of police officers in Britain, and the Superintendents' Association, representing the senior ranks, each has its spokesman in the House of Commons. They will be recompensed for this and will support the policeman's case in parliamentary debates.

There are other members of both the House of Commons and the House of Lords who act in similar ways as advisers or consultants. The names of 'interested' MPs, are listed in the House of Commons **Register of Members' Interests**. In recent years this sort of activity has grown dramatically and it is calculated that the amount paid by companies in consultancy fees to MPs increased by 50% in 1984. In 1985 there were no fewer than 310 'consultancies' listed in the House of Commons Register, with one Member declaring 21 companies among his 'clients'. The ethics of being an 'interested' MP have sometimes been questioned but the Speaker of the House of Commons has ruled on several occasions that, providing Members use discretion, it is a longstanding practice that has general acceptance.

From time to time a deputation will arrange to meet MPs in one of the lobbies, or meeting areas, in the Houses of Parliament to try to persuade them to support an interest group's point of view. This practice is called **lobbying** and may be accompanied by a march or demonstration in the area of Westminster.

Although lobbying in this sense is often practised in Britain, it is generally less effective than in countries such as the United States of America. In the United States members of the legislature, the Senate and House of Representatives, are more powerful figures than backbench MPs in Britain and, through their membership of Congressional committees, can influence public opinion and Presidential policy.

Having said this, there have been notable examples in recent years when skilful lobbying of MPs has resulted in humiliating defeats for the government. For example, the 1986 Shops Bill, which would have relaxed trading hours and paved the way for Sunday shopping, was defeated when Conservative backbenchers joined the other parties in their opposition to it. A combination of religious, commercial and trade union interests put considerable pressure on MPs and eventually won the day.

3.5 The Pressure Lobbies

In a different sense, the word lobby can also be used to describe a collection of groups which function individually for most of the time but which, together, represent one major interest.

For example, the **car lobby** in Britain can be said to include the car manufacturers, the trade unions in that industry, the petroleum producers, the car retailers, the car repairers, the tools and parts manufacturers and retailers, the owners of filling stations and the motoring organisations, such as the Automobile Association (**AA**) and the Royal Automobile Club (**RAC**). Collectively, they represent a huge and powerful interest which will consistently put forward the case for the motor car, calling for more expenditure on roads and opposing increased taxes on cars and fuel.

Another important grouping is the **farming lobby**, headed by the National Farmers' Union (**NFU**), which is reported to spend something like £2 m a year on public relations and political lobbying.

These two lobbies sometimes come into conflict with the **environmentalist lobby** whose aims are clearly different.

3.6 Pressure Groups in Action

'Interest' pressure groups and 'cause' pressure groups tend to operate in different ways.

Many of the interest groups have established over the years a kind of legitimacy and respectability, so much so that they are regularly consulted by government and have a more or less permanent 'open line' with appropriate government departments. Thus the NFU, in addition to having its spokesmen in Parliament, will have contacts with civil servants in the Ministry of Agriculture, Fisheries and Food. Similarly, the organisations representing the police will have contacts in the Home Office. These are sometimes referred to as the **inside** groups because of this ready access to government.

The cause groups, on the other hand, are often considered to be the **outside** groups and tend to be looked at more cautiously by governments. CND, for example, has consistently been a thorn in the side of the Ministry of Defence. These groups, therefore, resort more to open publicity, through the media and by demonstrations and marches. They operate more on public opinion than government directly.

All groups, however, tend to function on a day to day basis in broadly similar ways, some having a higher profile than others. In addition to making use of their contacts in Westminster and Whitehall, they will try to get their message across through advertisements, letters and articles in the newspapers, interviews on radio and television and sometimes by organising petitions, demonstrations and marches. Some groups will commission public opinion polls to show there is popular support for what they are trying to achieve. The many campaigns by CND, Greenpeace and Shelter are examples of the use of all these tactics.

3.7   The Importance of Pressure Politics

For good or ill pressure politics are well established in Britain, as in most other democratic countries, and are set to stay. How important are they? Do they help or hinder the democratic process?

Although many politicians accept them and, as we have seen, often work for them, when they get into government they usually see them as thorns in their sides. When he was Secretary of State for Defence in Margaret Thatcher's government, Michael Heseltine fought regular, and often bitter, battles with CND. James Callaghan, who headed the Labour government between 1976 and 1979, described pressure groups as 'a nuisance, if not a menace', and yet some years earlier he had been a spokesman in the House of Commons for the police. Even outside Parliament they have been criticised as having 'power without responsibility'.

Defenders of pressure groups see things differently. They claim that they add to and improve democratic politics. They justify them on several grounds. They say that having a vote just once every four or five years is not enough and that pressure groups allow people to state their case whenever they want to. They argue that pressure of this kind keeps governments on their toes, and that membership of a group provides a safety valve for social frustration.

The inside interest groups tend to have fewer critics than the outside cause groups. Indeed, as we have seen, the Whitehall civil service makes great use of interest groups for obtaining information and sounding out public opinion.

On balance, although some people argue that pressure politics can force a minority viewpoint on to a reluctant majority, it can be said that they provide a valuable opportunity for people who would otherwise be politically inactive to take part in the democratic process.

3.8   Pluralism or Corporatism?

Some students of politics have argued that the growth of pressure groups has tended to make Britain, like other Western democracies, a **pluralist** state. By this they mean that pressure groups have become so strong that political power, instead of resting firmly in the hands of government, has been distributed among competing groups and policy is determined by the groups which apply the most effective pressure.

Other observers of the political scene have identified a **corporatist** state in which the big economic lobbies, such as those we have looked at earlier, wield so much power that it is they, rather than governments, which decide national policy.

There is an element of truth in both views but each exaggerates the position. For example, between 1974 and 1976 in Britain, the Labour government headed by Harold Wilson agreed a 'social contract' with the trade unions whereby they agreed to moderate their wage demands if the government, in return, introduced legislation favourable to them. This agreement showed clear signs of a pluralist approach. On the other hand, there have been examples of corporatism when governments have changed policies to suit the big business and farming lobbies.

Politics has been rightly called 'the art of the possible' and all politicians, if they want to be elected, have to live with the facts of life as they find them. One of the significant political facts is that pressure groups have grown over recent years and show no signs of disappearing. Governments, therefore, ignore them at their peril and work with or against them. On balance, co-operation seems more sensible than opposition.

Questions and Assignments

1 What is an interest group?
2 What are the main types of interest group?
3 What is a pressure group?
4 What is meant by lobbying?
5 How do pressure groups operate?
6 Do pressure groups help or hinder the democratic process?
7 Draw up a list of 20 interest groups and 20 cause groups, showing against each what you believe its chief aims to be.
8 You have been asked to lead a group to fight a proposal by your local council to close a nearby swimming pool. Draw up a plan, setting out how you intend to conduct the group's campaign.

Chapter 4

Party Politics

Two parties have dominated British politics for more than two hundred years, Parliament witnessing classic battles between the Conservatives and Liberals and then Conservatives and Labour. The social structure and voting system both favour the two party system.

Today the Conservative Party draws most of its support from professional people and white collar workers, mainly in the south of Britain, and Labour from blue collar workers, mainly in the north. Each party stands for a different set of values, based largely on economic interests and social class, yet in the centre of British politics attitudes tend to overlap.

Organisationally, the Conservative, Labour, Liberal and Social Democratic parties are similar but differ in the distribution of power between the leaders and the rest of the members. Each party draws its financial support from obvious quarters, the Conservatives from business and industry, Labour from the trade union movement, and the Liberals and Social Democrats from individual members. Within each party are groups representing different factions and putting pressure on the leadership to support their points of view.

With the emergence of the Liberal/SDP Alliance two party politics seems under threat and the implications of this could be of constitutional as well as political importance.

4.1   The Nature of Party Politics

A **political party** is an association of people who hold similar views about what a country's social and economic priorities should be and come together to establish these priorities by gaining control of the machinery of government. It is this wish to govern which makes a party different from a pressure group.

One of the problems about membership of a political party is being able to agree with all its policies. As a member of the Conservative or Labour party, you may support its broad, basic aims, but you may have difficulty in accepting all the details of how they are to be achieved. That is why a party will often describe itself as a 'broad church', able to accommodate a wide range of opinions, and each party will have its centre and right and left wings. Each party will also have its own internal 'pressure groups'.

We should also make a distinction between a party member and a supporter. At the present time only about 20% of voters in Britain are paid-up members of a political party, and an even smaller percentage are regularly active in politics. Party supporters may give money but most do little more than vote. 25% or more eligible to vote do not even bother to do that.

4.2   The Domination of Party Politics

Most of the world's parliaments, or debating chambers, are circular or semi-circular in shape. The two chambers of the Palace of Westminster, as the Houses of Parliament in London are officially called, are not. They are long and narrow, obliging their Members to sit in rows of seats facing each other, with the president of each House, the Speaker in the Commons and the Lord Chancellor in the Lords, sitting between them at one end, rather like a referee. This physical setting emphasises the nature of party politics in Britain.

There was a period in the 1830s when some politicians were saying that parties in Britain were finished, but they were wrong, and the second half of the 19th century saw the dominance of two great parties, the Conservatives and Liberals, each led for a long time by figures who seemed head and shoulders above their contemporaries, Benjamin Disraeli and William Ewart Gladstone.

This Conservative-Liberal dominance lasted right up to the First World War and when the Labour Party was formed in 1900 it did not see itself as a serious challenger: it merely wanted working class representation in Parliament. Then, after a series of coalition governments, a split developed in the once powerful Liberal Party, some members wanting to continue their links with the Conservatives and the rest to return to being an independent party. At a momentous meeting of Conservative MPs at the Carlton Club in London, on 19 October 1922, the link with the Liberals was ended. In the general election in the following year the Conservatives won decisively and, with the Liberals shrinking to a fraction of their former size, the Labour Party became, for the first time, the official Opposition.

The swing of the political pendulum between government and opposition parties is shown in Figure 4.1.

Throughout this period the House of Commons still had a number of independent MPs, not tied to any particular party, but their numbers were dwindling.

It has now become impossible for an individual, however wealthy, to fight the great party machines, and the media, and particularly television, are now so concerned about dramatising issues between the main parties that independent views are crowded out. A party candidate can make clear promises to his electors, while the independent can guarantee nothing. After the 1959 general election only one independent MP remained. He was Sir David Roberston, who had left the Conservative Party earlier that year. He, in turn, was to disappear. Since then other politicians, at odds with their parties, have tried to sit as independent MPs but none has had any permanent success.

The two party system has now become so established that it is built into the constitution itself.

The Leader of the Opposition is officially recognised, has an office in the House of Commons, and a salary paid out of public funds. The procedural rules for debate and committee member-ship reinforce the two party division. For example, 17 debating days are set aside in the Commons for the Opposition and only 3 for the third largest party, the Liberals. All the select committee chairmanships are shared between the Conservative and Labour parties.

The voting system also assists the two main parties. For example, in the 1983 general election the Liberal/SDP Alliance won 25% of the total vote but less than 4% of the seats. In contrast, the Labour Party had 32% of the seats with 28% of the vote, and the Conservatives 61% of the seats with 42% of the vote.

4.3 The Origins of the British Parties

Sometimes it is possible to establish the beginning of a political party with pin point precision.

The **Labour Party** was founded in 1900 as a result of a meeting of trade unionists and representatives of a number of socialist societies. Prior to this Keir Hardie had led the **Independent**

Fig. 4.1

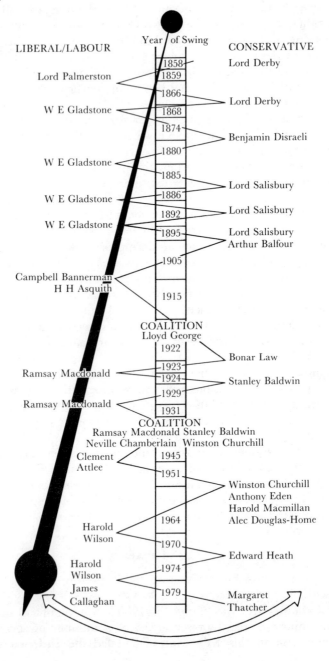

Labour Party and it was he who had been instrumental in bringing the unions into the Labour movement. Originally called the **Labour Representation Committee**, it soon became the Labour Party.

The **Social Democratic Party** had equally precise origins. It was formed on 26 March 1981 by four leading politicians, Roy Jenkins, Shirley Williams, David Owen and William Rodgers, who had all previously risen to Cabinet rank in the Labour Party. They had become disillusioned with what they saw as its drift to the left, and resigned. The 'gang of four', as they became known, with other dissenters and thousands of people who had never been active in politics before, founded the new party.

The origins of the other two main parties are a little more obscure.

The **Conservative Party** can be traced back to the Tories of the late 17th century, who supported the Duke of York's claim to the English throne against the Whigs. They were regarded as the 'conservators', because of their belief in and defence of traditional values, and came to be called the Conservative Party in the early 1830s.

The **Liberal Party** can be traced back to the Whigs. Like the Tories, they were originally mainly wealthy landowners and in the 1850s were joined by lawyers, businessmen and a number of people who described themselves as 'radical thinkers' to become the Liberal Party.

Although, from its start, the Labour Party was clearly to the left of British politics, the positions of the other two major parties were, until recent years, more difficult to identify. Under Disraeli, the Conservatives became identified with imperialism, or the expansion of the British Empire, while the Liberals, under Gladstone, were associated with free enterprise and individual freedom, but the two parties shared many social values.

Over the years all three parties have developed left and right wings so that on certain issues their views have overlapped. In truth, whether it likes it or not, any party, if it wants to form a government, must look to the middle ground of politics because it is there that the bulk of votes lie. The British people tend to be conservative, with a small 'c', and liberal, with a small 'l'.

4.4 The Characteristics of British Parties

On the continent of Europe party allegiances often reflect religious beliefs while in the United States of America they can mirror differences of race and colour. In Britain class, representing social and economic backgrounds, is the major factor. Politics in Northern Ireland falls into a different category. As the British population becomes more mixed, race and religion may well play a larger part but, for the present at least, they are largely in the background.

Britain is arguably still the most class conscious country in the Western world and this is reflected in the way people speak, how they dress, their eating habits, how they use their leisure time, the newspapers they read, the television programmes they watch and, perhaps most importantly, the way they are educated.

Although there have been changes during the past 40 years or so, the two main political parties, Conservative and Labour, continue to represent a class division. Labour is still the party of the working class and the Conservative Party that of the middle and upper classes. The Alliance parties tend to straddle this division.

Figure 4.2 shows the parties' share of the votes in the 1983 general election by social groups. From it will be seen that the Conservative Party drew half its support from the 'white collar' groups while nearly 80% of Labour's votes came from the 'blue collar' manual workers. In contrast, Alliance support was much more widely distributed.

Fig. 4.2

Parties' Share of Votes by Social Groups
1983 General Election

Social Group	Conservative	Labour	Alliance
Professional/Managerial	21%	6%	16%
Office/Clerical	29%	16%	21%
Skilled Manual	30%	37%	34%
Semi-/Unskilled	20%	41%	29%

Support for the parties also tends to be regionally based. The Conservatives are strongest in the South East, South West, East Anglia and parts of the Midlands and the Labour Party draws most of its support from the traditional industrial regions of South Wales, North West and North East England and Central Scotland, as well as most of the inner city areas. Liberal/SDP Alliance support has been much more evenly spread, and this is one reason why its share of the popular vote has not been reproduced in House of Commons seats. The 1983 general election revealed a clear north-south split between Labour and the Conservatives, with the less affluent parts of London being the exceptions to this pattern.

4.5 What the Parties Stand For

If politics in Britain is the art of the possible then it is difficult to identify the parties in ideological terms. In other words, it is impossible to say that Conservatives have always stood for one set of principles and nothing else or that Labour has always followed a particular line of thought and always will. Over the years there have been shifts in viewpoints by and within each party.

The Conservative Party has moved a long way from the days when Toryism meant rule of the old, landed ruling class. As it developed in the 19th and 20th centuries it took on board some of the attitudes of the Liberals who had split from their main party after the First World War. A number of viewpoints developed within the Party : strong government, but not too much of it; free market economics to let businessmen get on with their jobs with as little interference as possible; low personal taxation, but not at the expense of national defence and law and order; help for the poor and under-privileged providing it is not extravagant; public ownership only when it is absolutely necessary.

Some Conservatives might say that this is a splendid compromise between the Tory and the 'liberal' viewpoint. Others, such as Sir Ian Gilmour, might not wish to tie the Party down to any one particular stance, saying 'so far . . . as philosophy or doctrine is concerned, the wise Conservative travels light.' But not all his colleagues in the Party would necessarily agree with him.

Soon after she became Leader of the Party, in 1975, Margaret Thatcher made it clear that she was a 'conviction politician'. She had served in Edward Heath's government, from 1970 to 1974, and witnessed a series of 'U turns' on industrial and economic policy. She resolved not to tread the same path. Her convictions led her into monetarist, free market measures which tended to push her and her supporters to the right of the Party, to the dismay of some Conservatives who preferred to walk the middle ground.

Whether or not Mrs Thatcher is succeeded by another 'conviction' Leader or whether there is a return to the 'one nation' approach of Harold Macmillan, it is certain that the Conservative Party will still be able to accommodate a wide range of views without renouncing its basic foundations as the defender of private property and free enterprise.

The Labour Party is more clearly rooted in ideology, with a commitment in its Constitution to securing for the workers ' . . . the full fruits of their industry . . . upon the basis of the common ownership of the means of production, distribution and exchange', but, in practice, it has avoided committing itself to the full implications of that pledge.

It is, in theory as well as practice, more democratic than the Conservative Party, mainly because it has had to accommodate within its ranks three basic interests: the trade union movement; radical socialists, who aim to change the economic structure by fundamental means, such as public ownership; and social democrats, seeking to reform capitalism by making it fairer and more efficient, rather than by state control or ownership.

Within the past 30 years or so there have been frequent clashes between these three interests, with some social democrats feeling increasingly isolated, so much so that in 1981, as we have already seen, some broke away to form the Social Democratic Party. This does not mean that there are no longer any social democrats in the Labour Party: this line of thought still exists, but working within the party rather than outside it.

The present day Labour Party is much less dogmatic and ideological than its Constitution suggests, but with policies clearly different from those of the Conservatives. It sees public ownership as a means to an end, not as an end in itself, and the end is to maintain and improve the basic industries and services for the benefit of all. It seeks a fairer distribution of the nation's wealth and greater social equality. Unlike the Conservatives, it is prepared to divert the country's resources from what it sees as extravagant expenditure on defence to expenditure on social needs.

The Liberal/SDP Alliance produced a joint programme for the 1983 general election and since then the two parties have settled most of their former policy differences. This has been possible because the Liberal Party, since the 1920s, has moved a long way from the 'individual liberalism' of the 19th century towards the 'social liberalism' of Lloyd George and Beveridge. This brought it nearer to the 'social democrat' wing of the Labour Party and so made it easier for the 1981 defectors to join forces with it.

Fig. 4.3

The British Party Playing Field

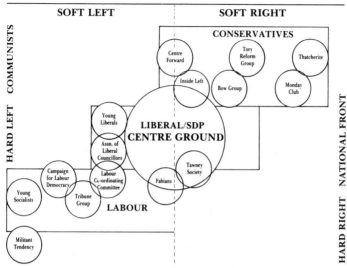

The British Party Playing Field, in Figure 4.3, is designed to show how the different viewpoints and allegiances within the parties overlap, with parts of the 'centre ground' occupied by all.

Fig. 4.4

Conservative Party Organisation

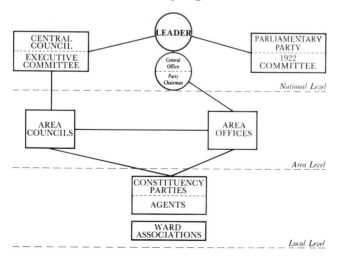

Fig. 4.5

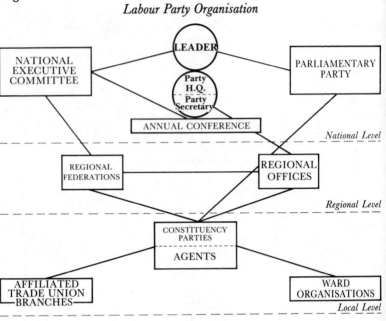

Labour Party Organisation

Fig. 4.6

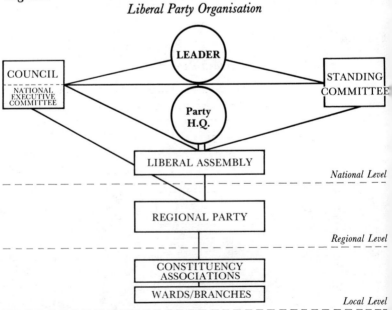

Liberal Party Organisation

Fig. 4.7

SDP Organisation

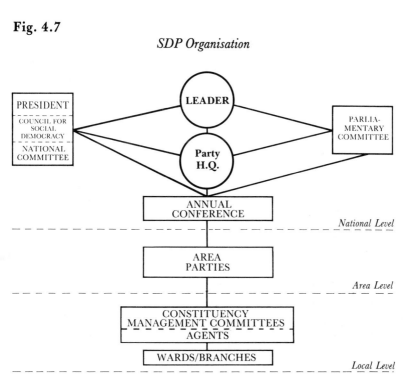

4.6   Party Organisation and Power

There are three common bases of power in all the British parties: the party in the country; the central organisation; and the party in Parliament. The main differences between the parties arise from the different distributions of power.

The structures of the four parties' organisations are, on paper, broadly similar, as Figures 4.4–4.7 show, but this similarity masks fundamental differences.

4.7   The Party Leader

Until 1965 the Conservative Leader was selected by a process of behind-the-scenes soundings of opinion within the Party. Influential figures were consulted and eventually an acceptable Leader emerged. The last to be chosen in this way was Sir Alec

Douglas Home, who took over from Harold Macmillan when he resigned the premiership because of ill health. Since then Conservative Leaders have been elected by MPs and Edward Heath was the first to be chosen by the new method.

The Leader of the Labour Party used to be elected annually by the Parliamentary Labour Party (PLP) but, after a long campaign, lasting nearly 10 years, members of the left wing, disillusioned with what they saw as the policies of compromise of Harold Wilson and James Callaghan, got enough support to force a change in the rules. After some often bitter arguments, a special conference decided, in January 1981, that in future the Leader would be chosen by an electoral college, with 40% of the votes cast by the affiliated trade unions, 30% by representatives of the constituency parties and 30% by MPs. The leadership, including the National Executive Committee (**NEC**), had recommended equal voting shares so the eventual result must be seen as a victory for the Party's left wing. The first Leader to be elected in this way was Neil Kinnock, in 1983.

The Leaders of both the Liberals and Social Democrats are elected by popular vote by all members of their parties.

The Conservatives normally like a strong leader and the first two people chosen by the current method, Edward Heath and Margaret Thatcher, have both used their powers to the full.

The Labour Party has always expected its Leader to pay due attention to the views of the Party at all levels and its structure tends to spread, rather than concentrate, power.

Although both the Liberals and Social Democrats make much of their belief in individual democracy, in specific circumstances the leaderships can be very strong and decisive. In 1977, for example, David Steel pushed a half-hearted Party into the Lib-Lab pact. Afterwards Steel himself admitted that it was 'not so much a Lib-Lab pact as a Steel-Callaghan pact'. Then when Roy Jenkins gave up the leadership of the Social Democrats in 1983 David Owen simply walked into the job, without any formal elections.

In any case the position of a leader changes dramatically when a party is in power. The leader becomes Prime Minister, with all the inbuilt authority and prestige attached to the office. Even the most democratically structured party inevitably has to shed some of that democracy when faced with the reality of power.

Figure 4.8 depicts the relative strengths of the four party leaders on the basis of what sorts of decisions the party structures allow them to make alone.

Fig. 4.8

Powers of the Party Leaders

	Conservative	Labour	Liberal	SDP
Chooses the Cabinet	Yes	Yes	Yes	Yes
Chooses the Shadow Cabinet	Yes	No	Yes	Yes
Controls Party Headquarters	Yes	No*	Yes	Yes
Approves the Manifesto	Yes	No	Yes	No
Makes Party Policies	Yes	No**	Yes	Yes

*The Leader works closely with the Labour Party Secretary
**When Prime Minister, the Leader makes policies with the Cabinet

4.8 The Parties in Parliament

The four main parties have parliamentary parties consisting of all their respective MPs. There are, however, differences between them.

The Parliamentary Labour Party (**PLP**) is the body which represents backbenchers. Its chairman is a leading figure and seen as an essential link between his fellow backbenchers and the leadership. The PLP has regular meetings of all members, including the Prime Minister, when the Party is in office, but they are primarily for the benefit of backbenchers. It also operates a number of subject groups which keep an eye on Party policies and has an influential **Liaison Committee**, which maintains contacts between the front and back benches and leading Party officials.

The Conservative equivalent of the PLP is the **1922 Committee**. It takes its name from the famous meeting at the Carlton Club in London in 1922 when it was decided to bring the Liberal-Conservative coalition under Lloyd George to an end. Like his opposite number in the Labour Party, the chairman of the 1922 Committee is seen as the Party's leading backbencher. The Committee provides a link between the back and front benches and is addressed from time to time by the Leader, but these occasions are usually in the nature of just 'pep talks'. The 1922 Committee can, on occasions, have a great influence on party policy, and the leadership ignores it at its peril.

The Liberal Party has a **Standing Committee** which goes beyond the bounds of Parliament. It consists of 30 members, representing all elements in the Party and has the job of co-ordinating policy. The relatively small number of MPs makes communication easier than in the bigger parties.

The Social Democrats have a **Parliamentary Committee** which includes all MPs plus representatives of SDP peers. There is also a House of Lords Committee comprising all SDP peers.

Figure 4.9 depicts the relative strengths of the parliamentary organisations of the four parties.

Fig. 4.9

Powers of the Parliamentary Parties

	Conservative	Labour	Liberal	SDP
Elects Leader	Yes	No*	No	No
Approves Party Manifesto	No	No	Yes	No
Makes Party Policies	No	No	Yes	Yes
Chooses Shadow Cabinet	No	Yes	No	No

*Shared with trade unions and constituencies

4.9   The National Conferences

Each party holds an **annual conference** at which policies and proposed policies are debated.

The Conservative Conference tends to be a much more stage managed affair than the others. At one time the Leader did not attend until the last day, so as to make his presence seem more important, but now the Leader attends most or all sessions. The final 'keynote' speech, however, is still given in an atmosphere which has been carefully built up to obtain the greatest dramatic effect.

The leaders' addresses at the other party conferences are much less contrived, but still intended to serve the purpose of raising the spirits of the delegates.

How important and influential are these conferences?

Clause VI of the Labour Party's constitution says 'the work of the Party shall be under the direction and control of the Party Conference which shall itself be subject to the Constitution and Standing Orders of the Party'. In contrast, the Rules and Standing Orders of the Conservative Party merely set out, in formal terms, who is entitled to attend and when and how the Conference should be convened. The Conservatives try to avoid 'washing their dirty linen' in public but the Labour Party prides itself on being openly democratic and is less dutiful towards its Leader.

The Liberal Party's annual conference, the Liberal Assembly, is generally less pretentious than those of the two big parties. Delegates are usually outspoken and the Leader takes part on equal terms with his parliamentary colleagues. Like the other leaders, however, he too makes the main keynote speech.

The Social Democrats set out to challenge the style and organisation of the conferences of the other parties and their first, in 1981, was described as a 'rolling conference', with a special train taking party leaders and their followers from Perth to Bradford and then to London. It certainly served the purpose of drawing attention to the new party. Subsequent conferences have been more conventional but usually held at less obvious venues, such as Salford in 1983.

A Conservative conference is not seen as a place for deciding policy, but more for 'displaying the Party's wares' to its supporters and the public at large.

The Labour Party gives much more weight to conference views and decisions, with strong groups of delegates from the various sections of the Party mandated to vote in specific ways.

The Liberal Party leadership normally gives considerable freedom to delegates to express their views and to convert them into conference resolutions, but it always reserves the right to take a realistic, practical view about accepting them. Debates on nuclear disarmament illustrate this.

The early conferences of the Social Democratic Party showed the leadership to be very much in the 'driving seat' but, as delegates become more experienced, things will undoubtedly change. There is also the likelihood of joint Liberal/SDP conferences in the future.

The power of delegates at party conferences depends very much on whether or not the party is in office. Prime Ministers and their Cabinet colleagues can always tell delegates that, in the real world of international politics, they cannot expect to tie a government down to a specific policy.

4.10   Party Central Organisations

At national level the Conservative Party has a **Central Council**, with representatives from the constituencies, prospective MPs, party leaders, officials and backbench MPs. It is too large a body to take effective decisions but it has an **Executive Committee**, numbering about 150, acting on its behalf.

The Labour Party's equivalent is the National Executive Committee (**NEC**). It is much smaller, with 28 members, representing all strands within the Party: the Leader and Deputy Leader, 12 from the trade unions; 7 from the constituencies, 1 representing the socialist and co-operative membership, 5 women representatives, and the Party Treasurer, who is usually a leading political figure elected annually by the Party Conference. The NEC controls party finance, is a disciplinary body, liaises with the PLP and supervises the central and local organisations. It is a powerful body within the Party.

At the head of the Conservative Party's central organisation is the **Party Chairman**. He is personally appointed by the Leader and is usually a prominent political figure. Recent holders of the office have been Cecil Parkinson, John Selwyn Gummer and Norman Tebbit. The Chairman will normally work closely with the Leader.

In the Labour Party the NEC controls the central organisation through a career officer, the **Party Secretary**. He can be a very influential person and, like the Conservative Party Chairman, will work closely with the Leader.

The Liberal Party equivalent of the Conservative Central Council is the **Liberal Council**, which normally meets quarterly. It includes representatives from all sections of the Party. It operates through a **National Executive Committee** which meets every two months.

The SDP equivalent of the Liberal Council is the **Council for Social Democracy**, chaired by the President, who is elected by popular vote. Day to day work is done by the **National Committee**, which meets monthly.

4.11   The Grass Roots of the Parties

As we shall see when we look at elections, it is at the grass roots levels, the **constituencies** and the **wards**, that the bulk of the undramatic, hard work of the parties is done. MPs and prospective parliamentary candidates have full time or part time agents looking after constituency matters, helped by unpaid volunteers. As a relatively wealthy party, the Conservatives can afford about 300 full time agents compared with less than 70 in the Labour Party and less than 30 for the Liberals.

Much of the success of the Conservative Party in the shire counties has been due to the efforts of party workers, many of them middle aged or older women, raising money through raffles, garden fetes and so on, distributing leaflets and canvassing voters. The Labour Party relies on similar support and hard work in the urban constituencies but usually its workers are younger and from a different social class. The Liberal Party has successfully used local politics as a launching pad for national elections and the Social Democrats are now working closely with them on the same lines.

Although the constituency organisations in the Conservative Party play little part in national policy making, they have a very free hand in selecting parliamentary candidates. The Party maintains a central list but the final choice of candidate is almost always made locally.

The Labour constituency parties have considerable power in the selection of prospective MPs and the re-selection of sitting MPs and there have a number of bitter clashes between moderate MPs and left wing local activists but in recent years the national leadership has been successful in disciplining local extremists.

4.12   Party Finance

The Conservative Party obtains its finance from donations from commercial and industrial organisations, various 'front' organisations, such as British United Industrialists, contributions from constituencies, individual donations and investments. In an election year it can amount to £10 m.

The Labour Party receives its funds from affiliated trade unions and individual subscriptions. In an election year the unions will usually set up an election campaign fund. Total monies, however, will be probably less than half those of the Conservatives.

The Liberal Party's even more modest income comes from constituency contributions and individual donations, which in an election year can be quite generous. The Social Democrats rely mainly on a substantial personal membership subscription. To 'take the pain' out of paying the subscription it was the first British Party to accept payment by credit card. Its funds, however, are modest, even compared with those of the Liberals.

4.13   Internal Party Pressure Groups

All the parties have their own internal groups, reflecting different shades of opinion and putting pressure on the leaderships for their own policy views. The Labour Party has the greatest number and the widest variety of such groups and they are all tolerated provided they do not attempt to be 'a party within a party'. It was this aspect that brought the **Militant Tendency** into conflict with the NEC and the party leadership.

Figure 4.10 lists the main pressure groups within the parties and their attitudes.

Fig. 4.10

British Party Pressure Groups

Name of Group	*Membership*	*Aims and Attitude*
Conservative Party		
Monday Club	The old right wing	Traditional values
Tory Reform Group	Progressives	Radical change
Bow Group	Liberal element	'One nation' Toryism
Inside Left	Supporters of Sir Ian Gilmour	Return to 'centrist' policies
Centre Forward	Supporters of Francis Pym	Similar to 'inside left'
Labour Party		
Tribune Group	Mainly 'soft' left wing MPs	Moderate, left of centre, policies
Fabian Society	Right wingers	Right of centre policies
Campaign for Labour Democracy	Followers of Tony Benn	Greater democracy in the Party
Labour Co-ordinating Committee	Left wingers	Campaigning on national issues
Young Socialists	Young left wingers	Extreme left wing policies
Militant Tendency	Extreme left wing	Based on 'Militant' newspaper

Liberal Party

Association of Liberal Councillors	Local activists	Experts in 'community' politics
Young Liberals	Young radicals	The Party's 'ginger group'

Social Democratic Party

Tawney Society	Party intellectuals	Similar to Labour Party Fabians

4.14   The Future of Party Politics in Britain

Three, or four, party politics now seems to be a reality and in the years to come is likely to have a profound effect on the British system. If the 'mould' is not yet broken it is certainly cracked.

The end of two party politics has constitutional implications and, eventually, may have an effect on the voting system. These matters will be discussed as we continue our study of the business of government.

One evident thing, however, is that parties are getting weaker rather than stronger. Their memberships are falling and their financial positions are less sound. While this is happening more and more people are looking to pressure groups, working outside the party system, for what they see as their political needs.

Questions and Assignments

1 What is a political party?
2 Why do two parties dominate British politics?
3 What are the main characteristics of the four British parties?
4 What do the four parties stand for?
5 From where do the four parties draw they finance?
6 Why are there pressure groups within parties?
7 Write, in not more than 500 words, the outline of a manifesto which could be used at the next general election to describe the policies of *either*
      the Conservative Party *or*
      the Labour Party.
8 Write a letter, in not more than 500 words, to a pen friend in the United States explaining the British party system.

Chapter 5

Voters and Elections

Parliamentary elections in Britain are based on single member constituencies and, as Parliament has a life limited to five years, a general election must be held within this period.

The minimum age for voting is 18 and to be a parliamentary candidate, 21.

Candidates are chosen by their constituency parties and are required to appoint election agents, who are responsible for the election campaign. A good agent, with a well organised team of workers, can be vital in winning an election.

The British voting system of first past the post is often criticised as being unfair because it tends to favour the larger parties and alternatives have been suggested. Most of the alternatives are based on the principle of proportional representation, which tries to match the percentage of votes cast for a party with the percentage of seats won. The main objection to a system of proportional representation is that it can result in weak governments. Although there is widespread support for electoral reform, the Conservative and Labour parties are both officially opposed to it.

5.1 Parliamentary Elections in Britain

To provide for the election of Members to the House of Commons the United Kingdom is divided into 650 **constituencies**, each returning one member. A constituency contains, on average, about 65000 electors. The size and shape of the constituencies are decided by four independent **Boundary Commissions**, which report regularly to recommend changes to keep them in line with population changes.

Each Parliament has a life of not more than five years so a **general election** must be held within that period or it will be automatically dissolved. At one time the maximum life was three and then seven years. In times of emergency, such as during the 1939–45 war, the life has been temporarily extended.

During this five year period the Prime Minister may ask the Monarch to dissolve Parliament but this request would normally only be made within about two years of the normal end of Parliament's life or if the government felt it was unable to obtain a majority of votes in the Commons. If the House of Commons passed a **vote of no confidence** in the government of the day the Prime Minister could immediately ask the House again for a formal vote of confidence and, if defeated a second time, would normally resign and ask for a dissolution.

When a Member leaves the House of Commons in between general elections a **by-election** is held. This will normally be the result of death or of the Member accepting what is called the Stewardship of the Chiltern Hundreds. This is an office of the Crown in name only but is the traditional way of resigning a seat.

5.2   Who are the Voters?

A voter in Britain must be 18 years of age or over, a British subject and be entered in the **electoral register** for a constituency. This register is compiled yearly. The people who are not eligible to vote are peers, aliens, prisoners serving prison sentences of more than 12 months for felony and anyone who has been convicted of corrupt practices at elections.

5.3   Who are the Candidates?

A parliamentary candidate must be a British subject, over the age of 21, and **nominated** by 10 electors, but not necessarily a resident of the constituency being fought.

Today, as we have already seen, it is virtually impossible to get elected as an independent MP so candidates need to be **adopted** by a political party.

It is, of course, possible to stand for election without party support and many people do, or they create their own party, as that frequent fighter of elections, Lord Sutch, has done with his one man Official Monster Raving Looney Party.

5.4   Selecting a Candidate

The first stage in the election process is to be chosen as a candidate by a constituency party.

In the Conservative Party the names of possible candidates can come from a central list held at Party headquarters, from personal sponsorship by a Party member, or simply by hopefuls putting their own names forward. In the Labour Party names can only be put forward by Party headquarters when there is a by-election. In general elections the involvement of headquarters is limited to providing a list of possible candidates for the constituency management committee to choose from.

If a seat is **safe**, in other words a party has a good chance of winning it, many names will be submitted. In this case a **short list** of possible candidates is drawn up and the people short listed appear before the constituency committee which makes the final decision.

5.5   Adopting a Candidate

The person selected has now been adopted by the constituency and from then on is the prospective candidate.

Once an election has been officially announced the candidate is nominated by having his or her name filed with the local **Returning Officer**, who is the local government officer responsible for running the election. To be nominated the candidate needs a proposer and seconder and eight additional sponsors, all registered locally as voters.

At the same time a deposit of £500 has to be made. If a candidate does not get at least 5% of the votes cast the deposit is forfeited. This is obviously intended to discourage frivolous candidates.

5.6   The Election Campaign

Nominated candidates are required by law to appoint an **election agent**, who, as we have already seen, can be full time or part time. It is an agent's job to run the campaign and to make sure that the limit of election expenses, laid down by law, is not exceeded. This ensures that wealthy candidates do not have an unfair advantage. The limit to election expenses is, however, confined to those of the candidate so enormous additional sums can be spent in national campaigns to promote the party

Each party will publish a **manifesto**, setting out the policies it will follow if it gets into government. Local agents produce their own leaflets based on points taken from the manifesto.

Nationally, the campaign is waged on radio and television, by press briefings and public meetings. The time for official party political broadcasts, on radio and television, is, by agreement between the parties and the broadcasting authorities, allocated in proportion to the number of MPs each party has at the time. In practice this clearly favours the larger parties.

At constituency level, the campaign is fought through public meetings, the distribution of leaflets, walkabouts by the candidate, and by **canvassing**. Parties attach great importance to canvassing, which means asking people how they intend to vote so as to estimate the support they are likely to get. By keeping lists of people who have said they will vote for their candidate, party workers can check at the entrance to polling stations to discover whether they have cast their votes, and, if they have not, can go to their houses to remind them and perhaps offer a lift to the polling station.

Running a successful campaign is a time consuming and tiring job but there is clear evidence that a good agent, backed by plenty of enthusiastic helpers, can make the difference between a candidate winning or losing. This is particularly true in **marginal constituencies**, where the gap between the first and second candidates is small.

On election day the polling stations, manned usually by local government officers recruited specially for the day, are open from seven in the morning until ten at night. An elector arriving at the polling station has his or her name checked off on the electoral register and is then given a voting card containing the names of all the candidates, in alphabetical order, with their parties. The voter then goes into a booth to mark X against the name of the chosen candidate. The card is then dropped into a sealed ballot box.

As soon as the polling stations are closed the ballot boxes are taken to a central point, usually a local school, where they are opened in the presence of the Returning Officer, and the candidates and their agents, and the votes on the slips are counted. People who expect to be away from home on polling day can vote by post. It is estimated that at a general election about half a million people vote in this way.

When all the votes have been counted the Returning Officer will declare the result. If the gap between the first and second candidates is small, the second candidate may ask for a recount. When everyone is satisfied with the result the candidate with the greatest number of votes will be declared the Member for that constituency.

5.7   The British Voting System

The system of voting in Britain is based on single member constituencies whereby the candidate who wins the largest share of the votes cast is automatically elected. It is usually called the **first past the post** system.

It has a number of merits. First, it is simple and easy to understand. Second, it keeps the election within one reasonably sized area, whereas some of the alternative methods require large, multi-member constituencies. Third, it usually produces a clear result in party terms.

It has disadvantages however. First, it favours the large parties at the expense of the smaller. Second, it cannot guarantee to produce a result whereby the percentage of votes cast for a party is broadly the same as the number of seats won. Third, in some constituencies electors may feel that the chance of their preferred candidate being elected is so small that they do not even bother to vote and so are disaffected. Figure 5.1 illustrates some of these disadvantages very well.

Fig. 5.1

Parties' Share of Commons Votes and
Seats in General Elections: 1945 – 1983

	Conservatives			Labour			Lib/Alliance*			Total	
	Votes		Seats	Votes		Seats	Votes		Seats	Votes	Seats
	(m)	%		(m)	%		(m)			(m)	
1945	9.6	40	213	11.6	48	393	2.2	9	12	32.8	640
1950	12.5	43	299	13.3	46	315	2.6	9	9	34.3	625
1951	13.7	48	321	13.9	49	295	0.7	2	6	34.6	625
1955	13.3	50	345	12.4	46	277	0.7	3	6	34.9	630
1959	13.7	49	365	12.2	44	258	1.6	6	6	35.4	630
1964	12.0	43	304	12.2	44	317	3.1	11	9	35.9	630
1966	11.4	42	253	13.1	48	363	2.3	8	12	36.0	630
1970	13.1	46	330	12.2	43	288	2.1	7	6	39.3	630
1974a	11.9	38	297	11.6	37	301	6.1	19	14	39.8	635
1974b	10.5	36	277	11.5	39	319	6.3	18	13	40.1	635
1979	13.7	44	339	11.5	37	269	4.3	14	11	41.1	635
1983	13.0	42	397	8.5	28	209	7.8	25	23	42.2	650

* Alliance fought its first general election in 1983
a February election   b October election

5.8   A Fairer Voting System?

Some critics argue that the first past the post method of voting is undemocratic. If the purpose of an election is to achieve as near to equality of the votes cast with the seats won, it is. If its purpose is to ensure that as many voters as possible get the MP of their choice then in some constituencies they do but in others they do not. If its purpose is to produce a clear result then it generally does. What is certain is that it would be possible to produce a fairer voting system, if that is what the majority of people want.

In the 1983 general election each Conservative MP was elected on the basis of less than 40000 votes, each Labour MP on rather more than 40000 votes, and each Alliance MP was backed by about 338000 votes. A fairer system, it is argued, would be based on the principle of **proportional representation (PR)**, which literally means securing a close relationship between votes cast and seats won. Let us look at a number of systems of PR and how they work in practice.

5.9   The Alternative Vote

The **alternative vote (AV)** is not theoretically a form of proportional representation in that it cannot guarantee a close relationship between votes and seats and, indeed, can sometimes produce surprising results. It does, however, go some way towards making the voting system fairer and is relatively simple and easy to understand. It is used, for example, in Australia.

It uses single member constituencies and the voter chooses a candidate by marking 1 against his name on the ballot paper. If he wants, he can also mark 2 against his second choice and so on, but this is not compulsory. First preference votes are then counted and if any one candidate collects more than 50% of all the votes cast he is automatically elected. If this does not happen the candidate with the least number of first choice votes is eliminated and the second preferences of those who chose him as No 1 are distributed among the other candidates. This process continues until one candidate emerges with 50+ %.

The main objection to AV is that it tends to help compromise candidates and Australian experience suggests that its results can sometimes be quite unpredictable, with the successful candidate being someone whom very few people want. Critics of it say that if we are to change our voting system we might as well choose something that is theoretically fairer.

5.10   The Second Ballot

The **second ballot** is a system used in France and is similar to AV.
A first past the post election is held and if no one gets more than
50% of the total vote, the candidate with the least votes is
eliminated and a second election is held within the next 10 days.

This system does not seem to be much better than AV and is
more costly to operate.

5.11   The Party List System

The **party list system** is used widely in Western Europe. The first
stage is the production of lists of candidates by each of the political
parties fighting the election. Each list shows names in descending
order of preference, as chosen by the party. An elector merely
votes for the party of his choice and then seats are allocated to each
party according to the total proportion of votes received. Thus a
party winning 30% of the votes would be entitled to 30% of the
seats and enough names would be taken from the party's list to fill
those seats.

Like AV, the party list system is not strictly speaking full PR. It
also tends to make the election very impersonal. Various formulae
have, therefore, been devised to adjust the AV method so that the
relationship between the candidate and the voter is more direct.

5.12   The Additional-Member System

The **additional-member system** makes use of party lists and is
used in West Germany for elections to the federal parliament, the
Bundestag. The elector casts two votes, one for a candidate and
one for the party of his choice. Half the Bundestag is then elected
just like the House of Commons in Britain and the other half, using
the party lists, is chosen so that the membership of the chamber
accurately reflects the national vote. The party lists, therefore, are
used to correct any unfairness in the first past the post system.

The main advantage of the additional-member system is that it
uses single member constituencies and so keeps the link between
the candidate and the elector. In 1976 the Hansard Society
recommended electoral reform in Britain based on this system, but
with the additional members coming not from party lists but from
the 'second bests' of the defeated candidates in each party.

5.13 The Single Transferable Vote

The **single transferable vote (STV)** is theoretically the best method of ensuring proportional representation and is used by many professional bodies in Britain and for district council elections in Northern Ireland.

The system uses multi-member constituencies but they can be as small as three members. All the candidates are listed on the ballot form, usually in alphabetical order, and the elector states his order of preference, from 1, 2 downwards. All the votes cast are counted and the 'electoral quota' is calculated, in other words, the minimum number of votes needed to be elected. The calculation is as follows:

$$\frac{\text{total number of votes}}{\text{number of seats} + 1} = \text{electoral quota}$$

Thus, in a three-member constituency with a total of 120 000 votes cast, the quota would be:

$$\frac{120\,000}{3 + 1} = 30\,000$$

and any candidate with 30 000 or more first preference votes would automatically be elected.

Let us suppose that of 12 candidates for the three seats only one obtained more than the 30 000 quota, in fact 31 000, or 1000 more than was needed. All the second preferences of voters who made him their first choice would be counted and their percentage distribution among the other candidates calculated. The 1000 'surplus' votes would then be redistributed on this percentage basis. If this redistribution brought another candidate up to to the 30 000 quota he or she would be elected and the process would be continued until all three seats were filled. If all the surplus second preference votes were used up and there were still seats to be filled then the bottom candidates would be progressively eliminated, with their second preferences redistributed among the other candidates on a proportionate basis.

5.14 Prospects for Electoral Reform

If there is electoral reform in Britain then STV is the most likely choice. Although the Hansard Society favoured the additional-member system it did not rule out STV. After considerable debate, the Liberal/SDP Alliance agreed to reform based on STV and there is support for it in all parties, although both the Conservative and Labour leaderships oppose it. In 1983 an all-party initiative 'The Campaign for Fair Votes' was launched but has not had a great impact.

The prospects of a third major party in Britain would be improved if PR were introduced and two party politics might become a thing of the past. It is understandable, therefore, that neither the Conservative nor Labour party would want to support such a change.

If at some point in the future a general election produced a **hung Parliament**, with no party winning a clear majority of seats, then PR might be put forward as the price for Liberal/SDP support of a minority Conservative or Labour government.

Questions and Assignments

1 What are the qualifications for voting in parliamentary elections in Britain?
2 What are the qualifications for being a candidate?
3 How are candidates adopted by the political parties?
4 What is meant by proportional representation?
5 What are the differences between the alternative vote, the second ballot, the party list system and the additional member system?
6 Exactly how does the single transferable vote operate?
7 Imagine you are a parliamentary candidate for the Conservative **or** the Labour **or** the Alliance party and write, in not more than 300 words, an election leaflet you would distribute to electors in your constituency.
8 This is a group exercise. Conduct an election, using six candidates, by secret ballot, based on the first past the post system and then on the single transferable vote and compare the results.

PART II

THE CENTRAL
GOVERNMENT PROCESS

Chapter 6
The Constitutional Foundations

Britain does not have a written constitution in the form of a single document. It is based instead on a number of documents, mainly Acts of Parliament, and a series of established practices, called conventions.

The legislative, executive and judicial powers are not kept separate as they are in many countries with written constitutions, such as the United States, but they are to some extent balanced against each other.

The most important single feature of the British constitution is what is called the supremacy of Parliament. This means that Parliament can pass or repeal any law it wishes and can override judicial decisions if it chooses. This makes the British Prime Minister and Cabinet potentially the most powerful in the world because, as long as they control a majority in the House of Commons, they can make any laws they like. There are, however, some practical limitations, notably legislation passed by the European Community.

6.1   The British Constitution

As we have already seen, Britain does not have a written constitution. It does not have a single document called a constitution but it does have a number of documents which over the years have acquired a constitutional importance.

In legal terms one Act of Parliament is no more important than another but in reality there are some which have, in effect, created the framework of the unwritten constitution. The Bill of Rights of 1688 laid down the powers of Parliament in relation to the Monarch. The Act of Settlement of 1701 carried this a stage further. The Parliament Act of 1911 restricted the powers of the

59

House of Lords and the Parliament Act of 1949 limited them further still.

In an earlier chapter we looked briefly at conventions, the unwritten understandings which bring flexibility to the constitution, and we also noted the doctrine of the supremacy of Parliament, which allows constitutional change to be carried out by simply passing an ordinary piece of legislation. In this chapter we will look at these and other aspects a little more closely as a prelude to our examination of the central government process which is the hub of the business of government.

As we do so we will realise that the British constitution is, to use an everyday expression 'double glazed'. In other words, it has two layers of institutions. It is a monarchy, which can be traced back by direct descent to King Egbert of the 9th century, but it is also a modern democracy. The 19th century writer, Walter Bagehot, who was at one time editor of 'The Economist' newspaper, in his celebrated book *The English Constitution*, described these two layers as the formal, or 'dignified', parts and the informal, or 'efficient' parts. The Queen represents the dignified parts and the Cabinet, led by the Prime Minister, the efficient. Thus we will see that many things which are done by the Crown are really the decisions of the government of the day.

6.2   Constitutional Conventions

Many of these conventions are concerned with this relationship between the Crown, as the formal head of the executive, and the Prime Minister and Cabinet, as the effective head. In a later chapter we will see how, by convention, cabinet government as we know it today evolved.

Some conventions are quite old, such as the Crown choosing a government from the party which has a majority in the House of Commons. Others are more recent, such as always having an MP from the opposition party as chairman of the Public Accounts Committee in the Commons.

Conventions are very much part of what Bagehot called the 'efficient' parts of the constitution. They make it work in practice. They give it flexibility. They provide the oil which lubricates the machinery of government.

If for practical purposes some aspect of government needs to change,a convention can be dropped or a new one added, but this will never be done lightly. It will be years before a new practice can be properly called a convention and the disappearance of one will also be a long, drawn out process. The British constitution is flexible but it is based on continuity rather than change.

6.3 The Separation of Powers

All constitutions of democratic countries have to deal with the allocation of power within a state and the three basic sources are the law making or **legislative** power, the **judicial** power and the **executive** power. Many constitutions, and that of the United States is a good example, try to keep these powers separate, so that no single person or group can control all three and have virtually unlimited power. As well as separating them, constitutions also try to balance one against the other, so that if the executive tries to do too much either the legislative or judicial power will block it. This process is usually called the balance or **separation of powers**.

In Britain the powers are not really separated. The executive, in the shape of the Prime Minister and government, is part of the legislature in Parliament and even the judiciary is partly based in Parliament. But there is a balancing of the powers in that those Members of the House of Commons who are not in government, in other words those in opposition and the backbenchers in the government party, can, if they choose to, block government policy, and even throw out the government. Although this happens rarely, mainly because of the loyalty of backbenchers to their party, and the government's inbuilt majority, the fact remains that the power is there if needed. There was a dramatic occasion in 1940, in the early years of the Second World War, when the Prime Minister, Neville Chamberlain so completely lost the confidence of the House of Commons that a Member of his own party, expressing the views of the whole House, said 'you have stayed in this place too long' and a vote of no confidence was passed. Chamberlain resigned and was replaced by Winston Churchill.

6.4 The Supremacy of Parliament

It is convenient to restate now the doctrine of the supremacy of Parliament because it is probably the most important feature of the British constitution. It is sometimes referred to as the sovereignty of Parliament. They are both the same thing.

By the supremacy of Parliament we mean that only Parliament has the right to make laws and this right is supreme and unlimited.

It can pass any laws it likes. It can repeal any law which it has made itself. It can override a judge's decision by making something he declared unlawful lawful, or something he said was lawful unlawful.

In 1971 Parliament passed the Industrial Relations Act for the Conservative government led by Edward Heath. One of the first things done by the Labour government of Harold Wilson, when it returned to power in 1974, was to repeal this Act and bring in legislation more sympathetic towards the trade unions. Soon after the Conservative government of Margaret Thatcher came into office in 1979 it repealed the Labour government's legislation and brought in its own.

The supremacy of Parliament makes the British government potentially the most powerful in the Western World because, as long as it has a majority in the House of Commons, a government can make and unmake any laws it wants. Some years ago the present Lord Chancellor, Lord Hailsham, described this unbridled power as 'an elective dictatorship'.

There are, however, some limitations on Parliament's power, most of which have international implications.

For example, Parliament cannot make changes which would affect the status of the Monarch or the line of succession without the approval of those Commonwealth countries which still accept the Queen as their head of state. Nor can Parliament pass a law which contravenes international law. If there is a conflict between British and European Community legislation the courts in Britain have agreed to give priority to Community law.

Questions and Assignments

1 What did Walter Bagehot mean by the 'dignified' and 'efficient' parts of government?
2 Give two examples of constitutional conventions.
3 What is meant by the separation of powers?
4 Are the powers separate in Britain?
5 What is meant by the supremacy of Parliament?
6 What practical limitations are there on the powers of Parliament?
7 Write a short article, of not more than 600 words, for a local newspaper or journal explaining that the British constitution is unwritten and showing what advantages this brings.
8 Explain what changes would have to take place if Britain became a republic.

Chapter 7

The Monarchy

Britain has a constitutional Monarch in the form of a hereditary head of state who reigns but does not rule. In other words, the monarchy is expected to operate within the bounds of the constitution.

The elected government acts in the name of the Crown and the personal powers which the Monarch used to have are now almost entirely used on the advice of the Prime Minister and the government. These are called the prerogative powers, and are formally used, on the Queen's behalf, by members of the Privy Council. Membership of the Privy Council is sometimes given as an honour to distinguished people but for practical purposes all Cabinet ministers are automatically made members. On taking up membership they are required to take the oath of secrecy and allegiance, and their membership is then held for life.

The Monarch has a close relationship with the government of the day, receiving all Cabinet papers and meeting the Prime Minister weekly for a report on the government's activities. It is at these weekly meetings that the Queen is said to have a constitutional right to be consulted, to advise and to warn, but there is a well established convention that any details of the conversations between the head of state and the head of government will never be made public.

The British monarchy is generally well respected in the outside world as well as being of great interest to visitors from overseas. Quite separate from her role as British head of state, the Queen is also head of the Commonwealth.

About 85% of the cost of the British monarchy is met from public funds but an objective observer would probably say that the nation gets value for money.

7.1   A Constitutional Monarchy

Britain has a constitutional Monarch carrying out the duties of head of state and leaving those of head of government to the Prime Minister. The role of constitutional monarch should not be seen as merely ceremonial although to the man and woman in the street this may be what it mainly appears to be.

The essence of the Queen's position within the constitution is that she provides the stability and continuity which seldom exists in politics. After all, it was a former Prime Minister, Harold Wilson, who once remarked that 'a week in politics is a long time'. Politicians come and go, making a greater or lesser mark on the nation's history, but the monarchy remains, providing a steadying influence as well as a focal point for the nation's patriotism.

Democracy is preserved in that the Monarch must always act within the framework of the constitution and must not only be above politics but must be clearly seen to be. The 'constitutional crisis', over a supposed disagreement between the Queen and Prime Minister about economic sanctions against South Africa, which some newspapers tried to create in the summer of 1986, emphasised, rather than questioned, the Sovereign's political neutrality. The Queen, as a person, may well hold strong political views but they are never revealed to the outside world.

7.2   The Royal Prerogative

The **royal prerogative** is the term used to describe the powers which have been left in the hands of the Monarch. At one time, of course, the Monarch was absolute and anything which he or she decreed was automatically the law of the land. Over the years, mainly because of the need for money, royal powers were transferred to Parliament so that they are now virtually only used at the request of the government of the day. These prerogative powers are used in the name of the Crown so when the Crown acts it is the government, led by the Prime Minister, which is really doing so.

The importance of the prerogative powers is that they can be used legally without needing to obtain the formal consent of Parliament, thus speeding up the time to take executive decisions, and allowing the government greater freedom of action.

Under prerogative powers the Crown can: enter into diplomatic relations with other states, or break them off; make treaties; control the armed forces; declare war; conclude peace; appoint judges; start criminal proceedings; pardon offenders; summon and dissolve Parliament; appoint the Prime Minister and other ministers; confer honours; create peers; and appoint Church of England bishops.

In reality, of course, all these powers are exercised by the government in the name of the Crown. Foreign affairs are in the hands of the Prime Minister, the Foreign Secretary and the Cabinet. Judges are appointed on the advice of the Prime Minister, who is, in turn, advised by the Lord Chancellor. Ministers are appointed on the advice of the Prime Minister and it is only on very rare occasions that the Monarch would have to make a choice for the holder of the top political office. Peers and bishops are also appointed on the Prime Minister's advice. Pardons are granted on the advice of the Home Secretary.

The Prime Minister has responsibility for recommending people for honours but the list of those to be rewarded for political services is first vetted by a group of three Privy Counsellors who are not members of the government. There are a few honours which are still personally awarded by the Queen: the Order of the Garter, the Order of Merit and the Royal Victorian Order.

7.3 The Privy Council

The usual way of using prerogative powers is by making an **Order in Council** and the body which formally approves an Order is the **Privy Council**. The Privy Council started with a small group of personal advisers to the Monarch during the 17th century.

Today, membership of the Council is given either as an honour or for convenience. As an honour it enjoys a high reputation and is granted relatively rarely. For convenience, all members of the Cabinet are sworn in as Privy Counsellors and are required to take the oath of secrecy and allegiance to the Crown. Past members of the Cabinet remain Privy Counsellors for the rest of their lives and are addressed in the House of Commons as the 'Right Honourable Member'. The total number of members of the Council today is about 300.

The royal assent to legislation and the formal approval of executive acts, using prerogative powers, are given in the name of the Crown by a small group of Privy Counsellors drawn from the government of the day.

The Privy Council Office, in Whitehall, London, is the administrative headquarters. Its political head, who is a member of the Cabinet, is the Lord President of the Council.

7.4　The Queen and the Government

The Queen receives all the important state papers, including those for the Cabinet. It seems certain that she does not see this as just a formality and actually reads them. She, therefore, knows as much about the government's business as the Prime Minister and probably more than other ministers, heavily involved in the work of their own departments. The Queen also has the advantage of continuity compared with the relatively short periods of office of the Prime Ministers with whom she deals.

She meets the Prime Minister once a week, when she is told about the activities of the government. In his study of the English constitution, Bagehot said that the Monarch has three rights in her relations with the Prime Minister: **the right to be consulted, the right to encourage, and the right to warn**. Much, of course, will depend on the circumstances but, again, there is evidence that the Queen does at times genuinely make use of these rights.

What actually takes place at the weekly audiences is, of course, kept absolutely secret. There is a well established convention that neither the Palace nor Downing Street will reveal anything. It is therefore left to the media to speculate on what goes on and on the warmth, or otherwise, of the relationship between Monarch and Prime Minister.

In her early years on the throne, the Queen had the benefit of guidance and advice from a man who was virtually an 'elder statesman' as well as Prime Minister, Sir Winston Churchill. Since then she has dealt with a variety of chief ministers and although the press write about her affection for Sir Alec Douglas Home, or her amusement at the gossiping of Harold Wilson, or her good relationship with James Callaghan, or the coolness between her and Margaret Thatcher, it is, of course, all pure speculation.

Day to day business between the Monarch and the Prime Minister is conducted by the respective offices in Buckingham Palace, or whichever royal residence is being used, and No 10 Downing Street. The Queen's closest adviser is her Private Secretary and relations with the media are in the hands of her Press Secretary. The Prime Minister also has a Private Office and a Press Secretary. Another important source of advice is the Cabinet Secretary. It is these officials who are expected to keep the machinery of communication running smoothly.

7.5　The Monarchy and the Outside World

Internationally, it is undeniable that the British monarchy is highly respected. It is the most successful surviving royal house in the world and has probably done something to make constitutional monarchies acceptable even in countries with left-of-centre governments, such as in Spain.

The Queen is also the head of the Commonwealth and this position is quite separate from that of British head of state. In this role, although she will obviously listen to the views of her ministers, she knows she has a far wider responsibility than that of the government in London. A decision by the British government to leave the Commonwealth or to disband it could, therefore, have serious constitutional implications.

On a more mundane note, the royal family is undoubtedly one of Britain's major tourist attractions, drawing people from all over the world to witness the great state occasions.

7.6   The Cost of the Monarchy

About 85% of the cost of the monarchy is publicly funded. Most of it is paid in an annual allocation by Parliament called the **civil list**. The civil list is intended to cover the cost of all the public duties associated with the monarchy. In 1985 it amounted to £3.98 million. In addition, the government pays for the upkeep of the royal yacht, the Queen's Flight, which is the name given to the aircraft used by the royal family, travel by train and the maintenance of the royal palaces.

Members of the royal family, other than the Queen herself and the Prince of Wales, receive annual allowances. The Prince of Wales obtains his income from the revenues of the Duchy of Lancaster, of which he is the hereditary owner. He keeps three quarters of this money and passes the remaining quarter to the Exchequer. The Queen's personal expenses as Monarch come from the **privy purse**. which is another form of hereditary income. Her private expenses, as an individual, come from her own resources.

All this may seem to be a high price to pay for what some cynics have described as a 'royal fairyland'. This expenditure must, however, be balanced against what a presidency would cost, because the pomp attached to a head of state would still be expected. Also, the 'hidden income' of the monarchy as a tourist attraction must also be included. On balance, most objective observers would probably say that the British people get value for money.

7.7   An Assessment of the Monarchy

A major advantage of having a hereditary Monarch is that the choice of head of state is kept out of politics. Because of this it can retain the mystique that this high office demands.

The monarchy has always had, and always will have, its critics because it is an institution which, by its very nature, is unable to answer back publicly. It has, however, largely done what it was intended to do: guarantee stability in the nation's affairs; encourage a sense of patriotism; give an example of responsible family values; and provide an ultimate check on the possible excesses of politicians.

If there were a referendum tomorrow on whether or not Britain should become a republic there can be no doubt that the public would vote for the retention of the monarchy.

Questions and Assignments

1 What is meant by a constitutional monarchy?
2 What is the royal prerogative?
3 Name six examples of prerogative powers.
4 What is the Privy Council?
5 What did Bagehot say were the rights of the Queen in relation to her ministers?
6 How is the British monarchy financed?
7 'If the royal family did not exist it would have to be invented'. Write an essay, of not more than 600 words, saying why you agree *or* disagree with this statement.
   Or the statement can be used as the basis for a debate, with one person, with a seconder, arguing for it and another two against it.
8 Take cuttings from a selection of newspapers over the past two weeks which make reference to the activities of the royal family, and analyse them on the basis of:
   1 whether they provide information about what they do as part of a constitutional monarchy, *or*
   2 whether they merely provide gossip.
   Present your conclusions in the form of the percentage of coverage which falls into category 1 and the percentage into category 2.

Chapter 8

The Judicial Process

Most democratic systems of government are based on the rule of law, but, in practice, although everyone may live under the same laws, some people are more privileged than others because of their backgrounds or wealth.

Justice is an ideal more than a reality, because it is difficult for people to agree on what is just or unjust, but the judicial process in Britain, and most democratic countries, does try to follow what are called the rules of natural justice.

In England and Wales there are two main sources of law: common law, which can be traced back to ancient customs, and legislation, passed by Parliament. It is the task of the judiciary to interpret and apply these laws.

A distinction is also made between civil and criminal law. Civil law applies when an individual has been injured in some way and seeks compensation. Criminal law is used when someone has committed an offence against society in general and needs to be punished.

The system of courts is based on this distinction, from the lower courts which deal with minor offences or small claims to the higher courts which deal with serious crimes or major actions for compensation. There is an appeals system built into the courts' structure, with the House of Lords as the final court of appeal.

For minor criminal offences people are normally tried by magistrates without a jury but for more serious contraventions they are tried by a jury with a judge presiding. Since almost anyone can be called to serve, the jury system is one of the most democratic, as well as one of the oldest, forms of obtaining justice.

Britain is one of the few countries in the world which has two kinds of practising lawyer: solicitors, who operate mainly in the lower courts, and barristers, who specialise in the higher courts, but critics say that this duplication is wasteful and unnecessary.

69

The judiciary is very conscious of the need to maintain its independence so judges have guaranteed salaries and are protected against political interference. There are, however, critics of the judicial process who argue that the Lord Chancellor, as head of the judiciary, is too powerful in his ability to appoint judges, and, because of his position as a member of the Cabinet, not politically neutral.

The high cost of going to court is also frequently criticised and the legal aid system has done little to blunt this criticism.

8.1   The Rule of Law

Countries which claim to be democracies usually pride themselves on living under the rule of law, and Britain is no exception. The idea of respecting the law, as opposed to the will of an individual, can be traced back in Britain to the rebellion of the barons against King John's personal rule. The outcome, of course, was the signing of the Magna Carta, at Runnymede.

The law which the barons wanted John to accept consisted of the old practices and customs which had developed over the years and become accepted as 'the law of the land'. These customs eventually became the basis of the common law of England.

The modern interpretation of the rule of law was set out in its clearest form, at the end of the 19th century, by an eminent constitutional lawyer, Professor A V Dicey, in a book called *Introduction to Study of Law and of Constitution*.

Dicey identified three features which he said guaranteed personal freedom within the constitution:

1 The absence of arbitrary power. In other words, governments and officials should only use their powers if they can show they have legal authority for doing so.
2 No one, whatever his position in life, is above the law. In other words, there is not one law for the rich and another for the poor, or one law for the official and another for the man in the street.
3 Individual rights are not guaranteed by some special law, as they might be in a written constitution. They are part of the ordinary law of the land.

Dicey was writing in the 19th century and was himself a strong believer in personal freedom. During his lifetime the activities of the state were very limited. Nowadays the business of government is vast.

If the underprivileged are to be helped then the better off will, inevitably, have to give up some of their privileges. If social and economic progress is to be made then some aspects of individual freedom are bound to suffer. A new airport may help the majority but harm a minority. A new motorway will be welcomed by the motorist but opposed by the environmentalist.

Some people will find certain laws objectionable and will not be placated by being told that the laws they object to have been properly made. So, although the principles of the rule of law may be fair, to some people the law itself may seem unfair.

Dicey's explanation of the rule of law said that no man should be above the law and that it should apply to everyone, regardless of his position in life. This sounds splendid in theory but in practice may be quite different.

The rich man who can afford an expensive lawyer will be better placed in presenting his case than the poor man. Indeed, the cost of litigation, as going to law is called, may be so great that some people will not even bother to pursue a claim.

Then we should not forget that Parliament is supreme and can make or unmake any law it chooses. It would be foolish to think that every Act of Parliament is perfect. Some Acts clearly benefit some people more than others. Some seem intended to protect the government itself. The Official Secrets Acts, which we shall look at in more detail later, have been condemned by politicians of all parties but are still part of the law of the land.

So, however valid the rule of law may be in theory, we should look cautiously at its practical implications. This is not to deny that it is an important and valuable concept.

8.2 Justice

Justice is a word as much used or misused as other words such as freedom, liberty or democracy. What might seem as just by one person could be seen as unjust by another, and yet we speak of the courts dispensing justice as if it were a certain and concrete commodity. We should, therefore, not become too obsessed about the meaning of the word and look more at how the idea, or concept, of justice operates in practice.

The courts of law in Britain have long operated on the basis of observing what are called the rules of **natural justice**, which apply and extend the concept of the rule of law. These rules contain four essential elements:

1 that no one should be a judge in his own case;
2 that, before a decision is taken, each side in a dispute should have an opportunity to present its case;
3 that both sides should be entitled to know the reasons why a decision has been reached;
4 that the decision should be based on the evidence presented to the court, and not on other factors.

These rules seek to achieve justice in a practical way and provide a better chance of ensuring a fair trial than any theoretical discussion of what is just or unjust.

8.3   What is the Law?

There are two main sources of law in England and Wales, **common law** and **statute law**. Common law is the law of custom and practice which has developed over the years and statute law is the law made by Parliament.

Both kinds of law are dealt with in the courts and have to be interpreted by judges. So as to avoid wild variations in their judgements, they try to be reasonably consistent and follow the practice of what is called **judicial precedent**. In other words, a judge, in trying to decide what the law actually means, will take into consideration decisions of judges in other cases. The collection of decisions, or judgements, of this kind is called **case law**.

Thus the law which the rule of law refers to comes partly from Parliament, partly from the common law and partly from the decisions of judges in cases they have tried.

8.4   Civil and Criminal Law

The courts have to deal with two kinds of law, **civil** and **criminal**. The difference between the two is based less on what people have done and more on what legal proceedings result from their actions.

If the purpose of taking someone to court is to punish them, then there should be a **criminal prosecution**. If the purpose is to obtain compensation then there should be a **civil action**.

Criminal cases are prosecuted by the Crown, or a public authority, because someone has offended against society at large. Civil cases are brought by the person who has suffered some injury to his person, his property or his reputation.

The penalties which are imposed in criminal cases are **fines**, which are paid into public funds, or **imprisonment**. The penalties in civil cases are **damages**, awarded to the person bringing the case.

The man in the street does not always appreciate the differences between the two types of law. A classic example is the frequently seen notice 'Trespassers will be prosecuted'. Normally trespassing, meaning intruding on to someone's property, is a civil offence which could result in an action for damages. It would be a criminal offence if there was an Act of Parliament which forbade anyone to enter some particular area or building, such as a defence establishment.

8.5 The Law Courts in England and Wales

Scottish law is different from English law in certain respects and so is the system of courts. Figure 8.1 gives a broad outline of the courts in England and Wales.

Magistrates' Courts are concerned with minor, or **petty**, criminal offences, for some of which a defendant, if he pleads guilty, may not even need to make a court appearance. They are

Fig. 8.1

The Court System in England and Wales

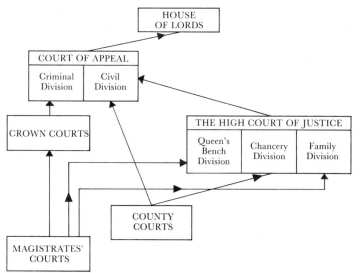

called courts of **summary jurisdiction**, which means that cases are heard without a jury. For more serious crimes an accused person will be **indicted** and tried before a jury in a higher court, with a judge presiding.

In the large towns and cities the magistrate will be a professional, paid **stipendiary**. Elsewhere, cases will be heard by two or more unpaid, non-professional magistrates called **Justices of the Peace** (JPs). They will be advised by a full time, professional Clerk.

County Courts hear civil actions for relatively small claims. Larger claims go to the High Court. County Courts were established in 1846 and, despite their name, have nothing to do with counties. Cases are normally heard by a judge sitting alone, but occasionally there may also be a jury.

Crown Courts have replaced the old Assizes and deal with serious criminal cases. There are six Crown Court regions, covering the whole of England and Wales, with a number of Courts in each. The presiding judge will often be one who travels, **on circuit**, to each Court in the region but the most serious crimes, such as murder, will always be tried by a High Court judge.

Crown Courts deal with indictable offences and cases will therefore be heard by a jury, with a judge presiding. Probably the best known Crown Court is the Central Criminal Court in London, popularly known as the Old Bailey.

The **High Court of Justice** deals with civil cases where substantial sums are involved. It operates in three Divisions.

The **Queen's Bench Division** hears mainly cases of contract or tort. If someone has promised to do something and fails to honour his promise he may well have broken a contract and could be sued. If someone who does not have a contract nevertheless acts in a way which harms you he may well have committed a tort. The Queen's Bench Division is presided over by the Lord Chief Justice.

The **Chancery Division** is concerned with estates and bankruptcy. The Lord Chancellor is its formal president but, because of his many other duties, he normally delegates the work to another High Court judge.

The **Family Division** is concerned mainly with petitions for divorce and sometimes disputes over wills. It is normally presided over by a High Court judge, but some cases are heard outside London by one of the circuit judges.

The **Court of Appeal** has two Divisions, one dealing with criminal and the other with civil appeals. As the name of the Court implies, it 'rehears' cases which have originally been tried in a lower court and in which one of the parties concerned has disputed the result.

The **Criminal Division** hears appeals from the Crown Courts. It is presided over by the Lord Chief Justice, with at least two other High Court judges.

The **Civil Division** hears appeals from the County Courts and the High Court. It is presided over by the Master of the Rolls, assisted by 14 Lord Justices of Appeal. They sit in odd numbers, with a minimum of three, and reach decisions by a majority vote.

The House of Lords, sitting as a **Judicial Committee** is the final court of appeal, hearing appeals from the Court of Appeal and the High Court. Its members are the Lord Chancellor, the 10 Lords of Appeal in Ordinary, usually called the Law Lords, any ex-Lord Chancellors and any other peers who have been judges. The minimum number at a sitting is three.

The dotted lines in Figure 8.1 show the various appeal routes which are available.

8.6 The Scottish Legal System

Scotland has kept a legal system which differs from that in England and Wales in several respects, and these differences are reflected in the distinctive court structure. Figure 8.2 gives an outline of this structure.

Scotland is divided into 12 **Sheriffdoms**, each with a **Sheriff**, supported by **Sheriffs-Substitute** who deal with much of the normal work of the **Sheriff Courts**. On the civil side the Sheriff Court is the Scottish equivalent of the County Court. Appeals from the Sheriff Courts can be made to the Sheriff himself, in the case of small claims, or to the **Court of Session**.

The Court of Session is the supreme civil court. It consists of an **Outer House**, with 5 judges, and an **Inner House**, of 10 judges, sitting in two divisions. Appeals against decisions of the Inner House can be made to the House of Lords.

Petty criminal cases are heard by **Police Courts** in the burghs and **Justice of the Peace Courts** in the counties. Most crimes are, however, tried by the Sheriff, sitting alone or, in serious cases, with a jury.

The highest criminal court is the **High Court of Justiciary**, consisting of the **Lord Justice General**, who is also Lord President of the Court of Session, the **Lord Justice Clerk** and the other 14

Fig. 8.2

The Court System in Scotland

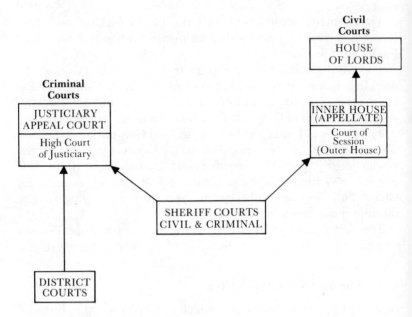

judges of the Court of Session. The High Court of Justiciary is based in Edinburgh, but judges also go out on circuit. There is no appeal from it to the House of Lords.

A feature of the Scottish system is the intermixing of the judiciary in the civil and criminal sides of justice.

8.7   Juries

The **jury system** represents one of the oldest, and in theory one of the most democratic, methods of obtaining justice.

Most people, between the ages of 18 and 65, who are on the electoral register are liable to be called for jury service. Peers, judges, barristers, solicitors and clergymen are exempt. People who have recently been convicted of a criminal offence resulting in more than three months' imprisonment may be disqualified, while those who have received prison sentences of more than five years are permanently disqualified.

Juries are more common in criminal than civil cases and consist of 12 people, except in County Court cases where there may be between 7 and 11. All members of a jury must be unknown to the person who is accused.

Jury members receive allowances for travel and subsistence and are sometimes housed in an hotel overnight, at public expense, when they need more time to reach a verdict. At one time their verdicts had to be unanimous but now, in certain circumstances, the presiding judge may be willing to accept a majority decision.

Although the jury system seems, on the surface, to be almost ideally democratic, it has its critics. How juries actually reach their verdicts is kept secret and there are suspicions that sometimes a few strong minded members, or even one, can influence the rest unfairly. Also, the whole jury can be swayed by a brilliant counsel, able to appeal to their emotions.

Nevertheless, there have been examples of brave, independent juries who have produced verdicts which seem based on plain, practical justice rather than on what the law might traditionally demand. The case of Clive Ponting, who was prosecuted under the Official Secrets Act and acquitted by a jury, is, perhaps, one example of this.

8.8   The Legal Profession

Britain is one of very few countries in the world, two others being South Africa and Sri Lanka, which have two different types of practising lawyer, **solicitors** and **barristers**.

Solicitors qualify by passing examinations set by the **Law Society**, which is a professional association, examining body and trade union, all rolled into one. Solicitors deal directly with the public and act as agents for barristers. A solictor cannot operate in the higher courts, which are the preserve of the barrister.

A barrister is a specialist lawyer who gains entry to the profession by passing what are called **Bar examinations** and becoming a member of one of the four **Inns of Court**: Inner Temple, Middle Temple, Lincoln's Inn or Gray's Inn. They are all in central London, not far from the Strand, where the Law Courts are located. The four Inns date back to mediaeval times and have the environment of colleges where young lawyers learn from senior colleagues who guide them in their studies, like Oxford or Cambridge tutors. In court they are referred to as **counsel** and address each other as 'my learned friend'. John Mortimer's

Rumpole of the Bailey is perhaps the most popular image of a barrister in Britain today.

After he has been practising for 10 years or more a barrister may, at the invitation of the Lord Chancellor's office, apply to 'take silk' and become a senior barrister, or **Queen's Counsel** (QC). The expression taking silk is used because, on becoming a QC, a barrister exchanges his gown of coarse stuff, or fabric, for one of silk. QCs form the top echelon of the legal profession and High Court judges are normally recruited from their ranks.

Together, solicitors and barristers constitute a powerful trade union and pressure group, maintaining a monopoly of the legal profession more complete than would be acceptable in the world of business.

The differences between the two branches of the profession, other than those already mentioned, lie in their different approaches to law. The training of solicitors, and the examinations they take, put stress on exact detail and down-to-earth information. The barrister, on the other hand, takes a broader, almost philosophical, view, although he will, eventually, become a specialist in some particular branch of the law.

Although solicitors present and defend cases in the lower courts, it is the barrister, and particularly the QC, who is the supreme advocate. Indeed, a successful barrister needs to be as much an actor as a lawyer. A former Lord Chancellor, Lord Gardiner, explaining why he became a barrister, said that he thought it would be easier to go on to the stage if he failed his Bar examinations than to go to the Bar if he was a failure on stage.

Barristers can earn very large amounts or less than a living wage, depending on how successful they are. One difficulty, of course, is that they have to obtain work indirectly, through a solicitor. Solicitors, on the other hand, can expect to earn a more regular and reliable living through the work they do outside the courts, such as the conveyancing of property. They also have the advantage of being able to deal directly with the public.

Solicitors greatly outnumber barristers, there being more than 44 000 of them compared with a total of about 4800 barristers.

8.9   The Judiciary

By the judiciary we mean all the men and women who sit in judgement in the various courts of the land, from the non-professional magistrates in the lower courts to the Law Lords at the top of the judicial ladder.

Lay magistrates, or Justices of the Peace, are usually prominent local citizens appointed by the Lord Chancellor. Anyone can recommend a person for appointment as a magistrate but recommendations generally come from local political parties or civic bodies. The actual reasons for selection are kept secret and, because of this secrecy, critics say that it is open to abuse.

JPs do not have to be legally qualified and receive only a short period of basic training. They do, however, have a qualified Clerk to advise them. There are now about 27 000 JPs, with an increasing number of women among them. Stipendiary magistrates are solicitors with at least seven years' experience.

Judges are appointed by the Crown on the advice of either the Prime Minister or the Lord Chancellor. The Prime Minister recommends the appointment of the Law Lords. the Lord Chief Justice, the Master of the Rolls and the President of the Family Division of the High Court. The Prime Minister, of course, also appoints the Lord Chancellor himself, as a member of the Cabinet. The Lord Chancellor appoints all the other judges, including the Recorders, who sit part time in the Crown Courts.

Judges, apart from some Recorders, are drawn almost exclusively from barristers, and the move from being a barrister to a judge is a dramatic change. He will normally have to accept a cut in salary, perhaps from £100 000 to less than £50 000, but, in compensation, will get a secure job for life, or at least until the compulsory retirement age of 72 for a circuit judge and 75 for a High Court appointment.

Instead of pleading a case he will be able to sit up on high and decide which side wins. Depending on the post, he may get an automatic knighthood and if he becomes an Appeal Court judge he will be made a member of the Privy Council. If he rises to the top he will sit in the House of Lords as a life peer, not just as a judge but as an ordinary member as well.

As a judge, he will enjoy many advantages: an office in the Law Courts, a seat at the high table in one of the Inns of Court, a two months' vacation in the summer, and all the prestige and attention which the office attracts. He may well become a national figure, such as Lord Denning or Lord Scarman, in demand to chair royal commissions and inquiries. There are now about 450 full time judges.

8.10   The Lord Chancellor

The Lord Chancellor is head of the legal profession and a very powerful figure. Being both a judge and politician, he seems to deny the existence of the principle of the separation of powers.

His duties and powers are vast. He is a senior member of the Cabinet, presides over the House of Lords and plays a major part in the selection of judges and magistrates. He occupies the oldest government office, five hundred years older than that of Prime Minister. His salary is higher than the Prime Minister's and on formal occasions he takes precedence. Like the Speaker of the House of Commons, he probably has, after the Queen, the best address in London: a house within the Palace of Westminster, next to the House of Lords itself.

8.11   The Law Officers

The **Attorney General** and his deputy, the **Solicitor General** are known as the **Law Officers** and their department as the Law Officers' Department. Both sit in the House of Commons and are members of the government.

They are the government's legal advisers and represent the Crown in court in important cases. In matters affecting the security of the state, such as cases under the Official Secrets Acts, the permission of the Attorney General must be given before a prosecution can be started.

Both the Attorney General and the Solicitor General, despite his title, are barristers by training and are expected to be politically neutral in their work as legal advisers and advocates, It is difficult sometimes, however, to preserve this neutrality and occasionally they can be drawn, perhaps unwittingly, into sensitive political areas, as the affair of the Westland Helicopter Company, in 1986, demonstrated.

The Attorney General supervises the work of the **Director of Public Prosecutions** (DPP), and answers questions about him in Parliament. The DPP is a civil servant and a barrister or solicitor of at least 10 years' experience. He approves or starts, on average, about 3000 prosecutions a year, mainly in serious criminal cases.

8.12   An Evaluation of the Judicial Process

We began this examination of the judicial process by restating the rule of law and suggesting that it formed one of the foundations of democratic government. We said that everyone, including public bodies and officials, should be subject to the law of the land, and not to the whim of an individual, and that no one, whatever his rank or position, should be above the law.

It seems sensible, therefore, to evaluate the judicial process by using these two essentials of the rule of law as our standard, or bench mark.

In all truly democratic countries one of the surest safeguards of individual freedom under the law is that there should be an independent judiciary. In countries with written constitutions this independence is normally clearly set out. In Britain it is achieved in practical ways.

Judges of the High Court and above cannot be removed except for misbehaviour in office. Their salaries are substantial and fixed by Act of Parliament and they are protected against civil proceedings for anything they may say or do during a case they are trying. Judges in the lower courts can be removed by the Lord Chancellor for 'incapacity' or 'misbehaviour', but removals are rare. The only judge dismissed so far in this century has been Lord Bruce Campbell, an Old Bailey judge who, in 1983, was removed after he had admitted a smuggling offence.

However independent they may seem as far as protection against dismissal is concerned, doubts have been expressed about the method of their selection. As we have seen, all senior judges come from the ranks of barristers and most of them from fairly privileged backgrounds. For example, during the present century approximately 80% of High Court judges have received a private, as opposed to a state, education. There are exceptions, of course, but the majority are conservative, in a non-political sense. This is understandable because of the route they have followed to get to the top of their profession.

The method of selecting magistrates for the lower courts has, as we have already said, also been criticised. It seems unduly secretive and produces JPs who are not necessarily typical of the community at large.

In recent years there have been calls, from inside and outside the legal profession, to alter the selection system by setting up a judicial appointments board, composed of people who are not in government. The present Lord Chancellor, Lord Hailsham, has resisted the idea.

Few people have really suggested that the Lord Chancellor's recommendations for appointments have been politically motivated, but they have tended to be conservative, with a small 'c'. For example, in 1986 out of 78 High Court judges only 3 were women and only 10 out of 374 circuit judges.

Another criticism of the judicial process is that it is very costly. Some years ago a High Court judge uttered the now famous remark: 'Justice, like the Ritz Hotel, is open to all'. His dry observation is as true, if not truer, today. For example, one day spent in the High Court is likely to cost each side at least £1500.

The idea that everyone is equal before the law does not make much practical sense if people are prevented, or dissuaded from going to law by the sheer cost involved. The legal aid system in Britain is really only designed to help the very poor, so the bulk of people, between the very poor and the very rich, are at a disadvantage.

Critics of the system argue that a profession divided into solicitors and barristers inevitably adds to legal costs, as, in many cases, there are two sets of lawyers' fees involved. However, the profession itself has so far opposed change.

In summary then, the judicial process in Britain seems to uphold the basic principles of the rule of law but, in practice, the position is less convincing. The average member of the public is suspicious of law and lawyers, partly because of the 'mystery' surrounding the legal process and partly because of the cost. A more radical and open minded approach to legal reform might remove some of these suspicions and go some way towards ensuring that the rule of law is everywhere a reality rather than a theoretical ideal.

Questions and Assignments

1   What do you understand by the rule of law?
2   What are the main sources of English law?
3   What are the main differences between civil and criminal law?
4   What is the distinction between a summary trial and one on indictment?
5   What are the differences between solicitors and barristers?
6   What are the main criticisms of the judicial process?
7   Write an article for your local paper, in not more than 800 words, arguing the case *either for or against* having two different kinds of lawyer, solicitors, and barristers.
    Alternatively this can be used as the basis for a debate on the motion: 'This House believes that having solicitors and barristers is an unnecessary burden on the legal system'.
8   Make a list of the main points in favour of *and* against trial by jury.

Chapter 9

Parliamentary Government

Parliamentary government in Britain has three distinctive features: a Parliament of two chambers, the House of Lords and the House of Commons, but with the Commons clearly superior in power and status, despite the Lords' description as the Upper House; a government drawn from, rather than separate from, the legislature; and a clear division of the legislature into government and opposition parties.

Although the House of Lords is wholly unelected, it is perhaps not as unrepresentative as might be thought because the active life peers are a reasonable cross section of parties and interests. It performs valuable legislative functions and its debates are generally of high quality. The House of Commons shares the task of considering and passing legislation with the House of Lords, except for financial matters from which the Upper House is excluded.

The chairman of the Lords is the Lord Chancellor and of the Commons, the Speaker, and both Houses have highly developed systems of party whips whose job is to maintain party morale and discipline.

Much of the time of both Houses is taken up with debates on legislation and government policy but there are daily opportunities for questioning ministers. Question Time in the House of Commons attracts particular interest, especially on the two weekly occasions when the Prime Minister attends. The value of parliamentary questions is, however, open to doubt.

An Act of Parliament starts life as a Bill and before it can become law it must pass through a five stage process in each House, during which both the principles and details are discussed.

The backbencher in Parliament is at a disadvantage compared with a minister, because of the lack of information and facilities at his disposal, but in recent years some attempts have been made to redress the balance, particularly by the establishment of Select Committees which can investigate and report on government activities.

The dominance of the party system in British politics has tended to replace parliamentary government with cabinet government and a major shift in power from the executive to the legislature is only likely to happen if future parliamentary elections produce a House of Commons more finely balanced in its party composition.

9.1   The Essentials of Parliamentary Government

Although Britain is often seen as the originator of parliamentary government, the 'Westminster model', as it is sometimes called, has features which, if not unique, are not as widely followed in the rest of the world as might be thought.

The word 'parliament' comes from old French and accurately describes the main activity, talking, but the United Kingdom Parliament is more than just a talking shop. It is a place where a lot of other business is carried out. Much of it is unseen by members of the public and only occasionally reported by the media.

The **first** distinctive feature of parliamentary government in Britain is that, although it is a **bicameral legislature**, in other wo. ' there are two chambers, or Houses, one, the House of Commons, is clearly superior in power and status, to the other, the House of Lords.

The **second** feature is that there is no attempt to keep the legislative and executive parts of government separate. The executive government is taken from and forms part of Parliament. Thus, in the House of Commons, out of 650 Members, the governing party will have upwards of 325, of which rather less than a third will be working members of the government.

The **third** distinctive feature, which we have already noted, is that Parliament, and the House of Commons especially, is divided on strict party lines, ensuring that the government can always get its business done as long as its side supports it in the voting lobbies.

These features make the British government, and hence the Prime Minister, potentially the most powerful in the western world, and certainly more powerful than the United States presidency, which, from time to time, has to trim its policies in the face of Congressional opposition.

9.2 The House of Lords

Membership

Members of the House of Lords are there on one of three bases. They have inherited their seats; they are there because they hold some national office; or they have been nominated to sit there. None of them has been elected.

Out of a total membership of over 1000, about 380 are appointees, or **life peers**. Then there are 2 Archbishops and 24 Bishops of the Church of England, who are there because of their positions. The rest are **hereditary peers**, and include 4 royal Dukes, 26 non-royal Dukes, 29 Marquesses, 157 Earls, 103 Viscounts and 474 Barons. Since 1958 women have been admitted and there are now about 65 women peers, or peeresses.

Unlike MPs, peers are not paid a salary, unless they are in government. They can, however, claim attendance allowances.

The Chamber

The chamber of the present House of Lords was first used in 1847. Most of the old Palace of Westminster, where Parliament used to meet, was destroyed by fire in 1834 and work began on the new Palace in 1840.

The chamber is 80 feet long, 45 feet wide and 45 feet high. As Figure 9.1 shows, at the southern end, facing the Press and Strangers' Galleries, is the **Throne**, where the Queen sits when she formally opens Parliament. In front of the Throne is the **Woolsack**, stuffed with wool from all the countries of the Commonwealth and symbolising the wealth of the old nation and Empire. The Lord Chancellor sits on the Woolsack, as speaker of the House of Lords.

Figure 9.1 also shows the seating arrangements for government, opposition and Alliance peers, as well as those who prefer not to be aligned to any particular party, the **cross benchers**.

The chamber is more ornate than that of the Commons and the colour scheme for seats, carpets and curtains, is red, whereas that in the Commons is green.

The Business of the Lords

The Lords meet on about 140 days each year, with breaks for Christmas, Easter and the long summer recess. Sittings are

Fig. 9.1

Chamber of the House of Lords

From an original drawing by Peter Heaton

normally on Tuesday, Wednesday and Thursday; often on Monday; and occasionally on Friday. Business usually begins at 2.30 pm on Monday, Tuesday and Wednesday, 3 pm on Thursday, and 11 am on Friday, finishing at about 9 pm, except on Friday when it will be earlier. Late, and even all night sittings, are, however, not unknown. Much depends on the volume of business to be dealt with.

As in the Commons, each day begins with Prayers and these will be followed by questions put to ministers and ministerial statements. Much of the time in the chamber itself will, however, be taken up with debates. Again as in the Commons, away from the main chamber there will be meetings of the House's many committees. The legislative process is similar to that in the House of Commons and will be looked at separately later.

Debates in the House of Lords tend to be much less partisan than those in the Commons and only occasionally will they end with a vote which is crucial. The quality of debates has also been judged to be better.

A major difference between the two Houses is that the Lord Chancellor, unlike the Speaker in the Commons, can get down from the Woolsack and speak not as the House's chairman but as a member of the government. When he has made his contribution he will return to his Woolsack place. Unlike the Speaker, he has no power to control debates: that is left to the peers themselves.

9.3   The Future of the House of Lords

From time to time calls are heard for the reform of the House of Lords, and even for its abolition, on the grounds that it is unrepresentative and out of touch with modern conditions. Even if these criticisms are justified, it is difficult to see how the business of government could continue effectively without the Lords or some alternative replacement. As things stand, a single House would find the legislative workload unbearable.

That apart, it can be argued that, far from being unrepresentative, it is, in fact, more representative than the House of Commons, now that it has so many active life peers. For example, in the 1983 general election the Conservatives, with just over 40% of the popular vote, obtained over 60% of the Commons' seats. In contrast, the proportion of Conservative peers was less than 50%: much nearer to the Party's popularity in the country. The Alliance parties were also more fairly represented, in relation to their national vote, in the Lords than in the Commons.

Is the House of Lords less in touch with modern conditions than the House of Commons? There is little evidence of this. For example, the Lords have agreed to have their proceedings televised since January 1985, while the Commons are still considering whether or not they should.

In recent years the Lords have shown themselves more independent in the tone of their debates than the Commons and have, on occasions, rejected government measures or forced a change of mind.

If some future government does not abolish it, should the House of Lords be reformed?

It would be possible to create a wholly elected chamber, perhaps representing major economic or regional interests, but a fully representative second chamber would more easily come into conflict with the Commons and create constitutional problems.

Supporters of the House of Lords argue that, in any case, it has been undergoing reform, in a gradual way, for many years and that its present active membership makes it the livelier and more expert of the two chambers.

9.4   The House of Commons

Membership

As we have already noted, the House of Commons consists of 650 elected members, each representing a constituency of about 65 000 voters. The Speaker is also an MP but, by convention, his election to Parliament is usually unopposed.

The Chamber

The present chamber of the House of Commons was opened in 1950. An earlier one, which was first used in 1852, was destroyed by German bombs in 1941 and rebuilt virtually in its original form.

Figure 9.2 shows the chamber, shorter than that of the Lords by 12 feet, which, despite the 650 Members, can seat only 437. It has been kept deliberately small—a quarter the size of the United States House of Representatives, which has fewer members—to preserve the intimacy of debates. The House is full only on

Fig. 9.2

Chamber of the House of Commons

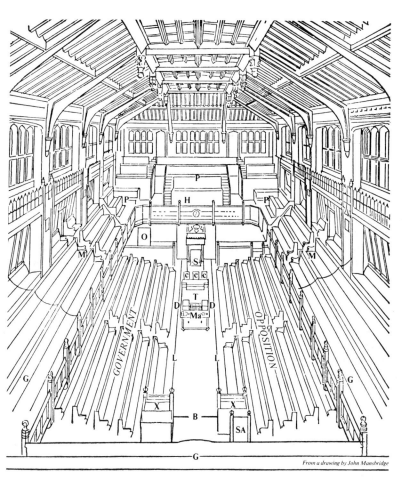

From a drawing by John Mansbridge

S	Mr Speaker	T	Table of the House	SA	Serjeant at Arms
P	Press Galleries	D	Despatch Boxes	M	Members' Galleries
H	*Hansard* Reporters	Ma	Mace	G	Visitors' Galleries
O	Government Officials' Box	L	Lines		
	(advisers to Ministers)	B	Bar of the House		
C	Clerks of the House	X	Cross Benches		

Reproduced with the permission of the Speaker of the House of Commons.

particular occasions, such as when the Chancellor of the Exchequer presents his budget, and then Members who have not found seats use the steps and gangways or cluster around the Speaker's chair.

The Speaker sits at the northern end of the chamber, in a chair presented by the people of Australia, and on the table in front of him rests the Mace, symbolising royal authority and signifying that the House is in session.

As Figure 9.2 shows, the chamber is starkly divided between government and opposition benches, with virtually no concessions to cross benchers. Members of the Alliance parties have to fit themselves into the opposition benches as best they can, the leaders normally sitting on a middle bench towards the southern end of the chamber.

The lines on the floor indicate the limits beyond which an MP should not step. These limits were originally drawn to make it impossible for a Member to attack another on the opposite side with his sword.

The leading members of the government and opposition face each other on either side of the Speaker's table and can move to the table to speak from one of the two despatch boxes. The original black boxes were destroyed in 1941 and replaced by two in puriri wood, a gift from the people of New Zealand.

The press and the official reporters who produce the daily account of proceedings, **Hansard**, sit in the galleries above the Speaker. Microphones hang above the MPs and small speakers are fitted into the backs of the benches so that Members can, if they wish, lean back to listen to them. There are similar facilities in the House of Lords.

Immediately behind the Speaker's chair, and to his right, is a sitting area known as **The Box**. It is technically outside the chamber and so civil servants are allowed to sit there, passing information and advice to ministers, on request, as they answer questions or speak in debates.

The Business of the Commons

The House of Commons normally sits from Monday to Friday for about 160 days each year, with breaks at Christmas and Easter and the long summer recess. A day's sitting is from 2.30 pm to 10.30 pm, Monday to Thursday, and from 9.30 am to 3 pm on Friday. The shortened Friday allows MPs to return to their constituencies for the weekend. Later, or all night, sittings occur from time to time. The House has also been known to sit on Saturday on special occasions. The last Saturday sitting was on 3 April 1982 when the Argentinian invasion of the Falkland Islands was debated.

As in the Lords, each day begins with Prayers and the rest of the business is set out in the **Order Paper** which is issued daily. Figure 9.3 is a reproduction of the front page of a House of Commons Order Paper.

Fig. 9.3

House of Commons Order Paper

No. 135   **TUESDAY 24TH JUNE 1986**   3931

ORDER PAPER

PRIVATE BUSINESS AFTER PRAYERS

CONSIDERATION OF BILLS ORDERED TO LIE UPON THE TABLE

1. Aberystwyth Harbour Bill.
2. Felixstowe Dock and Railway Bill.
        On consideration of Felixstowe Dock and Railway Bill, as amended : —

Saving for Wildlife and Countryside Act

Dr David Clark
Mr Andrew F. Bennett
Mr Peter Hardy
Mrs Ann Clwyd

NC1

To move the following Clause : —
        ' Nothing in this Act shall affect the operation of the Wildlife and Countryside Act 1981 as for the time being in force '.

Consent of Secretary of State required for certain works

Dr David Clark
Mr Andrew F. Bennett
Mr Peter Hardy
Mrs Ann Clwyd

NC2

To move the following Clause : —
        ' (1) The Authority shall not exercise the powers conferred by Section 6 of this Act without first obtaining the consent in writing of the Secretary of State in any case where—
                (*a*) the works include works of land reclaimed, and
                (*b*) the area of land which is to be reclaimed is to be used for purposes which require close and convenient access to a berth which is to be constructed within the area of jurisdiction of the Company.

        (2) The Secretary of State shall give his consent under this Section in any case where he is reasonably satisfied that—
                (*a*) further development of the land which is to be reclaimed will be commenced not later than one year after the date on which the works of reclamation have been substantially completed ;
                (*b*) no reasonably alternative site for that further development is available on other land within the area of jurisdiction of the company ; and
                (*c*) the area of land to be reclaimed is no greater than that which is reasonably required to accommodate that further development.

        (3) Where an application has been received by the Secretary of State from the Company for his consent under this Section, the Secretary of State shall, within the period of eight weeks following that receipt, give his consent or notify the Company of his decision to withhold it.

        (4) A consent given under this Section shall come into force as soon as it is given and shall remain in force for a period of one year or for such longer period as may be specified by the Secretary of State when he gives his consent and the duration of a consent so given may, at any time before its expiry, be extended for such further period or periods as the Secretary of State may specify by written notice given to the Company.'.
        10 H

Reproduced with the permission of the Speaker of the House of Commons.

A typical day's business might be:

2.30 pm   Prayers, followed immediately by Private Business. This consists mainly of **Private Bills**, which affect only a limited part of the country. For example, the Felixstowe Dock and Railway Bill.

2.40 pm   Questions.

3.30 pm   Public Business. This can include consideration of a **Public Bill**, which, when it becomes an Act will affect the whole country; or ministerial statements; or a debate initiated by the government or the opposition.

10 pm   Debate on the Adjournment.

10.30 pm   House adjourns.

The **Debate on the Adjournment** is a daily occurrence. Backbenchers ballot for the chance to open a short debate on a topic of particular interest to them or their constituents. The appropriate minister will make a brief reply.

The Speaker and Rules for Debate

The **Speaker** is a respected figure in the House of Commons and the importance of his office is emphasised by the pomp and ceremony which surrounds him. The office dates back to the 14th century but it was in 1679, when Charles II failed in his attempt to impose his own nominee on the Commons, that the Speaker became their spokesman and their guarantor of freedom of speech.

Mr Speaker, as he is usually called, enjoys several advantages. He lives in a large house within the Palace of Westminster; in order of precedence he immediately follows the Prime Minister and the Lord President of the Council; and is automatically given a peerage on retirement.

Within the Commons he calls MPs to speak by name and must, therefore retain a knowledge of every Member. He tries to keep his choice of speakers as impartial as possible, bringing them in from alternate sides of the House, but giving preference to leading party members and Privy Counsellors. With the assistance of the **Clerk to the House of Commons** and his staff, he rules on points of procedure and can, if he chooses, discipline MPs. He can require a Member to withdraw a statement if he considers it to be in 'unparliamentary language' and, if the MP refuses he can have him removed from the House. If he decides to do so he will move **name** the offender, whereupon the **Leader of the House** will move his suspension and the MP is then expected to leave. If he still refuses, the **Serjeant-at-Arms** will eject him.

The Speaker announces the results of votes, or divisions as they are called, and, if there is a tie, he has the casting vote.

During a debate an MP must not speak directly to another Member but always address the Chair. Nor must he refer to another Member by name but always by his or her constituency. Thus he will say 'Mr Speaker' first and call the other MP 'The Honourable Member for . . .', or 'The Right Honourable Member', if he is a Privy Counsellor, or 'Honourable and Gallant', if he was a serving officer, or 'Honourable and Learned', if he is a QC. If the other MP is in the same party he will be referred to as 'My Honourable Friend'.

All this may seem unnecessarily formal but it does serve a purpose. It keeps the emotional level reasonably low and prevents Members from verbally abusing each other. Nevertheless, some debates do become heated and barely veiled insults are hurled across the floor of the House in 'parliamentary language'.

When a vote is taken bells ring and Members have eight minutes to get to a **division lobby**. The Speaker, or his deputy, the **Chairman of Ways and Means**, names four **tellers**, two from each side of the House, to count the votes. As Members come out of the 'Ayes' or 'Noes' lobby one of the tellers calls out the numbers. As soon as the eight minutes have passed an order is given 'Lock the doors' and if an MP is not in the chamber, or not even in Parliament when a Division is called, he has to reach a lobby before the door is closed. The 'Ayes' lobby is at the southern end and the 'Noes' at the other end, behind the Speaker's chair.

9.5 Question Time

Questions are asked in the House of Lords but, because the majority of ministers, including the Prime Minister, are in the Commons, it is there that **Question Time** is more significant.

As we have seen, time is allocated for questions after Prayers, or Private Business, until 3.30 pm. The questions are printed on the Order Paper and the Speaker merely calls the name of the Member who then rises and calls the number of his question. The minister to whom it is put stands up and reads a reply which has been prepared for him by a civil servant. The MP who put the question can then ask a **supplementary question**.

Fig. 9.4

No. 135	Order Paper : 24th June 1986	3939

QUESTIONS FOR ORAL ANSWER—*continued*

Questions to the Prime Minister will start at 3.15 p.m.

The following Members have set down Questions for oral answer by the Prime Minister. With the exception of those set out in full after the Member's name, the Questions take the form :

To ask the Prime Minister, if she will list her official engagements for Tuesday 24th June.

*✷Q 1 **Mr Michael Hirst** (Strathkelvin and Bearsden):

✷Q 2 **Mr Peter Hardy** (Wentworth):

✷Q 3 **Mr Jack Straw** (Blackburn):

✷Q 4 **Mr Ken Eastham** (Manchester, Blackley):

✷Q 5 **Mr Gavin Strang** (Edinburgh East):

✷Q 6 **Mr Terry Lewis** (Worsley):

✷Q 7 **Mr Laurence Cunliffe** (Leigh):

✷Q 8 **Margaret Beckett** (Derby South):

✷Q 9 **Mr Tony Speller** (North Devon):

✷Q 10 **Mr Tony Blair** (Sedgefield):

✷Q 11 **Mr Reg Freeson** (Brent East):

✷Q 12 **Mr Toby Jessel** (Twickenham):

✷Q 13 **Mr Hugh Dykes** (Harrow East):

✷Q 14 **Mr James Pawsey** (Rugby and Kenilworth):   To ask the Prime Minister, if she has any plans to pay an official visit to the village of Ashow, near Kenilworth.

✷Q 15 **Mr Patrick Thompson** (Norwich North):

✷Q 16 **Mr John Townend** (Bridlington):

✷Q 17 **Mr Kevin McNamara** (Kingston upon Hull North):

✷Q 18 **Sir John Biggs-Davison** (Epping Forest):

✷Q 19 **Miss Betty Boothroyd** (West Bromwich West):

✷Q 20 **Mr Allen Adams** (Paisley North):

✷Q 21 **Dr Norman A. Godman** (Greenock and Port Glasgow):

✷Q 22 **Mr John Ward** (Poole):

✷Q 23 **Mr Chris Smith** (Islington South and Finsbury):

✷Q 24 **Mr Robert Maclennan** (Caithness and Sutherland):

✷Q 25 **Mr Bruce George** (Walsall South):

✷Q 26 **Mr George Foulkes** (Carrick, Cumnock and Doon Valley):

✷Q 27 **Mr Jim Callaghan** (Heywood and Middleton):

✷Q 28 **Mr Derek Fatchett** (Leeds Central):

✷Q 29 **Mr Alan Roberts** (Bootle):*

Reproduced with the permission of the Speaker of the House of Commons.

The supplementary question is more important than that printed on the Order Paper, because the minister can only guess at what it might be. His civil servants will, however, have tried to anticipate it and will have briefed him accordingly. They can also pass information to him, along the front bench, from The Box where they are sitting.

On Tuesdays and Thursdays the Prime Minister answers questions, between 3.15 and 3.30 pm, and it is then that the House is fuller and more excited. Again, the questions printed are not as important as the supplementaries. Indeed, as Figure 9.4, which is a reproduction of part of an actual Order Paper, shows, it is likely that well over 100 MPs will ask the same first question:

'To ask the Prime Minister, if she will list her official engagements'

In the allotted quarter of an hour probably no more that six or seven Members will be able to put their questions. The other hundred or so will have to wait for another day.

The Prime Minister will reply to the first questioner by giving details of the day's engagements. The reply to subsequent questioners will merely refer to the first reply, but it is the supplementaries which are important.

Questions are rarely intended to seek information. The idea is to surprise the minister and cause embarrassment. If an MP genuinely wants information he will put down a question for a written reply.

The value of Question Time as a check on the government seems increasingly doubtful and the half an hour per week of Prime Minister's questions is in danger of becoming a comic set piece, involving a battle of wits between questioner and answerer with each trying to score the most party political points. But parliamentary questions do at least keep ministers and civil servants on their toes, but at some expense. About 30000 questions are asked each year, at a cost of about £40 each.

9.6   The Party Whips

Discipline within the parties is maintained by **Whips**. Each of the main parties will have a Chief Whip and up to 10 to 12 Assistant Whips. All the Whips on the government side are paid as Treasury ministers but only the Chief Whip is paid on the opposition side. The term is thought to have been first used in 1769 by the MP, Edmund Burke, who saw them in terms of the whippers-in on the hunting field.

Although backbenchers may rebel against the tight discipline they try to impose, most would agree that the Whips perform very useful functions. They arrange parliamentary business and because their discussions are outside the chamber they are described as being carried on 'behind the Speaker's chair'. They cover an MP's absence from the House when a vote is to be taken by **pairing** him with someone on the other side who is also going to be away. They take soundings of backbench opinion and pass this information, through the Chief Whip, to the Prime Minister. Each week they circulate a memorandum to each of their MPs, outlining the business of the House for the coming week and underlining those items where they expect a vote to be taken. They may underline once, twice or three times. A **three line Whip**, as it is called, is expected to be treated very seriously and a Member who ignores it will be called to account for his behaviour.

The same principles apply in the House of Lords but the Whipping system is more relaxed and less obvious.

9.7   Leader of the House

In each of the two chambers there is a **Leader of the House** whose job is, with the help of the Whips, to make sure that the government's business moves smoothly through the parliamentary machinery. The Leader of the Commons holds a key post, with a seat in the Cabinet. The Leader of the Lords is also a Cabinet member and usually holds another post, such as Lord President of the Council.

Apart from overseeing and co-ordinating the government's business, the Leader plays an important part in the general work of the House, which is helpful to Members of all parties. For example, the revised system of Select Committees, which we will look at shortly, was introduced by Norman St John Stevas, in 1979, when he was Leader of the House of Commons in Margaret Thatcher's government. An earlier version had been set up, in 1966, by Richard Crossman, House Leader in Harold Wilson's administration.

9.8   Parliamentary Privilege

To allow them to speak as freely as they choose in Parliament, Members of both Houses are protected against legal actions, on the grounds of slander or defamation, by **parliamentary privilege**.

This means they can say what they like within the confines of Parliament but that protection vanishes when they speak outside.

Parliamentary privilege also protects Members against threats or intimidation from people outside. Someone who makes a threat may be summoned to appear before the House, to be reprimanded by the Speaker. A Member can also commit a breach of privilege if he or she refuses to comply with the orders of Parliament.

9.9   The Legislative Process

An Act of Parliament begins life as a Bill, drafted by specialist lawyers called **Parliamentary Counsel**. A Bill can start its journey in either House but must go through all the stages in each before it becomes law. A Finance Bill, or the financial parts of any Bill, are considered by the Commons only, as the Lords' control over money matters no longer exists. A minister in each House is given the job of piloting a Bill through its various stages.

A Bill is usually divided into Parts and the Parts into Clauses and Sub-Clauses. When it becomes an Act the Clauses are called Sections and the Sub-Clauses Sub-Sections.

The stages it must progress through in both Houses are:

First Reading	This is a formal reading of the Bill's title immediately before the full document is printed and distributed to Members. No vote is taken.
Second Reading	Members have copies of the Bill and a minister opens the debate by explaining the principles behind it. A vote is taken at this stage. If the vote goes against the minister the Bill is lost, otherwise it goes to the next stage.
Committee Stage	The Bill is sent to one of the **Standing Committees** for detailed, clause by clause, consideration. Occasionally, important Bills are considered by a **Committee of the Whole House**, in other words the main chamber with the Speaker's deputy in the chair.
Report Stage	It now comes back to the main chamber for approval of any amendments which have

	been made. If the Bill had been considered by a Committee of the Whole House, this stage is very much a formality.
Third Reading	This is the last chance to approve or throw out the Bill. If it is approved it goes, depending on where it started, to the Lords or the Commons. When all these stages have been completed in both Houses, the Bill is ready for its final stage.
Royal Assent	This is a brief, formal ceremony usually performed on the Monarch's behalf by a small group of Privy Counsellors.

Sometimes the government will wish to accelerate the passage of a Bill and can use one or more of a number of 'speeding up' devices. This is not done very frequently and is invariably objected to by the opposition parties.

The **Guillotine** is a cut off in the time for debate on a particular clause of a Bill. At the end of the allotted time a vote is taken and the debate moves on to the next clause.

The **Closure** ends the debate at a particular time and a vote is then taken.

The **Kangaroo** allows the chairman to jump clauses so that some are not debated at all and just voted on.

This staged procedure applies to two main types of Bill: **Government Bills** and **Private Members' Bills**. Private Members' Bills should not be confused with Private Bills, which have to follow a different, more legalistic, procedure.

9.10   Private Members' Legislation

Ten Fridays a year are allocated for Private Members' legislation. If a backbencher wants to introduce a Bill he can go about it in one of two ways. He can enter the ballot held each year to decide which Bills will be presented on Fridays, or he can use the **Ten Minute Rule**. Under this rule he can hand in a motion to introduce a Bill. If this is accepted, he will be called upon to speak by the Speaker, immediately after Question Time on Tuesdays or Wednesdays. The speech must be brief and is then followed by another short speech against the Bill. The House then votes and if the vote goes in favour of the Bill it is considered to have had its First Reading. It must then go through all the stages that apply to a Government Bill.

The odds against a backbencher getting a Bill passed are high and usually he will need the support of the government, which is in control of most of the parliamentary time. Nevertheless, Members are occasionally successful and some quite notable Acts have come on to the statute book through backbench initiatives. An Act to amend the law on divorce was introduced by David Steel, before he became Liberal Leader, and the Act which abolished capital punishment was introduced by a Labour Member, Sidney Silverman, in 1965.

9.11   Delegated Legislation

An Act of Parliament usually sets out the main points of the law and leaves the detailed application to **Regulations** and **Orders**, which are collectively called **delegated legislation**.

This means that ministers are given powers by an Act to make subordinate legislation without having to go through the full process which applies to a Bill.

Various devices and procedures have been established to ensure that delegated legislation is scrutinised so that it does not produce law which Members would find unacceptable. We shall look at these later.

9.12   European Community Legislation

Since the United Kingdon joined the European Community, on 1 January 1973, the sovereignty of Parliament, although still there in theory, is not always evident in practice.

Under the Treaty of Accession, Community law can take precedence over that of Parliament and appeals against United Kingdom legislation can be made to the **European Court of Justice**. There have been a number of successful appeals by British citizens when the two sets of law have been in conflict and this practice is likely to increase rather than diminish. The Community law which takes precedence is mainly in the economic and social fields.

9.13 The Select Committee system

In addition to the Standing Committees, known as A, B, C and so on, which are mainly concerned with the Committee Stage of legislation, there is now an impressive system of **Select Committees**. Some are long established and others have been introduced in recent years to help backbenchers exercise more control over government policies.

There are three main types: **Ad Hoc**, set up for a single, particular purpose; **Sessional**, which are mostly set up by Standing Order and renewed each year, but have become virtually permanent; and **Departmental**, which have been established since 1979.

Ad Hoc committees are disbanded once their work has finished but the others have become part of the established machinery of Parliament.

9.14   Sessional Select Committees

These committees are set up at the beginning of each parliamentary year and reconstituted in subsequent years. There are currently nine of them.

The **Public Accounts Committee** was originally introduced by W E Gladstone in 1861 and has continued more or less in its original form to the present day. It has 15 Members, drawn from both sides of the House, and, by convention, its chairman is always a prominent Member from the opposition party. Its purpose is to scrutinise and report on the government's accounts and it is assisted by an independent officer, appointed on similar terms to a High Court judge, called the **Comptroller and Auditor General**, and his staff. Although this Committee looks at money already spent, and is thus liable to 'close the stable door after the horse has bolted', it is a highly respected body and its reports have done much to keep successive governments on their toes.

The **Committee of Selection** consists of 11 Members, 6 from the government and 5 from the opposition side. As its name suggests, it selects members to sit on the various committees of the House.

The **Standing Orders Committee** is a specialist committee dealing entirely with Private Bills.

The **Committee of Privileges** has 15 of the most experienced Members, drawn from both sides of the House, and its job is to investigate and report back on alleged breaches of parliamentary privilege.

The **Public Petitions Committee** is another specialist committee dealing with public petitions. The practice of sending public petitions to Parliament has become outdated and has been largely replaced by people writing to their MPs or lobbying them.

The **Publications and Debates Reports Committee** helps the Speaker in the work of reporting and publishing accounts of parliamentary debates.

The **House of Commons (Services) Committee** oversees the domestic arrangments in the House, including the eating facilities.

The **European Secondary Legislation Committee** scrutinises all the delegated legislation which come from the European Community.

There is also a **Joint Committee on Statutory Instruments**, consisting of Members of the Commons and the Lords, which looks at UK delegated legislation, or statutory instruments, as they are officially called.

The **Committee of the Parliamentary Commissioner** considers reports from the Parliamentary Commissioner, or Ombudsman, on behalf of the House.

9.15   Departmental Select Committees

There are now 14 Select Committees, each covering the work of a major government department. As Figure 9.5 shows, at the present time 9 of them have Conservative and 5 Labour chairmen.

Fig. 9.5

House of Commons Departmental Select Committees in 1986

Committee	Chairman	Party	No of Members
Agriculture	John Spence	Conservative	11
Defence	Sir Humphrey Atkins	Conservative	11
Education	Sir William van Straubenzee	Conservative	11
Employment	Ron Leighton	Labour	11
Energy	Ian Lloyd	Conservative	11
Environment	Sir Hugh Rossi	Conservative	11
Foreign Affairs	Sir Anthony Kershaw	Conservative	11
Home Affairs	Sir Edward Gardner	Conservative	11
Scottish Affairs	David Lambie	Labour	13
Social Services	Renee Short	Labour	11
Trade & Industry	Kenneth Warren	Conservative	11
Transport	Harry Cowans	Labour	11
Treasury	Terence Higgins	Conservative	11
Welsh Affairs	Gareth Wardell	Labour	11

The purpose of these Committees is to give Members, and particularly backbenchers, a better check on government activities. The average MP is at a great disadvatange in his questioning of ministers, who have all the knowledge and expertise of the civil service at their disposal. Although the powerful Congressional Committees in the United States have provided a useful model, the British variety, mainly because of the differences between the constitutions of the two countries, are not nearly as strong.

Departmental Select Committees have powers to send for papers and records but cannot insist that ministers or civil servants appear before them: they can only ask. The Committees' reports vary in their impact, some passing almost unnoticed and others attracting considerable attention.

Perhaps the most significant report in recent years was by the Defence Committee, in 1986, on the government's handling of the future of the Yeovil based helicopter company, Westland, which, to help it out of a grave financial crisis, wanted to enter into partnerhip with an American conglomerate, United Technologies, manufacturers of Sikorsky helicopters. The events between December 1985 and January 1986, which resulted in the resignation of two Cabinet ministers, Michael Heseltine and Leon Brittan, became known as the 'Westland Affair' and were investigated by the Defence Committee.

The Committee's report was highly critical of some aspects of the Affair and particularly the roles of the Secretary of the Cabinet, Sir Robert Armstrong, and the Prime Minister's Press Secretary, Bernard Ingham. The report demonstrated that, however little a Departmental committee's investigations might achieve in practical terms, the political impact can be considerable.

9.16   An Assessment of Parliamentary Government in Britain

The theory behind parliamentary government is that the nation freely elects its representatives to form a Parliament, out of which an executive government is formed which is accountable to it. The theory goes on to argue that the government can only carry out its policies and remain in office as long as it can command the support of Parliament. The reality is a little different.

Because of the dominance of party politics, a general election is more about choosing a government than choosing a House of Commons, and once a government is in power it can almost automatically assume that it will be able to carry through its major policies. It may have to concede here or there but not on important issues.

To some extent, therefore, parliamentary government in Britain has been replaced by Cabinet government or, some would even say, Prime Ministerial government. Is parliamentary government then a relic of the past and has it become a cover for something more like presidential government?

A completely honest answer would be Yes, and No.

We should be wary of jumping to long term conclusions on the basis of recent events. It was only just over seven years ago that a Labour government, led by James Callaghan, was defeated in the House of Commons by one vote, 311 to 310, on a question of confidence. Two years earlier the same government had held on to power by arranging a deal with the Liberal Party, and three years before the Lib-Lab Pact, as it was called, a Conservative Prime Minister, Edward Heath, had unsuccessfully tried to remain in office by trying to fix a similar deal.

So the evidence is that Parliament, in the shape of the House of Commons, is not always the obedient servant of the Prime Minister and the Cabinet: much depends on the state of the parties. If, after the next general election, no party obtained an overall majority and there was a 'hung' Parliament, the government which emerged after all the political 'wheeling and dealing' would have to pay more attention to the ordinary MPs than some governments in recent years have done.

This does not mean that there will no longer be Cabinet, or Prime Ministerial, government. It means that House of Commons' support will not always be completely reliable: the government will have to listen more to what MPs have to say and respond accordingly.

But whatever the future composition of the House of Commons may be, it cannot itself afford to be complacent. There are many aspects of its work and organisation which could be usefully improved.

The physical accommodation for MPs is inferior to that in any other major Western country and this stems mainly from an over-reverence for tradition. Not only does the main chamber have insufficient seating for the entire membership, there is no provison for minority parties or groups, and they could well be more numerous in future years.

Working facilities for backbenchers are poor in comparison with those for legislators in other countries. A member of the House of

Representatives of the US Congress would not tolerate for a minute the conditions which British MPs accept.

We pay our MPs less than a third of that paid to a US Congressman, about a half of that paid to a member of the French National Assembly or the Australian House of Representatives, and appreciably less than the salary of a member of the lower House in either Canada or West Germany. Provision for House of Commons secretarial services is also relatively inferior.

An overstressed respect for tradition shows itself in the inefficient and time wasting voting methods in the House of Commons. In the passage of a major Bill hours can be spent unnecessarily in the numerous Divisions which are bound to occur.

Question Time could become more significant if it were used less as an arena for party political point scoring and more as an opportunity for making the government account seriously for its policies.

These criticisms may seem insignificant and superficial but they reflect a deeper problem facing parliamentary government in Britain today. There is a real danger that MPs may feel themselves so lacking in power and so poorly regarded that they fail to perform the task of representing their constituents and overseeing the work of government as they should and as they were intended to.

Questions and Assignments

1 What are the three main features of parliamentary government in Britain?
2 What does an Order Paper of the House of Commons contain?
3 Why do so many MPs ask the Prime Minister the same question?
5 What stages does a Bill have to go through before it becomes an Act?
6 What Select Committees are there in the House of Commons?
7 Using the same first question: 'To ask the Prime Minister, if she will list her official engagements', think of 10 possible supplementary questions you might ask, bearing in mind the news which is current at the time.
  This assignment can also be used as a group exercise with some members asking questions and others replying.
8 Draw up a report, in not more than 800 words, that you believe a firm of management consultants would present to the Leader

of the House of Commons, indicating what steps might be taken to improve its efficiency.

The report should be in this format:

To: The Leader of the House of Commons

From: (The name of the consultants)

Subject: House of Commons Reform

Areas requiring reform:

Conclusions:

Recommendations:

Chapter 10
The Prime Minister and the Cabinet

Cabinet government started with a small group of advisers to the King and developed into a committee of senior politicians of the ruling party. The chairman of this committee has been described as a 'first among equals' but this is not an accurate description of a modern Prime Minister. He or she has considerable power, particularly in appointments to the Cabinet itself and to other public offices.

The full Cabinet, of 20 or so, usually meets at least once a week but in recent years much of its work has been delegated to its many committees and subcommittees, which together make up the Cabinet system. It is served by the Secretary of the Cabinet who runs the Cabinet Office and is now also head of the civil service. Prime Ministers not only make great use of the Cabinet Office but have also built up their own personal staff, so that there is now what can best be described as a Downing Street Centre, working directly for the Prime Minister.

The Cabinet has always operated on the principle of collective responsibility, which means that all members must support its collective decisions or resign. Collective responsibility applies equally to the Prime Minister but in the final analysis it is his or her personal authority which counts.

10.1 The British Political Executive

Earlier we looked at the principle of the separation of powers which said that government is likely to be more democratic if its three parts, the legislature, the judiciary and the executive, are kept separate. In Britain this strict separation does not exist since the executive is drawn from the legislature.

There is a real difference, however, between sitting on the opposition side of the House of Commons, or on the back benches on the government side, and sitting on the front government seats, with all the access to power that this gives.

Former ministers have remarked on the dramatic change which takes place when their party goes out of office and they have to leave their Whitehall offices, give up their official cars, and no longer have the civil service administrative machine at their beck and call. They then realise that the gap between the front and back benches is much greater than it seems on the surface.

Thus, although ministers, as part of the political executive, sit in the legislature, they are in many ways separate from it and in outlook and understanding perhaps closer to the permanent executive, the civil service.

In this chapter we will look at the top of the political executive: the 20 or so politicians who form the Cabinet and decide policies. In the next chapter we will look at the central departments and the hundreds of thousands of civil servants whose job it is to advise on those policies and to implement them.

Fig. 10.1

The Pyramid of Political Power

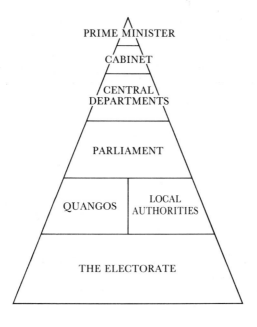

Like most large organisations, government is like a pyramid, with a few people at the top, taking responsibility and making major decisions, and more people below, putting those decisions into effect, their numbers increasing as the bottom of the pyramid is reached. Figure 10.1 provides a broad picture of this pyramid of power.

At the top of the pyramid is the Prime Minister and the Cabinet so our study of the political executive must start at this point.

10.2   The Origins of Cabinet Government

The word cabinet used to mean private room and it was in their private rooms that Kings and Queens of England had meetings with their closest advisers. Henry VIII, although an absolute ruler in many respects, still felt it necessary to take advice from leading figures in the country. This group of advisers was called the **King's Council.** Towards the end of his reign it became known as the Privy Council, in the sense that its discussions and the advice given to the King were strictly private. Elizabeth I continued the practice but, as the Council grew in size, businesslike meetings became more difficult so the Monarch started holding discussions with a select few in a private room, or cabinet. Thus the chief ministers became known as the Cabinet.

As long as he had sufficient personal funds the King could carry out whatever policies he chose, even against the advice of his Cabinet, but over the years, as he needed more and more money, he had to ask Parliament to authorise the levying of taxes. Members of Parliament then demanded a greater say in how the country was run in return for their co-operation, so power began to shift away from the Monarch towards Parliament.

After 1688, when Parliament removed James II because of his Roman Catholic leanings and replaced him with William III from Holland, the power of the Monarch declined quickly and that of Parliament increased. The Cabinet became not so much the King's advisory body as a group of leading parliamentarians.

The King continued to attend Cabinet meetings but relied increasingly on his ministers' judgement. During the reign of George I, between 1714 and 1727, this dependence was centred on one man, Sir Robert Walpole, who held appointments as First Lord of the Treasury and Chancellor of the Exchequer. Walpole became recognised as the King's first minister, or **Prime Minister.** George I took little interest in domestic politics and, in any case, did not speak English, so Walpole took charge of policy. By the time Victoria came to the throne, in 1837, Cabinet government as it is known today was clearly established.

10.3   Cabinet Government Today

The Privy Council still exists but, as we have seen, its functions are now more formal than political. A full Council is summoned only on the death of the Monarch or when he or she announces an intention to marry.

The Cabinet nowadays consists of 20 or so ministers who are mostly MPs, with a few members in the House of Lords. The exact size is decided by the Prime Minister. Most Cabinet ministers are in charge of major government departments but a few will have no specific, or a mix of, responsibilities, such as the Lord President of the Council or the Lord Privy Seal. Figure 10.2 shows the Cabinet of Margaret Thatcher in September 1986.

Fig. 10.2

The Thatcher Cabinet of September 1986

Prime Minister, First Lord of the Treasury & Minister for the Civil Service	Margaret Thatcher
Lord President of the Council, Leader of the House of Lords & Deputy Prime Minister	Viscount Whitelaw
Lord Chancellor	Lord Hailsham
Secretary of State for Foreign and Commonwealth Affairs	Sir Geoffrey Howe
Secretary of State for the Home Department	Douglas Hurd
Chancellor of the Exchequer	Nigel Lawson
Secretary of State for Education and Science	Kenneth Baker
Secretary of State for Northern Ireland	Tom King
Secretary of State for Energy	Peter Walker
Secretary of State for Defence	George Younger
Secretary of State for Scotland	Malcolm Rifkind
Secretary of State for Wales	Nicholas Edwards
Secretary of State for the Environment	Nicholas Ridley
Lord Privy Seal and Leader of the House of Commons	John Biffen
Secretary of State for Health and Social Security	Norman Fowler
Secretary of State for Employment	Lord Young
Secretary of State for Trade & Industry	Paul Channon
Chancellor of the Duchy of Lancaster*	Norman Tebbit
Secretary of State for Transport	John Moore
Minister of Agriculture, Fisheries & Food	Michael Jopling
Chief Secretary to the Treasury†	John MacGregor
Paymaster General‡	Kenneth Clarke

* Norman Tebbit was made unpaid Chancellor of the Duchy of Lancaster so that he would be in the Cabinet. His main job was Chairman of the Conservative Party, for which he was paid out of Party funds.
† The Chief Secretary to the Treasury was the Chancellor of the Exchequer's Number 2.
‡ The Paymaster General was the Employment Secretary's Number 2.

10.4   The Prime Minister and the Cabinet

Some of the views of Walter Bagehot, who wrote what is now a classic book *The English Constitution*, have already been noted. He also had something to say about the Cabinet and the Prime Minister.

He likened the Cabinet to a buckle which joins the legislative part of government to the executive. He pointed out that, while Parliament made laws and civil servants and other officials carried them out, the members of the Cabinet straddled the two arms of government, being both members of the legislature and the executive.

Far from criticising this arrangement, Bagehot saw it as something useful. It seemed to confirm the value of representative democracy. The people cast their votes and elect a House of Commons and the party which wins most seats forms the government. The leader of the government party becomes Prime Minister and he or she chooses a Cabinet from among the leading members of that party. As long as the Prime Minister and the Cabinet can count on the support of a majority in the House of Commons they can remain in office. If they lose that support eventually they must go.

Bagehot saw the Prime Minister as the leading member of a team of equals: *primus inter pares*, or first among equals.

The Prime Minister and the Cabinet are still accountable to the House of Commons and can be removed on a vote of 'No confidence' but, as we have seen, this has happened on only a handful of occasions in recent years. Party discipline and big parliamentary majorities ensure that the Cabinet can count on the Commons' support.

As for the Prime Minister's relationship with the Cabinet as being just a first among equals, that is certainly no longer true.

10.5   The Power of the Prime Minister

Most of the powers of the Prime Minister are based on conventions, rather than law, but they are real enough for all that.

The first, and obvious, power is the choice of the Cabinet. Members are appointed by the Queen on the Prime Minister's advice and can be dismissed just as easily. Of the 22 members of the Cabinet which Margaret Thatcher formed when she first became Prime Minister in 1979 only 8, including herself, remained in the 1986 list, shown in Figure 10.2. Of that 8, only 3 had retained their original posts: the Prime Minister herself, the Lord Chancellor and the Secretary of State for Wales. Figure 10.3 shows the extent to which Prime Ministers have used their powers of appointment and dismissal since 1945.

Fig. 10.3

Cabinet Appointments 1945–1986

Prime Minister	Period in Office (Years)		Cabinet Appointments (Number)
Clement Attlee	6¼	(1945–1951)	50
Winston Churchill	3½	(1951–1954)	33
Anthony Eden	1¾	(1954–1956)	12
Harold Macmillan	6¾	(1956–1963)	62
Alec Douglas Home	1	(1963–1964)	11*
Harold Wilson	5¾	(1964–1970)	73
Edward Heath	3¾	(1970–1974)	41
Harold Wilson	2	(1974–1976)	27
James Callaghan	3	(1976–1979)	35†
Margaret Thatcher	7 +	(1979–1986 +)	40

* Sir Alec Douglas Home inherited a Cabinet from Harold Macmillan and therefore did not form a completely new administration.

† James Callaghan inherited a Cabinet from Harold Wilson.

Of the 20 ministers who left Mrs Thatcher's Cabinets between 1979 and 1986, 9 resigned, for a variety of reasons, and 11 were dismissed. Although, as Figure 10.3 shows, her Cabinet changes were fewer, on average, than those of her post-war predecessors, of the original 21 who formed her first Cabinet in 1979 only 7 were still members in September 1986.

The Prime Minister's powers of ministerial appointment extend beyond the 20 or so first rank ministers and include about another 80 members of the government.

Then there are more than 20 civil service department heads whose appointments fall directly into the hands of the Prime Minister. Not all will, of course, be appointed by the same Prime Minister, but it is interesting to note that during Mrs Thatcher's first administration, between 1979 and 1983, 23 of the 27 Permanent Secretaries, as the departmental heads are called, retired, allowing her to choose their successors. Furthermore, a minister cannot of his own accord dismiss his Permanent Secretary. He must first obtain the Prime Minister's approval.

The Prime Minister also has enormous powers of patronage. Twice a year lists of honours are published under the authority of the Crown. As we have seen, the Queen awards a very limited number in a personal capacity but the great bulk of honours she confers are in response to recommendations from an advisory committee. It is unlikely that the Prime Minister would have the time, or even the inclination, to influence the majority of the committee's recommendations but, undoubtedly, the more senior honours, of knighthoods and above, can well come within No 10 Downing Street's control.

Harold Wilson's last honours list, in 1976, was widely criticised because some awards were thought to have been made to unusual people. Margaret Thatcher has used her powers of political patronage to a much greater extent than her immediate predecessors. Of the ten companies which made direct cash contributions to the Conservative Party during the 1983 general election year, the chairmen of seven of them were given knighthoods or peerages during Mrs Thatcher's period of office, as Figure 10.4 shows. This is not to suggest that honours cannot, or should not, be given for 'political services', as the honours list usually puts it. The list is provided as just another example of Prime Ministerial power.

Fig. 10.4

Top Ten Donors of Cash to
The Conservative Party in 1983

Company	Name of Chairman	Amount Donated	Year of Peerage or Knighthood
British and Commonwealth Shipping	Lord Cayzer	£94050	1982
Hanson Trust	Lord Hanson	£80000	1983
Racal	Sir Ernest Harrison	£75000	1981
Plessey	Sir John Clark	£55000	1971
London & Northern	J Mackenzie	£54000	—
Distillers	J M Connell	£50000	—
Trafalgar House	Sir Nigel Broackes	£50000	1984
Rank Organisation	Sir Patrick Meaney	£45000	1981
Taylor Woodrow	Lord Taylor	£44035	1982
Trusthouse Forte	Lord Forte	£41100	1982

Additionally, as we have already noted, the Prime Minister recommends the appointment of Church of England Archbishops, Bishops and Deacons; senior judges; Privy Counsellors; and specific people, such as the Poet Laureate, some senior university officers and heads of public boards and corporations.

In terms of power and influence, therefore, a Prime Minister is today clearly well above any of his or her Cabinet colleagues.

10.6   The Cabinet at Work

The full Cabinet usually meets once a week, for up to three hours before lunch on Thursdays, in the Cabinet Room at No 10 Downing Street. It can meet, and has met, more frequently, the extra day usually being Tuesday. In times of emergency it has met on other days as well.

The seats around the Cabinet table are set out in order of importance, with the Cabinet Secretary on the Prime Minister's immediate right and the most influential ministers sitting opposite or nearby. Exactly how Cabinet meetings are conducted is officially secret but enough has been said or written by former ministers to allow a reasonably accurate picture to be built up.

The Prime Minister is, of course, chairman and the method of chairing depends greatly on personality. Clement Attlee, who was Labour Prime Minister between 1945 and 1951, was said to be the perfect chairman, allowing everyone who wanted to speak to do so and then summing up quickly and fairly at the end. Prime Ministers with strong personalities might seem able to dominate their Cabinets if they choose to but much depends on their compositions.

Most Cabinets contain politicians who are important figures in their own right and Prime Ministers have to have been in office a long time before they can say that everyone around the Cabinet table is their own personal choice. Even Margaret Thatcher, after winning two consecutive general elections and being in power for more than seven years, had to appoint some Cabinet colleagues who did not necessarily share all her views, particularly on economic and social policies.

Even though a Cabinet of about 20 may not seem an over-large committee, there is a limit to how much can be successfully covered in three hours or less per week. It is possible to get through the agenda only because a limited number of members will speak on a particular item. The Social Services Secretary will obviously be more knowledgeable and better briefed about the Health Service, for example, than any of his colleagues, while the Foreign Secretary will be regarded as the expert on foreign affairs. Most ministers, however, will be content to 'fight their own corners' on most occasions and put their main efforts into protecting what they see as their departmental interests, and particularly their departmental budgets. Sometimes, when they share a common interest, a group of ministers may support each other and try to persuade the rest of the Cabinet to go along with them.

If a Prime Minister wants agreement on a particular policy and senses that the Cabinet is divided, there are various ways in which he can get their support. Harold Wilson, when he was Prime Minister in 1966, was faced with a financial crisis in which the pound was under pressure in international money markets. Some Cabinet members wanted to devalue sterling but Wilson and the Chancellor of the Exchequer were unwilling to do so. The Prime Minister got what he wanted by inviting each would-be devaluer in turn to make his point and gradually the case for devaluation crumbled and eventually collapsed.

Margaret Thatcher is said to have adopted a tactic whereby she stated her own views strongly and then challenged other members of the Cabinet to disagree with her. This approach, allied to a strong personality, would be daunting for any except the most confident minister.

A more subtle, and more effective, way for a Prime Minister to ensure Cabinet support is to by-pass the full Cabinet and rely more on committees, or even 'ad hoc' groups. This became very much a feature of Mrs Thatcher's approach and style and eventually contributed to the resignation of Michael Heseltine, in January 1986.

10.7   The Cabinet Committee System

Behind the full Cabinet there is now an important network of committees and subcommittees. Until recent years little was known of their existence, let alone their names and membership, but now, through academic research and unofficial 'leaks', a reasonably clear picture has emerged.

There were short-lived committees and subcommittees as long ago as the 19th century but it is only since 1945 that a permanent system has been established. There are now about 25 standing committees and subcommittees and about 100 which are temporary and 'ad hoc'. The most important standing committees are **Defence and Overseas Policy**, chaired by the Prime minister; **Economic Strategy**, again with the Prime Minister in the chair; **Home and Social Affairs**, chaired by the Home Secretary; and **Legislation**, with the Lord President of the Council in the chair.

Although Prime Ministers can, and occasionally do, invite non-Cabinet ministers to attend full cabinet meetings, it is not a regular practice. The membership of Cabinet committees and subcommittees, however, includes junior as well as senior ministers, and some subcommittees are chaired by the Secretary of the Cabinet, or one of the departmental Permanent Secretaries, and consist entirely of civil servants.

As we have already noted, during her period of office, Margaret Thatcher placed more reliance on committees and subcommittees than on the full Cabinet itself. For example, she called, on average, 40–45 Cabinet meetings a year, which was about half the number of her predecessors in the 1960s. The reason stemmed from her style of government, preferring quick and sharp decision taking to wide and long discussions.

More importantly, under her government decisions reached in one of the standing committees were regarded as having been reached by the Cabinet itself. This means that some Cabinet decisions were taken without some members even being consulted.

10.8   The Cabinet Office

Before the present century the Cabinet had no secretarial staff, indeed, some people argued that it would be unconstitutional if it did. There were no agendas and no minutes of proceedings were kept. The Prime Minister used to summon a meeting as and when he thought it necessary and after it had finished would tell his colleagues what had been agreed, based entirely on his own recollections. At the start of the First World War a secretariat was set up but, even then, Prime Minister Asquith did not allow anyone other than Cabinet ministers into the Cabinet room. In 1916, however, Prime Minister David Lloyd George appointed a permanent secretary and now there is a **Cabinet Office** headed by the **Secretary of the Cabinet**, who is also head of the civil service.

Although the Cabinet normally meets at No 10 Downing Street, it can, in theory, meet anywhere. Lloyd George on one occasion had a meeting in Inverness, so that he would not have to interrupt his Scottish holiday. There have, occasionally, been whole day meetings at Chequers, the Prime Minister's official residence in Buckinghamshire.

The Cabinet Office services the Cabinet and all its committees and subcommittees. It organises meetings; prepares agendas; decides, with the Prime Minister, which issues should go to the full Cabinet and which to a committee or subcommittee; and prepares and distributes Cabinet papers, including minutes.

The Secretary of the Cabinet has become a powerful figure. He is not only close to the Prime Minister in the work that he does, he is also physically nearby, the Cabinet Office being linked to No 10 by means of a green baize door. Margaret Thatcher placed great reliance on her Cabinet Secretary, Sir Robert Armstrong, making him head of the civil service and, in an unprecedented move, asking him to remain in his post beyond his normal retirement age so as to preserve the continuity she obviously desired.

As a unit, the Cabinet Office is more than just a secretariat. It includes the Central Statistical Office, the Management and Personnel Office, which deals with civil service recruitment, training and efficiency, and an Historical Section, which maintains government records.

10.9   The Downing Street Centre

Soon after he became Prime Minister, in 1970, Edward Heath set up a high level 'think tank', the **Central Policy Review Staff** (CPRS). It consisted of 16 graduates from a variety of academic disciplines, headed by Lord Rothschild, who had previously been in charge of Shell Petroleum. It was attached to the Cabinet Office and was intended to advise the Cabinet collectively, particularly on the government's overall strategy.

After Heath had departed subsequent Prime Ministers continued with the CPRS, under different chairmen, but Margaret Thatcher was obviously not keen to use it and, in July 1983, it was disbanded. She preferred her own **No 10 Policy Unit**, which she staffed with people who shared her political views. She also sought advice from outside bodies, such as the **Centre for Policy Studies**, which she and Sir Keith Joseph had set up in 1975, while in opposition.

There is now a strong, if not large, **Downing Street Centre**, which includes the Prime Minister's Private Secretary, and Press Secretary. The Chief Whip is also a contributor to this central advisory unit, keeping the Prime Minister in touch with backbench opinion and assisting her in the choice of ministers and junior ministers. Other Prime Ministers have felt the need to strengthen their personal staff and Harold Wilson, for example, had an even larger Downing Street office than the present one.

10.10   Collective Responsibility

As the modern Cabinet evolved so the convention of **collective responsibility** evolved with it. The convention simply means that any policy agreed by the Cabinet is a collective one and must be supported by all members. If a minister feels unable to go along with a particular decision he should resign.

There have been several examples of ministers leaving the cabinet because they have been unable to support a particular collective view. The most recent was in January 1986 when Michael Heseltine, Secretary of State for Defence, resigned because he disagreed with Cabinet policy on the future of the Westland Helicopter company. However, his reasons for doing so were perhaps not as clear cut as that. He seemed as much concerned about the way Mrs Thatcher was running the Cabinet.

Soon after Heseltine's departure Leon Brittan, the Trade and Industry Secretary, also resigned. His resignation, however, had less to do with collective responsibility and more with individual responsibility for the work of his department, and this is something we will look at in the next chapter.

Earlier examples of ministerial resignations provide better evidence of the operation of the doctrine of collective responsibility. In 1966 Frank Cousins, Minister of Technology, objected to the Labour government's prices and incomes policy and left the Cabinet. Two years later, Lord Longford resigned because he could not agree to cuts in education funding.

Although resignations of this kind have been comparatively few, most people agree that the convention of collective responsibility still exists and that it applies to all members of the Cabinet, including the Prime Minister.

Unusually, in 1975, the Labour Prime Minister, Harold Wilson, temporarily suspended the application of the convention on the issue of membership of the European Community. Although he himself wanted to remain in the Community, he realised that some members of his Cabinet did not, so agreed to allow them to differ and even campaign against staying in. A referendum eventually confirmed Britain's continuing membership. The fact that Wilson felt it necessary to do this supports the view that the convention still has force and meaning.

10.11   Cabinet or Prime Ministerial Government?

Since the 1960s there has been considerable discussion about the increasing power of the Prime Minister in relation to the Cabinet and some writers have suggested that Cabinet government is in danger of being replaced by Prime Ministerial government, if this has not already occurred.

Clearly a Prime Minister is better placed to know more about the totality of government policies than an individual minister, but, equally clearly, a minister will know more about his own department than a Prime Minister ever could. So the question might be one of balancing the value of overall as compared with detailed knowledge.

In the final analysis, however, the power of a Prime Minister depends upon his personality, upon the extent to which he wishes to impose his views on the Cabinet, and upon his standing within the country and the party he leads. If he has a strong personality, has a clear idea of what he wants his government to achieve, and enjoys a high reputation within his party, all the ingredients for Prime Ministerial government are there.

Once she had settled in after the 1979 general election, Margaret Thatcher began to show some of the requisite qualities of a dominant Prime Minister and the successful Falklands campaign confirmed the strength of her position. Winning the 1983 general election with a huge Commons majority made her virtually unassailable.

But it would be unwise to read too much into this. The office of Prime Minister is not as institutionalised as, for example, the United States presidency. It rests mainly on conventions. Because of this, a shift in power from the Cabinet to the Prime Minister at some particular time does not necessarily mean that this is a permanent movement. A different personality at the top coupled with a Cabinet of stronger individuals could change the relationship almost overnight.

All that can be said with certainty is that the British system, because it is based so much on flexible practices and understandings, provides an ideal environment for a forceful Prime Minister to dominate his Cabinet if he sets out to do it, and if his colleagues allow him to get away with it.

Questions and Assignments

1 How did the present day Cabinet evolve?
2 What are the Prime Minister's main sources of power?
3 What are the purposes of Cabinet committees?
4 What are the functions of the Secretary of the Cabinet?
5 What is meant by collective responsibility?
6 How far is it true to say that Cabinet government has been replaced by Prime Ministerial government?
7 If you were given the task of reducing the size of the present Cabinet to 11, including the Prime Minister, which of its members would you leave out? Explain why you have discarded some and kept others.
8 'I could not waste any time having internal arguments.' Mrs Thatcher made this remark in an interview in November 1983. In not more than 800 words, argue the case for **and** against this approach to Cabinet government.

Chapter 11

The Central Departments

Most Cabinet ministers are responsible for major central departments of state and are styled either Secretary of State or Minister. They are supported in their departments by a political hierarchy of Ministers of State and Parliamentary Secretaries and by permanent civil servants headed by the senior official called the Permanent Secretary. The Permanent Secretary is not only the full time head of the department but the minister's chief adviser.

Each minister is also supported by a Private Office, containing his Principal Private Secretary, a civil servant who is constantly at his side, and his Parliamentary Private Secretary an MP or peer who assists him in Parliament. Some people argue, however, that a minister's Private Office should be strengthened by including outside advisers as well as career civil servants, on the lines of the ministerial cabinets in the French system of government.

The relationship between the minister and his permanent secretary is vital to the smooth running of the department and, although ministers rarely have a choice in the appointment of their permanent secretaries, most seem to work harmoniously together.

The relationship between ministers and their civil servants also rests on the convention of ministerial responsibility, which states that a minister is responsible for everything that happens in his department, whether he is aware of it or not, and is accountable to Parliament for what is done on his behalf. Ministers have, from time to time, accepted responsibility for their civil servants' errors and misdeeds and have resigned, but there have been other instances when they have ignored criticism and remained in post. The convention, therefore, seems to rest more on political expediency than principle.

Central government operates through a civil service machine, consisting of about 600000 people, about a quarter of them based in London and the rest in other parts of the country.

Since the middle of the 19th century British civil servants have been recruited and promoted on the basis of merit, and have consequently established an international reputation for honesty and political neutrality. In recent years, however, this neutrality has at times been strained and former senior officials, as well as those within the service, have expressed concern about this unwelcome trend. The fact that the head of the civil service is also Secretary of the Cabinet has, in particular, been questioned, on the grounds that his loyalties have sometimes been stretched in competing directions.

11.1   Departments of State

There are currently 15 major **Departments of State** headed by Cabinet ministers and 16 more minor or sub-departments for which, with one or two exceptions, non-Cabinet ministers are responsible.

The full list, with a broad indication of each department's functions, is given in Figure 11.1.

Fig. 11.1

Central Government Departments, 1986

Major Departments

Department	Functions	Responsible Minister
Ministry of Agriculture, Fisheries & Food	Policies for agriculture, horticulture, fishing & food	Minister of Agriculture, Fisheries and Food
Ministry of Defence	Defence policy & control of armed services	Secretary of State for Defence
Department of Education & Science	Promotion of education and science	Secretary of State for Education & Science
Department of Employment	Manpower policies, labour legislation, payment of unemployment benefits, work permits for immigrants, small businesses, tourism, careers services	Secretary of State for Employment

Department	Functions	Responsible Minister
Department of Energy	Policies for all forms of energy	Secretary of State for Energy
Department of the Environment	Planning policies, local government, new towns, housing, inner cities, protection of the environment, sport and recreation, conservation, historic buildings and ancient monuments	Secretary of State for the Environment
Foreign and Commonwealth Office	Conduct of Britain's overseas relations	Secretary of State for Foreign & Commonwealth Affairs
Department of Health & Social Security	National Health Service, local authority personal services, public health and hygiene, social security system	Secretary of State for Health & Social Security
Home Office	Administration of law and order, including criminal justice, police, prison and probation services, electoral matters, civil defence, fire services, regulation of firearms and dangerous drugs, gaming and lotteries, immigration, race relations, broadcasting, sex discrimination	Secretary of State for Home Affairs
Northern Ireland Office	Central government functions in Northern Ireland	Secretary of State for Northern Ireland
Scottish Office	Central government functions in Scotland	Secretary of State for Scotland
Department of Trade and Industry	Industrial and commercial policy, export promotion, competition policy, company law, consumer protection	Secretary of State for Trade and Industry

Department	Functions	Responsible Minister
Department of Transport	Land, sea and air transport, shipping and ports, HM Coastguard service, motorways and trunk roads	Secretary of State for Transport
HM Treasury	Economic strategy, control of manpower and pay in the civil service	Chancellor of the Exchequer
Welsh Office	Central government functions in Wales	Secretary of State for Wales

Minor Departments or Sub-departments

Lord Chancellor's Department	Administration of the Supreme Court, judicial appointments, law reform
Office of Arts and Libraries	Promotion of the arts, public libraries and museums
HM Customs and Excise	Customs and excise duties, value added tax
Export Credits Guarantee Department	Insurance and credit facilities for exporters
Central Office of Information	Government publicity and information
Board of Inland Revenue	Administration of tax system
Law Officers' Department	Legal advice to the government, representation of the Crown in court cases
Management and Personnel Office (Part of Cabinet Office)	Organisation, management and efficiency of the civil service
Ordnance Survey Department	Official surveying and mapping
Overseas Development Administration	Overseas financial aid and technical assistance
Parliamentary Counsel's Office	Drafting of government Bills

Paymaster General's Office	Government banking services and payment of public service pensions
Office of Population Censuses and Surveys	Administration of Marriage Acts, registration of births, marriages and deaths, population estimates
Procurator General and Treasury Solicitor's Department	Legal services for government departments
HM Stationery Office	Government printer and publisher
Office of Tele-communications	Monitoring of British Telecom and other operators

11.2   Departmental Ministers

As we have seen, the majority of Cabinet ministers are responsible for major central departments, some of them, such as Defence, Employment and Social Services, being big spenders and others, such as the Treasury and Trade and Industry, mainly co-ordinators and controllers. In each major department there is a political structure consisting of ministers of various ranks and below them a non-political structure of civil servants.

The departmental head is either a **Secretary of State** or a **Minister** and he will be assisted by one or more **Ministers of State**, depending on the size of the department. A Minister of State is of immediate sub-Cabinet rank, but will occasionally be given a Cabinet seat, and will normally be responsible to the Minister or Secretary of State for a major sector of the department. Sometimes a Minister of State will be in complete charge of a small department.

The next rank down is the **Parliamentary Secretary**. If the head of the department is styled Secretary of State then, to avoid confusion, Parliamentary Secretaries are called Parliamentary Under-Secretaries. One of the main jobs of a Parliamentary Secretary is to deputise for a Minister in Parliament, answering questions or piloting a Bill through its various stages. It is usual to have a Parliamentary Secretary in both Houses of Parliament. Figure 11.2 shows the distribution of ministers and junior ministers in the major central departments: the larger the department, the larger the number of junior ministers.

Fig. 11.2

Ministerial Composition of the
Major Central Departments

Department	Cabinet Minister/ Sec. of State	Minister of State	Parliamentary Sec./ Under-Sec.
Agriculture, Fish & Food	1	2	1
Defence	1	2	2
Education & Science	1	—	2
Employment	2	—	2
Energy	1	1	2
Environment	1	2	3
Foreign & Commonwealth	1	4	1
Health & Social Security	1	2	3
Home Office	1	2	2
Northern Ireland Office	1	2	2
Scottish Office	1	1	3
Trade and Industry	1	3	3
Transport	1	1	1
Treasury	2	—	2
Welsh Office	1	1	1

11.3 Departmental Organisation

Figure 11.3 shows the typical organisation of a central department. The Secretary of State or Minister will have overall responsibility and Ministers of State will be in charge of major parts, or even, as in the Department of the Environment, for example, sub-departments such as Local Government, or Housing and Construction.

Below the political level, shown by the dotted line, the civil servants will be led by a **Permanent Secretary** who is also the Minister's principal adviser. Below the Permanent Secretary will be Deputy Secretaries, each responsible for a Division and, at the same level, specialist posts such as an establishments officer, concerned with staffing, an accountant, a solicitor, and perhaps a scientist or a statistician. Much will depend upon the nature of the Department's work. The next level down will consist of Branches, each headed by an Assistant Secretary. The structure of civil service grades is shown in Figure 11.4.

Fig. 11.3

Organisation of a Central Department

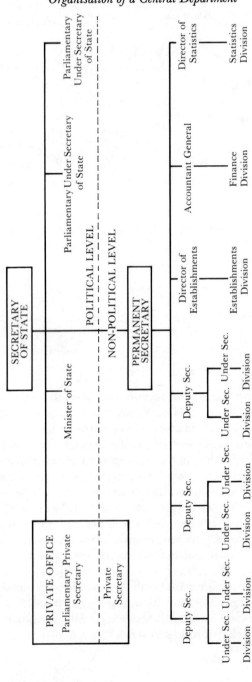

This is the structure of a typical department. Individual departments will vary in detail.

11.4 The Minister's Private Office

Each minister has a **Private Office** which is his own personal secretariat. It consists of his **Principal Private Secretary**, who is a civil servant, and his **Parliamentary Private Secretary**, who is an MP, supported by secretarial and clerical staff.

The Private Secretary occupies a key post. He is the minister's closest assistant and will accompany him everywhere. He will see more of him than the Permanent Secretary. A Private Secretary does not normally move when there is a change of minister so he may well work for several ministers, even from different political parties. Private Secretaries are usually potential 'high fliers', hoping to rise to a top post in the service.

The Parliamentary Private Secretary acts as the minister's unpaid 'Man Friday' in the House of Commons. Although this may seem a thankless task, it can be a step on the ladder to higher political office. It certainly gives a young MP excellent first hand experience of how government operates.

11.5 Is a Private Office Enough?

Some ministers engage political advisers as temporary civil servants. In this way they get advice from people who share their party political viewpoint, as a balance to the 'neutral' advice from the permanent civil servants. Quite often these advisers are academics or they may be brought in from industry or commerce.

The practice of using political advisers, although followed earlier by some politicians, only became properly established after 1974 when Prime Minister Harold Wilson agreed that any cabinet minister could appoint up to two advisers. When Margaret Thatcher became Prime Minister, in 1979, she put a limit of one adviser per minister. The attitude of the permanent civil servants to temporary advisers seems to vary but, on the whole, they are, at best, lukewarm to the idea. In France the equivalent of the British minister's Private Office is larger and more high powered. It is called the minister's **cabinet**, using the French pronunciation of the word, and consists of a mix of political advisers and civil servants who meet with the minister and collectively discuss and agree policy. Together they provide him with much more information and expertise than is available to his British equivalent and so put him in a stronger position when he presents policies to the Prime Minister and the Cabinet.

In recent years there have been calls from several quarters to introduce French style cabinets into the British system of government, although some people have pointed out that things operate differently in France and that it may not be possible to transplant such a device successfully. French civil servants, for example, unlike their British counterparts, may not spend all their working lives as public servants. It is possible for them to move easily in and out of the non-political and political worlds.

A former head of Mrs Thatcher's Policy Unit, Sir John Hoskyns, has recently argued that each minister should have a **private executive office** of up to eight people, rather like a French ministerial cabinet. This office would provide the minister with research facilities and better information and thus improve his own powers of decision taking.

The idea is gaining support within the political parties but whether it will ever be adopted is a matter of speculation.

11.6   The Minister and the Permanent Secretary

The working relationship between a minister and the permanent secretary is probably the most crucial element in the successful operation of a government department. The permanent secretary is the department's long term chief and the minister its political head. If the two do not function in reasonable harmony the effectiveness of the department may well be put at risk.

The popular view of the relationship has been very much influenced by the excellent television series 'Yes Minister', in which a clever and unscrupulous civil servant skilfully manipulates a rather naive and innocent politician. There is undoubtedly an element of truth in the picture the programmes have presented but there is also some distortion.

The average permanent secretary is an intelligent, well educated individual who has made the civil service his lifetime career. The average minister may be less intelligent and less well educated and is likely to be in his post for only a few years. If the politician is clearly incompetent or does not have a decisive enough approach to his job, it is inevitable that the civil servant will climb into the driving seat and run the department for him.

There is little evidence, however, that permanent secretaries actually want to do this. It should also be remembered that ministers, whatever their backgrounds, have had to fight their way up to the top and, accustomed to the rough and tumble of politics, are not as innocent as they are sometimes depicted to be.

Permanent secretaries, in contrast, on entering the civil service, settled for being always the No 2 in the background. If they had wanted to be No 1 then, presumably, they would have entered politics themselves.

Nevertheless, however intelligent and competent a minister might be, his time is obviously limited. He has Cabinet papers to read and meetings to attend. He has his duties in the House of Commons and in his constituency. If he is sensible, therefore, he will concentrate on major matters of policy within his department and leave the rest to his permanent secretary and his staff.

The minister – permanent secretary relationship, if it is to work, must be a true partnership. Once a genuine trust has developed the minister will see his permanent secretary as a source of wisdom and experience and he, in turn, will instinctively wish to support him in what he trying to do. Both will have the success of the department as their prime objective.

Ministers normally inherit permanent secretaries rather than choose them and occasionally a clash of personalities may occur. Richard Crossman, a former Labour minister, has written extensively about his relationship with his permanent secretary, Dame Evelyn Sharp, which was not always harmonious. Another former Labour minister, Shirley Williams, has expressed mixed feelings about her experience with civil servants. However, any differences are usually resolved. If a minister feels that the gulf between him and his permanent secretary is too great he may feel obliged to go to the Prime Minister and ask for a change. That this happens very rarely is evidence that the partnership usually works.

11.7   Ministerial Responsibility

Cabinet ministers are expected to share collective responsibility for all government policies. They are also individually responsible for the work of their departments.

Individual ministerial responsibility is, like so many aspects of the British system of government, based on a convention. The convention says that anything which is done by civil servants in the name of the Crown is done with the minister's authority, so he must take responsibility for it whether he knows about it or not. The purpose of the convention is to create responsible and accountable government, through elected politicians, while the permanent servants of the State remain neutral and clear of politics. In practice, however, the convention does not seem to work consistently.

Perhaps the best known post-war example of its operating effectively was the resignation, in 1954, of the Minister of Agriculture, Sir Thomas Dugdale, because some senior civil servants in his department had acted improperly over the sale of land on Crichel Down in Dorset. Although they had proceeded without his knowledge or authority, the minister accepted full responsibility.

Twenty-eight years later, in 1982, the man who had been Dugdale's Parliamentary Secretary, Lord Carrington, himself resigned as Foreign Secretary because he had allowed the dispute between Britain and Argentina over the Falkland Islands to drift into war. His two junior ministers, Humphrey Atkins and Richard Luce, resigned with him.

Two years later, in 1984, despite a highly critical report on mistakes and failures at the Maze Prison in Belfast, which resulted in 19 Republican terrorists escaping, neither the minister responsible for the prison, Nicholas Scott, nor his chief, the Northern Ireland Secretary, James Prior, offered to resign.

More recently, in 1986, as we have already seen, the Secretary of State for Trade and Industry, Leon Brittan, resigned after he had admitted 'leaking' a private letter by the Solicitor-General in order to embarrass a fellow minister, Michael Heseltine, in the middle of what became known as the Westland Affair.

In this case the issue seemed reasonably clear cut, as the minister had apparently acted on his own initiative. Other aspects of the Westland Affair were, however, more doubtful. A report of the House of Commons Defence Committee was highly critical of two civil servants, the Secretary of the Cabinet, Sir Robert Armstrong, and the Prime Minister's Chief Press Secretary, Bernard Ingham, yet neither appeared to be disciplined for their actions, nor did their political chief accept responsibility.

Over the years some ministers have accepted responsibility while others have not, so commentators have questioned whether there is any point in retaining the convention. From the viewpoints of both ministers and civil servants there are advantages in its retention. Ministers can, apparently, choose to accept responsibility or not, depending on particular political circumstances. Civil servants, on the other hand, are able to carry out their political masters' orders without fear of harming their professional careers. There is, however, a danger that some civil servants may become so associated with the policies of a particular government that their political neutrality may be put in doubt. We will look more closely at this danger later in this chapter.

11.8 The Civil Service Machine

There are currently just over 600 000 civil servants in Britain, of whom 100 000 are classed as industrial staff, in other words they work in state-owned industrial establishments of one kind or another, and the rest non-industrial, performing a variety of clerical, administrative and technical jobs in London and all over the country. Approximately half of them are women.

The departments employing the most civil servants are the Ministry of Defence, about 150 000, and the Departments of Health and Social Security, Inland Revenue, Employment, and the Prison Service, who have about 310 000 between them. The rest are spread comparatively thinly across the other departments. Although Whitehall is seen as the hub of the civil service machine, three quarters work outside London, following a deliberate policy in the 1960s and 1970s to disperse to places of high unemployment, such as the North East of England and South Wales.

The civil service reached a peak of nearly 1 million around 1960 and has more or less steadily contracted since then. Since 1979 there has been a planned reduction to a target of 593 000 by 1988.

Civil servants are officially defined as 'servants of the Crown, other than holders of political or judicial offices, who are employed in a civil capacity, and whose remuneration is paid wholly and directly out of moneys voted by Parliament'.

The bulk of non-industrial civil servants comprise an Administration Group, divided into a series of grades, from clerical assistant at the bottom to permanent secretary at the top. Figure 11.4 shows the various grades, with the basic entry qualifications and the promotion opportunities.

11.9 Origins of the Modern Civil Service

Until the middle of the 19th century entry to the civil service was based on patronage and favouritism and corruption was widespread. In 1854 a report by Sir Stafford Northcote and Sir Charles Trevelyan

Fig. 11.4

Civil Service Administration Group Grades

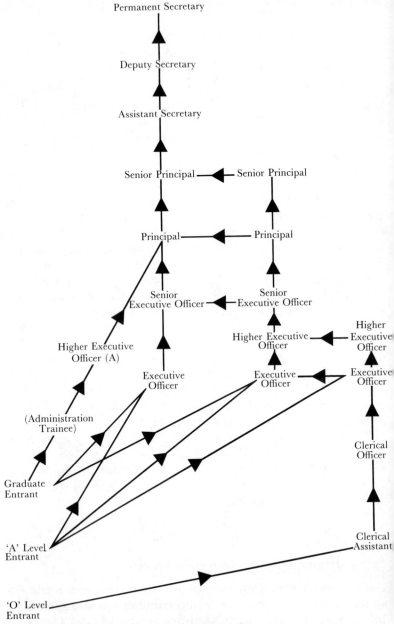

The arrowed lines show the entry and promotion paths.
The fast entry and promotion route is on the left, through the Administration Trainee Competition.

recommended a wholesale reorganisation so as to base the service on competitive selection, objective promotion and political neutrality. A **Civil Service Commission** was established in 1855 to supervise recruitment on the basis of merit and in the years that followed the British civil service became the envy of the world.

The Treasury, as the controller of the nation's purse strings, came to dominate the service and the main grades within it were called Treasury Classes. There were, however, critics of the Treasury's domination who argued that it had too negative an approach and was concerned more about saving money than improving quality.

In response to these criticisms, a committee was set up in 1966, under the chairmanship of Lord Fulton, Vice-Chancellor of Sussex University, to advise on improvements in structure, recruitment and management. The **Fulton Report** which was published in 1968 made a number of recommendations including the creation of a new **Civil Service Department** to take over the Treasury's role; the replacement of Treasury Classes by a single, unified grading structure; the establishment of a **Civil Service College**; the introduction of 'accountable management' into the service; and a greater openness in decision taking.

It is now nearly 20 years since the Fulton Committee reported and most, but not all, of its recommendations have been implemented. A Civil Service Department was created in November 1968 but abolished in November 1981, control of the service returning to the Treasury in conjunction with the Cabinet Office. A Civil Service College was opened at Sunningdale in Berkshire but it has not really lived up to the expectations of its supporters. Treasury Classes have been replaced by the grading structure set out in Figure 11.4 but many years elapsed before this was finally achieved. The Fulton concept of 'account-able management' seems based more on theory than practice and, far from there being more openness in decision taking, the reverse seems to have happened in recent years, with the Westland Affair as a striking example of an attempt at a ministerial 'cover up'.

The British civil service still enjoys a high reputation but there are other national public services which might justifiably claim to be better. The most senior part of the French civil service, for example, is certainly better trained and probably functions more effectively. It would be wrong, however, to blame the British civil service itself for its faults, the politicians who control it are as much responsible.

11.10   An Evaluation of the Central Government Machine

The Fulton Committee hoped that its recommended reforms would transform the central government machine and make it more efficient, more adaptable and more accountable. It placed its greatest emphasis on ending what it called the 'cult of the generalist'. It wanted to replace the arts-educated, non-specialist all-rounders, who had consistently risen to permanent secretary level, with a new breed of business-minded professionals who would inject a sharp dose of managerial accountability into the service. The reforms that have come have generally been a pale shadow of what Fulton wanted. What are the reasons for this?

There are mainly three. First, the people at the top of the service, whom the Fulton Report criticised, are the very people who were given the job of making the changes and very few people are able to change themselves unless forced to do so.

Second, top civil servants are, understandably, conscious of the need to be as politically neutral as possible and to protect their ministers, whatever party they represent, from criticism in Parliament or the world outside. Because of this they will err on the side of caution and be resistant to change.

Third, the career civil servant has made running the government machine his life's work, whereas the politician comes and goes, usually spending, at most, a few years in one ministerial post. It is not surprising, then, that the experienced official becomes a little cynical about radical ideas and changes of policy when he knows that he will have to live with these changes long after the politician has departed.

Nevertheless, most former ministers concede that, when in office, they were well served by a loyal, and generally efficient, machine, able and willing to do their bidding once they had made their policies clear.

One disturbing feature in the relationship between ministers and civil servants has developed in recent years and threatened to weaken the traditional neutrality of the service. It revolves around the degree to which a civil servant should always be loyal to his minister. A possible conflict of interest became most apparent during and following the trial of Clive Ponting, a senior official in the Ministry of Defence, who was prosecuted and acquitted in 1984 for an offence under the Official Secrets Act.

After his acquittal, Mr Ponting said he believed that a civil servant must ultimately place his loyalty to Parliament and the public interest above his obligation to the government of the day. This view seems broadly in line with that of Sir William Armstrong, as he then was, when he was head of the civil service in the government of Edward Heath. He argued that officials should be concerned more with 'the continuity of the realm rather than for the success of the party'.

The head of the civil service under Margaret Thatcher, Sir Robert Armstrong, however, issued a code of conduct for civil servants, in 1985, which stated that an official's duty 'first and foremost' is to his minister. If he is asked to do something of which he seriously disapproves then the official should go to his superior and, if necessary, to the permanent secretary. If this does not resolve the problem then he should resign, but remain silent.

The **First Division Association** (FDA), which represents about 8000 top civil servants, has reaffirmed the traditional neutrality of the service, arguing in an issue of **FDA News**, published in April 1986, that civil servants are 'servants of the Queen in Parliament'. This reaffirmation has to some extent brought it into conflict with the views of the Secretary of the Cabinet who is also head of the civil service.

Two former heads of the civil service, Sir Douglas Wass and Lord Bancroft, have also publicly expressed their disquiet about the possible politicisation of the service, which has evidently had some adverse affect on morale.

Another aspect of the debate has focused on Sir Robert Armstrong who has the delicate task of being head of the nation's civil servants as well as Secretary of the Cabinet and, as such, one of the Prime Minister's closest and most senior advisers. There is growing support for a move to return to the situation when the two offices were separate, because of the strains of competing allegiances which a joint holder inevitably experiences.

Questions and Assignments

1 What is the political structure of a central government department?
2 What does a permanent secretary do?
3 What is a minister's Private Office and what is its purpose?
4 Why is the relationship between a minister and his permanent secretary so important?
5 What is meant by the convention of individual ministerial responsibility and how does it operate in practice?

6 What could be done to improve the central government machine?

7 Using the information provided in Figure 11.1, suggest how you might reduce the number of major central government from 15 to 10.

8 Set out, in not more than 300 words, the terms of reference you would give to a new Committee of Inquiry set up to study and improve the British civil service, based on your views of what is wrong with the present day service.

PART III

THE DECENTRALISED GOVERNMENT PROCESS

Chapter 12

Government Off Centre

Although major policy making in Britain is centralised, its implementation is highly decentralised, by either a delegation of administrative decision making or a devolution of minor policy formulation.

Several of the major central departments, such as the DHSS, have strong regional and local networks and the Scottish and Welsh Offices are responsible for a range of functions which in England are carried out by a number of separate departments.

Northern Ireland used to enjoy the greatest degree of decentralisation until the growth of sectarian violence resulted, in 1972, in direct rule from London, under a newly appointed Secretary of State and Northern Ireland Office.

In the 1970s several attempts were made to introduce systems of devolved government for Scotland and Wales, giving each its own elected Assembly, but they did not attract sufficient support and were eventually dropped. The extent to which power will be devolved in the future is likely to depend upon the composition of the House of Commons after the next general election.

12.1 Away from Whitehall

On the surface the British system of government looks highly centralised. Parliament is firmly based in London, so are the Prime Minister and the Cabinet, and the civil service is usually associated with Whitehall, that wide street linking Westminster to Trafalgar Square.

Yet, as we have seen, out of some 600 000 civil servants, more than 400 000 work outside London and, if all the other public servants up and down the country are added, there is a total workforce of well over 2 million based and operating outside the capital city.

They are all, however, ultimately controlled, in one way or another, by London. The truth is that major policy making is centralised while its implementation is highly decentralised.

12.2   Delegation or Devolution

There are two main forms of decentralisation: by the **delegation** or the **devolution** of powers. Delegation involves a passing down of administrative decision making while devolution means the passing down of policy making.

When delegation is practised the scope of what can be done is narrowly defined and if a person or body to whom power is delegated wants to extend it the approval of the centre must first be obtained. When power is devolved the limits set are wider and the room for manoeuvre is greater. An example from the business world best illustrates the difference between the two forms of decentralisation. Delegation is similar to setting up a branch of a company away from headquarters. Devolution is like setting up a new company within a total corporate structure.

Imperial Chemical Industries (ICI) has a divisional structure, based mainly on products: Paints, Fibres, Alkalis, and so on, and powers are devolved to chief executives of these divisions. Within each division, however, power is delegated downwards for day to day management.

In British government, as Figure 12.1 shows, delegation can take place within one department or across a number of departments. Devolution can be to appointed or to elected bodies.

12.3   Decentralisation by Delegation

The Department of Health and Social Security (DHSS) is a good example of decentralisation by delegation. Major policies are determined nationally and then implemented through regional and local offices. The Department of Employment is organised in a similar way.

The Department of the Environment (DOE) and the Department of Trade and Industry (DTI) also have regional offices, with regional directors empowered to take major decisions within the broad framework of Whitehall policies. A regional director in the DTI, for example, can authorise a development grant to a firm for up to £2 million. The Scottish, Welsh and Northern Ireland Offices, on the other hand, implement a range of policies covering the activities of more than one department.

Fig. 12.1

The Decentralisation of Government

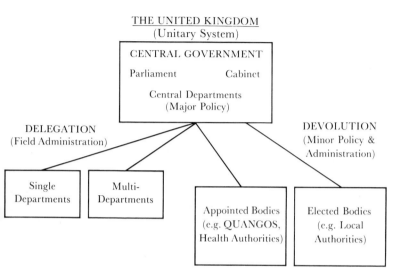

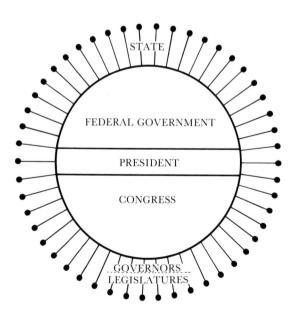

12.4   Decentralisation by Devolution

The National Health Service (NHS) is probably the best example of a devolution of minor policy powers to appointed authorities. In England a wide spread of powers has been devolved by the DHSS in London to 14 Regional Health Authorities (RHAs), and from them to 193 District Health Authorities (DHAs), as Figure 12.2 shows.

Fig. 12.2

Structure of the National Health Service in England

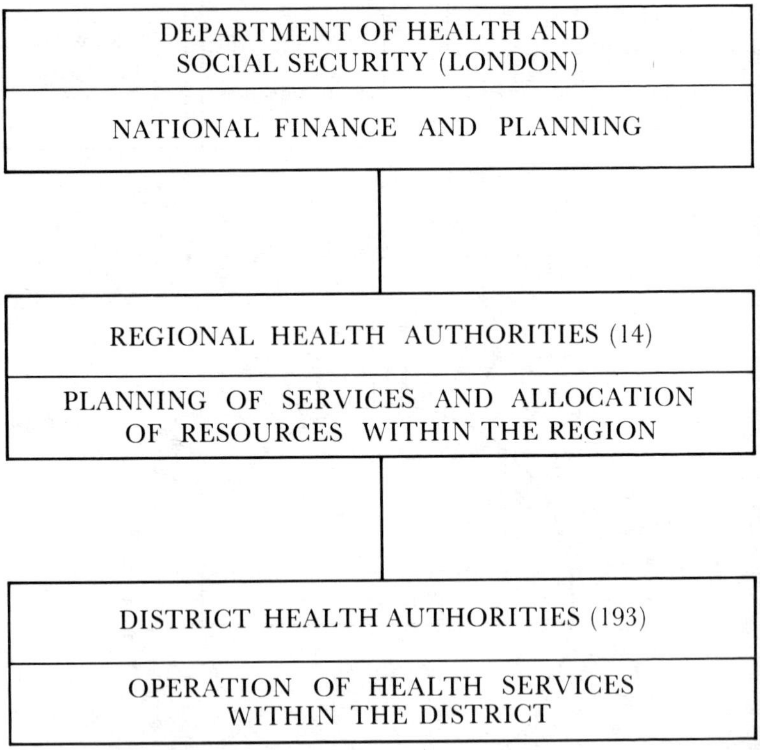

DEPARTMENT OF HEALTH AND SOCIAL SECURITY (LONDON)
NATIONAL FINANCE AND PLANNING

REGIONAL HEALTH AUTHORITIES (14)
PLANNING OF SERVICES AND ALLOCATION OF RESOURCES WITHIN THE REGION

DISTRICT HEALTH AUTHORITIES (193)
OPERATION OF HEALTH SERVICES WITHIN THE DISTRICT

The system of local authorities in Britain demonstrates the concept and practice of devolution to elected bodies. We will look more closely at the system in the next chapter.

12.5   Government in Scotland

The first Secretary for Scotland was appointed in 1885. He was redesignated Secretary of State for Scotland in 1926, but the Scottish Office did not take over the bulk of its responsibilities until 1939.

The Scottish Office is now a 'mini-government', led by the Secretary of State who is, of course, a member of the Cabinet. It now employs over 6000 civil servants, most of them operating from St Andrew's House in Edinburgh. The structure of the Office is shown in Figure 12.3.

Fig. 12.3

Structure of the Scottish Office

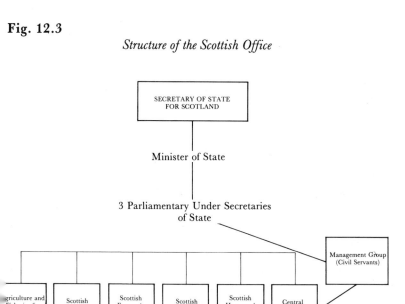

It will be seen from Figure 12.3 that as far as Scotland is concerned the Secretary of State combines the portfolios of the Departments of Education and Science, Health and Social Security, Trade and Industry, Environment, Transport, as well as the Home Office and the Ministry of Agriculture. It is a formidable array of powers, but all are ultimately subject to the control of the Cabinet in London.

There are also special arrangements for Scotland within Parliament. In the House of Commons there is a **Scottish Grand Committee**, consisting of 72 Scottish MPs, with sufficient English MPs added to maintain the overall party balance, which considers Scottish affairs and deals with the Second Reading Stages of Bills or parts of Bills which are concerned exclusively with Scotland. There is also a Select Committee on Scottish Affairs.

12.6   Government in Wales

Wales enjoys a smaller degree of devolution. The Welsh Office was established in 1964 and most of its 1000 civil servants are based in Cardiff. The Secretary of State, supported by a Minister of State and a Parliamentary Under Secretary, is responsible for primary and secondary education, town and country planning, water, roads, tourism, new towns, urban grants and, with the English minister, agriculture in Wales.

There is a **Welsh Grand Committee** in the House of Commons, with similar functions to its Scottish equivalent, and a Select Committee for Welsh Affairs.

12.7   Government in Northern Ireland

Following a history of conflict between the Catholic Irish and the Protestant Scottish Presbyterian settlers, the United Kingdom government was forced to accept, after the First World War, the principle of self-determination. The Government of Ireland Act, 1920, provided for Home Rule based on a division of the country into 6 counties in the North and 26 counties in the South.

Two parliaments were set up, one in Dublin and one in Stormont, near Belfast, but in 1922 a complete partitioning was agreed under the Treaty of Ireland Act, creating the Irish Free State, which eventually became the Republic of Eire.

From 1922 onwards the Northern Ireland parliament was dominated by one party, the Unionists, representing the Protestant majority who favoured union with Britain. They consistently won two thirds of the seats and determined policies in the Province. The Catholic minority felt increasingly discriminated against, enduring the worst housing and the highest levels of unemployment, and their dissatisfaction gradually expressed itself in violence in the 1960s, under the influence of the self-styled Irish Republican Army (IRA) which wanted a united Ireland, under what would be Catholic majority rule.

The violence increased to such a degree that in 1969, at the request of the Northern Ireland cabinet, British troops were sent to the Province from the mainland. At first their arrival was welcomed by the Catholics but, as violence grew on both sides, the prospects for a political solution worsened and in March 1972 the Conservative government of Edward Heath announced that the British Cabinet would take full responsibility for Northern Ireland's affairs until order was restored.

The Stormont parliament was dissolved and a new Northern Ireland Office set up to apply direct rule. The first Secretary of State for Northern Ireland was William Whitelaw. Since then many politicians, from both the Conservative and Labour parties, have carried this cross.

Several attempts were made in the 1970s to establish a new Northern Ireland Assembly, but with no lasting success. The most recent move by Margaret Thatcher's government to find a political solution has involved greater co-operation with the government in Dublin, through the *Anglo-Irish Agreement*, but this has been vehemently opposed by the hard line Unionists, led by Ian Paisley. The Province thus remains under direct rule from London.

The Northern Ireland Office consists of seven major departments: Finance, Agriculture, Commerce, Education, Environment, Health and Social Services and Manpower Services. The civil servants are based mainly in the Province so the Secretary of State and his two Ministers of State have to divide their time between Belfast, Westminster and Whitehall.

Direct rule is seen as a temporary arrangement but it is likely to continue until a long term political solution to Northern Ireland's problems can be found.

12.8 The Prospects for Political Devolution in the United Kingdom

If the United Kingdom remains a unitary State there will always be limits to the degree of devolution which is possible. As a unitary State, the national Parliament at Westminster will always be sovereign. This is in contrast to a federal system, such as in the United States of America, where the federal government in Washington DC is given specific powers by the Constitution, which apply to the whole nation, leaving other matters to the individual states, each with its own Governor and legislature.

It would be possible, however, to devolve more political power from the centre in the United Kingdom without destroying the unitary nature of the State. The political system in Northern Ireland prior to 1972 represents the greatest degree of devolution which has yet been achieved, giving the Province its own parliament and cabinet drawn from it, and might be used as a model.

In the 1960s it seemed that this kind of devolution might spread to Scotland and Wales. A great deal of resentment had built up at what was seen as the over-centralising attitude of the government in London and politicians with nationalist labels began to win seats in the House of Commons, particularly in by-elections. A growing cultural movement based on nationalism combined with one based on economic forces in both Scotland and Wales.   The arrival of North Sea oil off the Scottish coast accelerated the process.

The Labour government of Harold Wilson responded to the nationalistic calls in the traditional way of 'buying time' by setting up a Royal Commission on the Constitution, in 1969. The Commission took nearly four years to report by which time the Conservative government of Edward Heath had the task of receiving its recommendations and deciding how it should act on them.

Unfortunately, the views of the Commission's members were not unanimous and did not present the government with a clear line of policy. In any case, the deterioration of the political situation in Northern Ireland, the rise in world oil prices and the miners' strike posed more pressing problems.

In the event, the Heath government went out of office and Harold Wilson returned. In 1975 his government published a White Paper called 'Our Changing Democracy', proposing forms of devolution for Scotland and Wales.

There was to be an elected assembly for Scotland with legislative powers in the fields of social services, law, education and the environment, and a cabinet-type executive drawn from it and accountable to it.

The Welsh Assembly would be mainly a debating chamber, without law making powers, and the Welsh executive would be a committee of it, with only slightly more functions than those of the Secretary of State for Wales. The sovereignty of Parliament at Westminster would be preserved by its having the right of veto over either Assembly.

In 1976 the Labour government, now with James Callaghan as Prime Minister, presented a Bill based on the White Paper's proposals but, after it had passed its Second Reading Stage, it ran into opposition from both sides of the House and was eventually withdrawn.

In 1977 two Bills were introduced, one for Scotland and one for Wales. They contained similar proposals, with modifications, to those presented earlier. The Bills were eventually passed and received the Royal Assent in the summer of 1978. It had been agreed beforehand, however, that neither Act would be implemented unless a referendum revealed a clear majority for change. Two referenda were held, on 1 March 1979, and Parliament had decided beforehand that the Bills would only go ahead if at least 40% of the voters were in favour. The Welsh result was a clear rejection and, although there was a majority in Scotland in favour, it was less than 40%. In consequence, both Acts were dropped and never became law.

Since 1979, despite high regional unemployment in Wales and Scotland, the calls for devolution have not been strong and the Welsh Nationalist Party (**Plaid Cymru**), and the Scottish Nationalist Party (**SNP**) have fared badly in parliamentary elections. Devolution proposals however, form part of the policies of the Alliance and Labour parties and a future Parliament might well see another attempt to implement some form of change.

The situation in Northern Ireland is different and a solution more difficult to find. In addition to a level of unemployment much higher than that in mainland Britain, there are the problems of giving a religious minority a fair share of power, and of achieving some sort of amicable relationship with the Republic of Eire.

As in all communities where there is sectarian violence, an ultimate solution must be political but of all the possible approaches none has yet found majority support.

As a first step, some people would argue for a withdrawal of British troops but if this happened there is no guarantee that a bloodbath would not result. The British government has favoured power sharing, between Protestants and Catholics, but this has been tried and has not worked. The Protestant Unionists would like to have a return to the self government they enjoyed before 1972, or even a complete integration with Great Britain, but the Catholics, and the IRA, would resist this. At the other extreme, the Catholics would probably accept full integration with Eire, but this would be vigorously opposed by the Protestants. An intermediate solution might be the creation of a federal State, with the federal government based in Dublin and a considerable devolution of political power to state governments in the North and the South.

In the 19th century the Liberal Prime Minister, William Gladstone, once said that it was his mission in life to find a solution to the Irish problem, which was almost as vexing then as it is now. If a contemporary politician could do what all his predecessors have tried to do and failed, he would undoubtedly achieve a permanent place in history.

Questions and Assignments

1 What is the difference between delegation and devolution?
2 What are the main functions of the Secretary of State for Scotland?
3 What are the main functions of the Secretary of State for Wales?
4 What is meant by direct rule in Northern Ireland?
5 Why were the 1978 devolution proposals for Scotland and Wales not put into effect?
6 Outline four possible ways of ending direct rule in Northern Ireland
7 Using a major town or city as the focal point, draw up a list of not more than eight regions in England which, in your view, could be given their own elected assemblies under a system of devolved regional government. Each region should correspond broadly in population size and should have a communications network which would allow easy movement of people and goods within its boundaries.

    You will need to consult a map and gazetteer to carry out this assignment.
8 Make a list of all the politicians who have held the post of Secretary of State for Northern Ireland since 1972, indicating the posts they previously held and the appointments, if any, they were given afterwards.

Chapter 13
The Local Government System

The term local government is a little misleading because it is really only another form of decentralised government. Although local councils are elected bodies, they are subject to the will of Parliament and can be changed, or even abolished, by the government of the day.

The local government system is mainly a product of the 19th century but several large reorganisations during the 1960s and 1970s have created the present structure. The most recent change resulted in the abolition of the County Councils in the large city conurbations, including the Greater London Council (GLC). The end of the GLC has meant that London is the only major capital city without a system of government covering its whole area.

Local government in Britain is concerned essentially with providing services for the local community, the main ones being personal, environmental, amenity and protective services. Most local authorites are also engaged in some kind of trading activity. Nearly 10% of the nation's spending is done by local government, or about a quarter of total public expenditure.

Like central government, local authorities operate through departments, with a full time chief officer heading each. The departments are controlled by committees of elected councillors and the committees are themselves accountable to the full Council.

The money local authorities need to finance the services they provide comes partly from rates, which are local taxes on property owners, grants from central government, borrowings and from income from trading activities. Rates are a simple, but some people would say unfair, form of taxation and, since more than half their incomes come from grants, local authorities have become increasingly dependent on central government.

At one time party politics operated in only the large urban councils but it is now universal. This has sharpened interest in local affairs, but political activity is still much lower than it is nationally. It has also brought some local authorities into conflict with a central government that does not share their political views.

The position of local government in Britain would be improved if it had a better system of local funding and perhaps, if, through proportional representation, its politics became less polarised.

13.1   The Nature of Local Government in Britain

Local government in Britain is really another form of decentralised government from London. Lawyers call the elected local bodies 'creatures of statute'. In other words, they were established by Act of Parliament and can just as easily be wound up. The ending of the **Greater London Council** (GLC) and the other Metropolitan County Councils on 1 April 1986 is evidence of this.

What makes the local authorities, as they are called, distinctive is the fact that they are elected bodies and have power to levy taxes as well as limited opportunities to make local laws. But all these powers are subject to the will of Parliament and so, ultimately, to the will of the government of the day.

13.2   The Development of Local Government

Although it is possible to trace the history of local government back to mediaeval times, the present system is really a product of the 19th century. The structure is based on a distinction between rural and urban areas, with London receiving different treatment, and, because of its different geography and population distribution, with an alternative arrangement for Scotland.

The various local authorities in England and Wales were established by Act of Parliament in the following sequence:

> 1835 – Town Councils
> 1888 – County Councils for the counties, County Borough Councils for the larger towns and the London County Council for Greater London
> 1894 – District Councils for the rural areas
> 1899 – Metropolitan Councils for the boroughs within the County of London

Changes in the inter-war years had made the populations of some of the authorities disproportionate to the rest and there were calls for reform but nothing was done before the outbreak of war in 1939.

After 1945 the pressure for reform returned and eventually the Redcliffe-Maud Royal Commission was set up to look at local government in England. It presented its report in 1969. Meanwhile, a separate inquiry had been made into London government by the Herbert Royal Commission, which reported earlier, in 1960.

The Redcliffe-Maud Report had recommended a streamlined system for England, with 58 single-tier authorities, each with a population of between 250000 and 1 million, except for densely populated areas where there should be additional top tier bodies concerned with planning and environmental services above a bottom tier responsible for personal services.

There was considerable opposition to the proposals from the existing County Councils and District Councils and after the 1970 general election, the Conservative Government of Edward Heath announced its plans, which accepted the suggestion of two tiers in the metropolitan areas but also retained two tiers in the rest of the country.

The Herbert Report was more warmly received and most of its proposals were put into effect.

A wholesale reform was eventually carried out by the London Government Act of 1963 and the Local Government Act of 1972.

13.3 The Reformed Local Government Structure

The new structures which were brought into effect in 1965 for London and in 1974 for the rest of England and Wales are shown in Figure 13.1.

It will be seen that in England and Wales, outside London, the top tier authority was the County Council and the bottom the Parish Council or Meeting. In between there were District Councils.

The 47 Non-Metropolitan County Councils were mostly the old, historic shires, each based on an established county town. The Metropolitan County Councils comprised the six largest city conurbations: Greater Manchester, Merseyside, West Midlands, Tyne and Wear, South Yorkshire and West Yorkshire. Within each of these Metropolitan Counties there were 36 Metropolitan District Councils, with populations ranging from about 170000 to over 1 million in the case of Birmingham.

The Non-Metropolitan Counties have populations varying from just over 100000 for Powys in Wales,or just over 110000 for the Isle of Wight, to over 1.5 million for Essex, Hampshire and Kent.

Fig. 13.1
Reformed Local Government Structure for England and Wales

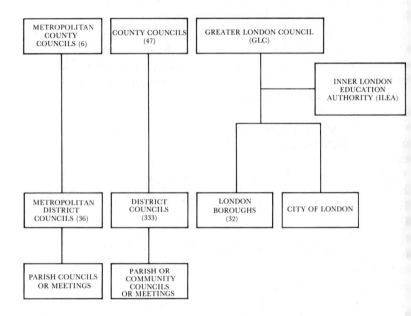

The Non-Metropolitan Districts are a mixture of town and country and include mainly rural areas as well as large established towns. Not all Districts have Parish Councils. If a Parish has 200 or more electors it is compulsory to have a Council. Otherwise it is optional.

In London the GLC covered an area of nearly 800 square miles with a population of some 7 million. Within its boundaries were 32 London Boroughs plus the City of London, that square mile of mainly financial institutions which has retained its independent status, including its own distinctive police force. To co-ordinate education services in the densely populated central area of London a new body, the **Inner London Education Authority** (ILEA) was formed, as a committee of the GLC.

13.4   Have the Structural Reforms Worked?

Despite the large scale structural reforms of the 1960s and 1970s, dissatisfaction has continued. Under the revised structure, old counties, such as Rutland and Huntingdonshire, disappeared, to the disappointment of some of their residents. Small, old boroughs lost their status and became parishes, to the dismay of some of their leading citizens.

The politicians, too, were not overwhelmingly happy with the changes. The Labour Party disliked the domination of the shire counties in matters such as education and planning services, and would like to restore power to the larger District Councils.

The Conservative government, led by Margaret Thatcher, soon after taking office in 1979 became concerned about what it regarded as the high-spending Labour Councils, particularly in the Metropolitan Counties. Their behaviour was putting national economic policies, based on tight public spending limits, at risk.

The GLC, under its articulate and publicly attractive leader, Ken Livingstone, became a particular target for criticism. Eventually a pledge was belatedly inserted into the Conservative Party's manifesto for the 1983 general election that the GLC and the other Metropolitan County Councils would be abolished. The legislation for this was eventually passed, after opposition from some unexpected quarters, and from 1 April 1986 they ceased to exist.

The new, revised structure for England and Wales, excluding London, is shown in Figure 13.2. The revised arrangements for London are shown in Figure 13.3.

The 1986 changes have required the transfer of functions from the Metropolitan County Councils to the Metropolitan District Councils but in the case of London the disappearance of the GLC has produced additional problems, resulting in the creation of a **London Residuary Body** (LRB), to pick up all the loose ends which were left. It also resulted in the creation of a number of 'ad hoc' bodies to administer services for which no home in the London Boroughs could be found.

The LRB is a wholly appointed organisation, intended to have a life time of five years, but this may have to be extended if another reform of London government does not intervene. In 1987 it is expected to spend more than £600m, of which £354m will be used to pay interest on debts. Although it will be able to recover 80% of this in charges, it will still need to collect £100m from the London Boroughs.

Fig. 13.2
Local Government Structure for England and Wales from 1 April 1986

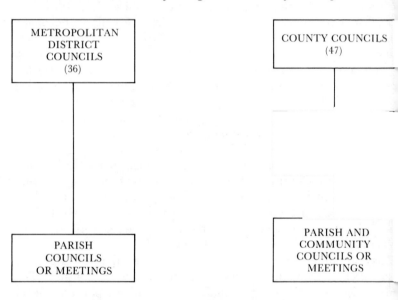

Perhaps the biggest job facing the LRB is disposing of about 10 000 buildings once owned by the GLC, including the massive County Hall, sitting on the south bank of the Thames, near Westminster Bridge and facing the Houses of Parliament.

Fig. 13.3
London Government from 1 April 1986

Figure 13.4 shows how the old GLC functions have been redistributed since April 1986.

While it was in being, the GLC had its critics and its defenders. It deliberately provoked the Conservative government of Mrs Thatcher by displaying a banner outside County Hall, clearly visible from the Houses of Parliament, giving up-to-date figures of

Fig. 13.4

*Redistribution of GLC Functions from
1 April 1986*

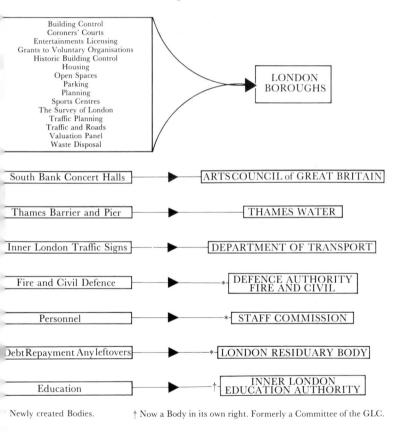

Newly created Bodies.   † Now a Body in its own right. Formerly a Committee of the GLC.

rising unemployment, and by financing what some people saw as left wing and radical minority cultural activities.

Nevertheless, there is a sizeable body of opinion which questions the wisdom of abolishing it without putting something in its place to co-ordinate those Greater London services which stretch right across the region. After all, London is now the only major capital in the world that does not have an authority responsible for all the spread of public services and activities which any large city is bound to require. The retention of the ILEA, to co-ordinate education in the centre of the conurbation, demonstrates that London, because of its size and complexity, demands treatment which is different from that in the rest of the country.

13.5   The Business of Local Government

Local authorities were created essentially to provide services for their local communities. They were given elected councils so that the people being served could have some say in what was provided. Figure 13.5 shows the range of services provided and how they are distributed among the various councils.

Fig. 13.5

*The Distribution of Local Authority
Services in England and Wales*

Service	Metropolitan District Councils	County Councils	District Councils	London Borough Councils
Strategic Planning		*		*
Local Planning	*		*	*
Transport & Roads	*	*		*
Education	*	*		*
Social Services	*	*		*
Housing	*		*	*
Fire Service	*	*	*	New Authority
Police Service	*	*		Home Secretary
Trading Standards	*	*		*
Environmental Health	*		*	*
Libraries	*	*		*
Museums	*	*	*	*
Leisure Facilities	*	*	*	*
Tourism	*	*	*	*
Cemeteries	*		*	*
Footpaths	*	*	*	*
Smallholdings	*		*	*
Allotments	*		*	*

The services provided fall into four main groups:

Personal Services:
education, social services, health services, housing

Environmental Services:
public health services, refuse collection, highways, planning controls

Amenity Services:
sports and leisure centres, libraries, concert halls, theatres, museums, sponsorship of the arts

Protection Services:
police service, fire service, trading standards

Many authorities are also engaged in **trading services** for which they charge the public and make profits which help to increase their incomes. For example, Doncaster has a racecourse, Hull a telephone service, Manchester and Luton have airports and Birmingham a bank.

13.6 Local Government in Scotland

There was a major reorganisation of the local government structure in Scotland in 1975, resulting in the creation of a two tier system, with a third, bottom tier, equivalent to the parishes in England and Wales. The structure is shown in Figure 13.6.

Fig. 13.6

Local Government Structure in Scotland

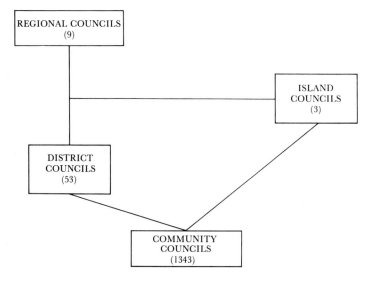

The revised structure has not been an unqualified success. Some critics have complained that the Regional Councils are too remote and some that the division of functions between the Regions and the Districts is confusing. This attempt at regionalism seems, however, to have silenced the calls for devolution, but this may be only a temporary situation.

13.7   The Management of Local Government

Local authorities, like central government, operate through departments. They differ, however, in their supervision at a political level. Whereas central departments have a minister at the head, local departments are controlled and answerable to committees. On these committees across the nation sit some 100 000 elected councillors, part time and unpaid. It is because these local politicians, unlike those at Westminster, are part time that they are very dependent on the advice of their full time officials.

Fig. 13.7

Local Authority Committee Structure

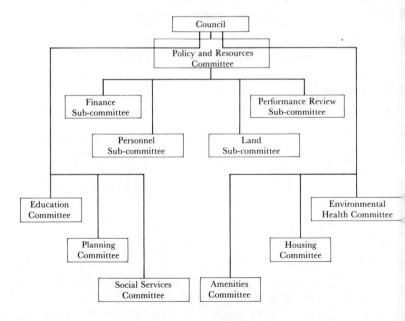

Sample structure based on the Bains Report.

Another difference between central and local government lies in the backgrounds and training of the permanent heads of departments. Permanent secretaries are 'generalists', with little or no professional training, whereas most local authority chief officers, as they are called, are specialist professionals, with engineering, legal, medical, or some other technical qualifications.

Local chief officers advise the councillors on policy matters and their advice is generally accepted but ultimately, of course, any local policies are subject to the overriding views at Westminster and Whitehall. Local councillors tend, therefore, to be more concerned about **how** a service is provided than **whether** it should be provided.

For example, there are obligations placed on local authorities by Education Acts to provide certain education services, and the Secretary of State for Education and Science can, through circulars, memoranda and letters, indicate how he would like certain aspects of the services to operate. Nevertheless, individual authorities can interpret these directions in different ways and can,

Fig. 13.8

Local Authority Management Structure

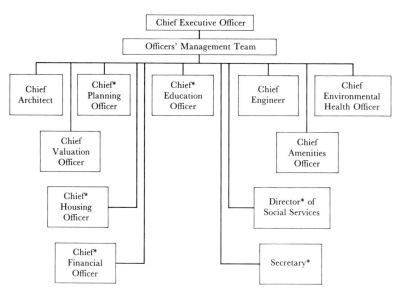

Based on the Bains Report.

* Member of Officers Management Team.

within limits, vary the distribution of resources between the various services. One can put more into nursery or primary education while another can give a priority to further education. All are ultimately constrained, however, by the financial limits which central government may impose.

Departmental committees usually meet monthly. A councillor is in the chair and the chief officer of the department attends to report on its work. The committee later reports to the full Council. The committee, and particularly its chairman, is therefore the link between the department providing the service and the general public.

A typical committee structure of a local authority is shown in Figure 13.7 and a typical management structure in Figure 13.8.

13.8　The Finance of Local Government

About a quarter of all public spending in Britain is done by local authorities. It amounts to nearly 10% of the nation's annual income, or Gross Domestic Product (GDP), as it is called. By any standards, this is very big business, and the biggest single item of spending is on education: about a third of the total.

The income to cover this expenditure comes from four main sources: rates, central government grants, borrowing and trading services.

Rates are a local tax on property. With some exceptions, each property in the local authority area is independently assessed and given what is called a **rateable value**. This is based on the rent it could command in a theoretically free market. The total of all rateable values in the area is then calculated and this forms the basis for deciding what annual rate should be charged. An example will best illustrate this.

Total rateable value for the area	£56.5 million
Product of 1p rate (rateable value divided by 100)	$\dfrac{£56.5}{100} = £565\,000$
Rate income required for the year	£50 million
Annual rate	$\dfrac{£50\,000\,000}{565\,000}$
	$= 88.49\text{p in the } £$

This means that if the rateable value of your house is, say, £350 you will pay £350 × .8849 = £309.71 in rates for the year.

Rates are a simple kind of tax, easy to calculate and easy to collect but they have been criticised on a number of grounds.

First, they assume that a person's ability to pay can be judged by the house he lives in: the bigger and more expensive the house the higher its rateable value and hence the greater the rates to be paid.

Second, they take no account of the income coming into a household. An elderly woman may be living alone in a large house and so pay high rates, whereas four younger wage earners may all live together in a small house and pay low rates.

Third, as property is not revalued every year, the rateable value remains the same, even though its market value may have risen. So if the amount required by the local authority goes up it can only be obtained by increasing the rate in the £, thereby raising the overall price level.

Fourth, rates are such an obvious form of tax they tend to be resented. Value added tax, for example, is 'lost' in the final price of goods and services so that the ordinary shopper tends not to notice it.

Many attempts have been made to find a replacement for rates, including a local income tax, but no alternative has yet won sufficient support from a party in government able and willing to do something about it. The Conservative Party, under Margaret Thatcher, has fought and won two general elections with promises to abolish rates and has not yet been successful in doing so.

Grants from central government are of two kinds. Some are paid to support the cost of **specific** services, such as policing or road maintence. The other main source of central support is the **block** grant. This is calculated individually for each authority and takes account of the pattern of past spending by the council and the amount of income which can be expected if the local rate is set at a particular level. If a council decides to raise its rate above the level central government would like, then the amount of the block grant is reduced accordingly.

Grants have become an increasing proportion of the income of local authorities and, as a result, made them more and more dependent on central government.

Capital projects, such as new buildings, are usually financed by **borrowing**. This is also tightly controlled by central government through the practice of **loan sanction**. This means that approval for the loan must be obtained from Whitehall before the money can be borrowed and the work started.

The one source of income which is mainly free from central government interference is **trading revenue**. The amount of this will, of course, vary from authority to authority. Seaside resorts, and other towns catering for tourists, will obviously have better opportunities for increasing their income in this way than those which are primarily industrial.

Looked at as a whole, the financial state of local government is not healthy and it desperately needs a major source of income which will help to make it less dependent on central government.

The broad distribution of income and expenditure of local authorities is shown in Figure 13.9.

Fig. 13.9

UK Local Authority Income and Expenditure 1984

Income	Amount (£m)	% of total	Expenditure	Amount (£m)	% of total
Grants from central government	19986	52	Education	12687	33
			Social services	3089	8
Rates	13074	34	Police, fire and law courts	3915	10
Rents, dividends and interest	3077	8	Housing and amenity services	2083	6
Trading surpluses	248	1	Recreation and cultural services	1295	3
Other income	1771	5	Transport services	1332	3
			General public services	933	3
			Grants and subsidies	4836	13
			Interest on debts	4031	11
			Other net expenditure	3955	10
TOTAL	38156	100	TOTAL	38156	100

13.9   Politics in Local Government

At one time party politics only featured in the large, urban local authorities but in the past 20 or 30 years it has spread to all of them, urban or rural. However, public interest is much lower locally than nationally. Turnouts at local elections reflect this, seldom rising to more than 40% of the electorate, compared with more than 70% nationally.

Within a Council each of the main parties will have a group, with a leader to co-ordinate its activities. Since control of policy and administration is through committees, it is important for a party to secure committee chairmanships, and the majority party will do this. At one time local councillors were looked on as second-best politicians, compared with those at Westminster, but in recent years some of them have become national figures, particulary in the bigger cities. Men like Ken Livingstone of London, David Blunkett of Sheffield and Derek Hatton of Liverpool have become household names.

Some people, particularly in the shire counties, have regretted the introduction of party politics into local government and hoped that it might go away. It is clear, however, that this will not happen. Although at times local authorities have been brought into conflict with central government, because of differing political views, politics has helped to increase public awareness of local issues, to the benefit of ratepayers.

Local politics has also become a platform for entry on to the national scene. The Liberal Party has been particulary effective in developing what it calls 'community politics'. This has involved showing a genuine interest and concern about local issues and taking steps to deal with ratepayers' problems. Community politics has persuaded electors to vote not only locally but in national elections as well.

13.10 The Future of Local Government

It is possible to argue that local government in Britain is now at its lowest ebb. The financial basis is unsatisfactory and the political composition of some Councils has brought them into open conflict with the government at Westminister. At the same time, restrictions on public spending have made themselves very evident locally, mainly because it is at the local level that most of the services the government provides are actually carried out.

Because of this, there is a danger that local authorities will become no more than agents for Whitehall departments, and decison taking will be even more bureaucratic and remote than it is at present. But too much should not be read into current events. A new Parliament could well result in an improved central-local relationship.

Apart from a change in the rating system, another reform might usefully be introduced. Local government would appear to be an ideal place to introduce proportional representation. It might help to de-polarise attitudes and increase public interest. It is used in local elections in Northern Ireland so this could become a model for the mainland.

Questions and Assignments

1 Why is the term local government misleading?
2 Why were the GLC and the Metropolitan Counties abolished?
3 What are the main services which local authorities provide?
4 What are the main sources of income for local authorities?
5 Why are rates criticised?
6 What are the chief objections to central government grants?
7 By using information available in your local library, or by approaching your local council offices, produce a list of district councillors, showing:
   (*a*) which party each belongs to
   (*b*) which committees each sits on
   (*c*) which committees, if any, each is chairman of
8 By referring to local newspapers, list three current local issues which local politicians have raised and write a a report, in not more than 600 words, on them, which would be suitable for publication in a newspaper.

Chapter 14
The Central-Local Government Interface

The relationship between central and local government ought to be one of partnership but in recent years it has often been one of conflict.

Since 1979 the Conservative government has pursued an economic policy requiring tight controls on public spending and this has clashed with the plans of some local authorities, particularly in deprived inner-city areas, to improve local amenities. The fact that these local councils have been Labour controlled has aggravated the situation.

The central-local partnership has, however, been threatened in the past. For example, Labour governments have clashed with Conservative councils over such things as the introduction of comprehensive education.

Finance lies at the heart of the conflict. As long as local authorities are dependent on central government for the bulk of their income, the relationship will be one sided. In 1976 the Layfield Committee on local government finance recommended the introduction of a local income tax to give councils an independent source of revenue but no party in power has yet taken up the idea.

If the status of local authorities is to be restored some guarantee of their independence must be reaffirmed.

14.1 Partnership or Conflict?

Local authorities were set up by Act of Parliament to carry out functions for which they are better equipped than central government. The relationship between the two ought to be one of partnership but in recent years it has deteriorated into one of conflict.

Why have local government at all? Why not just have local offices of the big central departments? It is there so that people living in the locality can have some say in what is done with what is essentially their money.

Yet since 1979 there has been a growing clash between local authorities and the centre and the way in which it has happened is an object lesson in how not to run a partnership.

14.2   The Growth of Big Brother

After winning the 1979 general election, the Conservatives, under Margaret Thatcher, set about reducing inflation. A major part of their economic strategy lay in controlling public spending. Since local authorities accounted for about 25% of the total, it was inevitable that they would be subjected to a squeeze.

In 1981 the grants system was amended so as to give more power to central government, enabling it to cut grants to high spending authorities. Controls on loans were also tightened and, with borrowing becoming more difficult and more costly, the rate of council house building fell. Some Labour controlled councils decided to ignore the central government curbs, finding extra money by raising rates. This prompted the government to introduce **rate capping** in 1985, making it illegal for councils to exceed a certain limit on rates. Thus the inherent clash between a Labour local council and a Conservative central government was aggravated.

As the squeeze on local spending and borrowing tightened, even Conservative led councils began to protest and the threatened partnership became a genuine conflict.

There were, additionally, the problems of infrastructure decay in the inner cities and high unemployment in the old industrial areas which added fuel to the fires of resentment. The big metropolitan authorities decided to rebel and flex their muscles.

For example, Ken Livingstone in London and David Blunkett in Sheffield adopted policies of reducing public transport fares to encourage people to use the subsidised services. These moves were in direct contrast to Mrs Thatcher's ideas of allowing market forces to work unimpaired, so that supply and demand, and not social considerations, would decide the price of everything.

The outcome of the battle went, of course, beyond cuts in grants and rate capping and resulted in the total abolition of the large metropolitan authorities, such as the GLC, which had shown the greatest defiance.

So, by the mid-1980s, central government had, whether it had intended it or not, become 'big brother' and local democracy seemed threatened.

14.3 What Can Be Done to Restore the Partnership?

Although the central-local relationship has deteriorated in recent years, the problems are not completely new. It is a long time since there was a true partnership. For example, Labour governments have battled in the past with Conservative councils about the ending of selective secondary education and the introduction of comprehensive schools.

If Britain had a written constitution then perhaps the powers of local authorities would be more clearly defined and protected but, without such a safeguard, the partnership must rest on mutual respect and understanding.

Most MPs are woefully ignorant about local government and when they become ministers that ignorance sometimes turns into disbelief. Richard Crossman, who was in Harold Wilson's Labour government, recalled that when he became Minister of Housing and Local Government he was surprised to find that his department did no house building itself and relied entirely on the efforts of local authorities.

The key to a possible solution lies in finance. As long as local authorities are so dependent on central government for financial support any partnership must be an unequal one.

14.4 The Layfield Committee on Local Government Finance

In 1976 a Committee chaired by Sir Frank Layfield, a barrister who had considerable knowledge of local administration, reported to the Labour government led by James Callaghan on how the financing of local government could be improved. The Committee recommended that local authorities should be given powers to raise 25% of their revenue through a local income tax, and that central government financial support should be limited to not more than 40% of total income.

Since the Report was published no political party in power has chosen to grasp the nettle of rates reform and so the partnership has become more one sided and the grip on local government by the centre tighter.

14.5 A Needed Reaffirmation

If local councils are to avoid becoming mere branch offices of central government then a reaffirmation of their independent existence is needed. There have been numerous inquiries into the structure of local government but its purpose and status within the British political system has been taken very much for granted.

Something needs to be done urgently to restore confidence in the local democratic system by guaranteeing local authorities' independence within clearly defined limits, whatever their political complexions, and whether or not these happen to be popular with the government of the day in London.

Questions and Assignments

1 Why is there not a genuine central-local government partnership?
2 Why were the GLC and the Metropolitan County Councils abolished?
3 What is rate capping?
4 Why did Harold Wilson's government clash with Conservative local authorities?
5 What did the Layfield Committee recommend as a replacement to rates?
6 How might the independence of local government be guaranteed?
7 Draw up a 'Charter for Local Government', setting out what you think should be the main points on which the independence of local authorities should be based, e.g. the right to raise money locally up to a limit of x% of their income; the right to make laws within their own localities; and so on.

   Bearing in mind the overriding power of Parliament to make and unmake laws, how would you go about guaranteeing such a Charter?
8 Write a letter to your local MP asking him or her to explain why a local income tax has not been introduced.

Chapter 15

The Fringe of Government

The public sector includes all the organisations and activities which, in one way or another, are paid for out of public money. It includes, as well as central and local government, all the institutions set up, or sponsored, as government 'fringe' bodies, as well as those parts of industry and commerce which are state owned.

The publicly funded organisations outside the industrial sector have been labelled 'quasi non-governmental organisations', or quangos, and there are several hundred of them, each with its own sponsoring central department. Each has been set up to promote, co-ordinate or regulate some function which the government does not want to involve itself with directly.

The industrial fringe organisations are normally called the nationalised industries. Most of them were set up between 1945 and 1950 by the Labour government under Clement Attlee, the form of organisation chosen being the public corporation, which aimed at combining commercial freedom with public account-ability.

The Conservative Party has always had mixed views about the nationalised industries but generally tolerated them until after 1979 when Margaret Thatcher became Prime Minister. She has always been firmly opposed to public ownership and soon after taking office embarked on an ambitious programme of pri-vatisation.

Although the Labour Party is in principle committed to public ownership by its Constitution, the present leadership has taken a moderate and practical line, saying that, in office, it would treat each case on its individual merits. The Alliance parties are likely to follow a broadly similar approach.

The future of the nationalised industries in Britain is, therefore, very much dependent on the outcome of the next general election.

15.1   The Public Sector

It has become commonplace to speak of the private and public sectors as if they were two completely distinct and separate parts of Britain: almost as if there was a 'Berlin Wall' or 'Iron Curtain' separating them. In the private sector everything is free enterprise and competition while in the public sector everything is subsidised and run by bureaucrats. The truth is a little different.

Where the private sector ends and public sector begins has become a little hazy. Everyone knows a government department and a civil servant when he sees them. Everyone knows that a town hall is full of local government officers, but when you fly on holiday with British Airways or British Airtours does it matter whether you are in the private or the public sector? Is travelling in a bus owned by the local council so very different from travelling in one owned by a private company? Does a car made by Austin-Rover look so very different from one made by Ford? Did you know that Renault and Alfa Romeo cars are both made by companies which are state owned?

And yet through the eyes of Westminster and Whitehall the public sector is very real and and its boundaries are very clear. This is because they see it in financial terms. The Chancellor of the Exchequer frequently rises to his feet in the House of Commons and complains, with feeling, about the size of the **public sector borrowing requirement** (PSBR).

The PSBR is simply the difference between what a government obtains in income and what it spends. In other words, the amount it needs to borrow. What it collects in taxes and duties plus what it borrows is the total amount it spends in the public sector.

The public sector, therefore, in the eyes of the Treasury at least, includes all those organisations and activities which, in one way or another, need to be financed from public funds.

As we have said, some parts of the public sector are clearly defined, such as central departments and local authorities. It is the rest which we will now consider: what has usefully been called the **fringe of government**. Some of it is based in London but much of it is spread across the country.

15.2   What is the Fringe?

The Civil Service Department, in 1978 before it was disbanded, published a report which it called a 'Survey of Fringe Bodies'. The Report said there were 252 of such national bodies and it defined them as 'organisations which have been set up or adopted by Departments and provided with funds to perform some function which the Government wished to have performed but which it did not wish to be the direct responsibility of a Minister or a Department'. In another part of the Report, fringe bodies are described as 'government at arm's length'.

In the same year that the Civil Service Department's Report was published a group of academics met at Essex University to discuss public administration. They talked about the many bodies which had grown up on the fringe of government and looked for a word which would accurately describe them. Eventually they decided they were 'quasi non-governmental organisations', in other words, a kind of, but not quite, government organisation. The description **quango** seemed appropriate. The word stuck and has now found its way into most dictionaries.

So we can say that the fringe of government, or quangos, whichever term you prefer, includes all the organisations which are not part of central or local government but which perform functions the government wants done but does not care to do itself. The quangos are, therefore, paid to do the government's work for it.

15.3   The Government Sponsored Quangos

It would take up too much space to consider all the 252 bodies listed in the Civil Service Department's 1978 Report so we will select some of the best known, remind ourselves of what they do and see which government departments keep their eyes on them.

In any case, not all the original 252 fringe bodies still exist. Soon after coming into power in 1979, Mrs Thatcher commissioned a high ranking civil servant, Sir Leo Pliatzky, to look at them with a view to doing some pruning. Sir Leo spent some months of study and finally recommended that some could usefully be dispensed with. As a result, 250 jobs disappeared and £11.6m was saved.

Figure 15.1 lists the main quangos, indicating what each does and which is the sponsoring department.

These are only some of the more significant quangos. The Civil Service Department list represents probably not much more than a quarter of the total. A lot depends on what definition of a fringe body you choose to use.

Fig. 15.1

Quangos in Britain

Name of Quango	Functions	Sponsoring Department
Advisory, Conciliation and Arbitration Service (ACAS)	Settling industrial disputes by conciliation and arbitration	Employment
Arts Council of Great Britain	Sponsoring art by awarding government grants	Education & Science
British Broadcasting Corporation	Providing radio and television services	Home Office
British Council	Sponsoring and providing assistance to Third World countries and promoting British ideas abroad	Foreign & Commonwealth
British Film Institute	Promoting the production of British films	Education & Science
British Tourist Authority	Promoting tourism in Britain	Trade & Industry
Central Midwives Board	Co-ordinating and supervising the work of midwives	Health & Social Security
Civil Aviation Authority	Supervising and regulating civil aviation in Britain	Trade & Industry
Commonwealth Institute	Promoting cultural activities for the Commonwealth	Foreign & Commonwealth
Countryside Commission	Promoting and protecting the countryside	Environment
Criminal Injuries Compensation Board	Dealing with claims for compensation resulting from criminal injuries sustained	Home Office
Crown Agents for Overseas Governments and Administrators	Providing financial, commercial and professional services for overseas governments	Foreign & Commonwealth
Design Council	Promoting good commercial and industrial design	Trade & Industry
Economic and Social Research Council	Encouraging and promoting social science research	Education & Science

Name of Quango	Functions	Sponsoring Department
Equal Opportunities Commission	Promoting equal opportunities for men and women	Home Office
Forestry Commision	Managing state forests	Agriculture
Gaming Board for Great Britain	Regulating gambling	Home Office
Health Education Council	Promoting health education	Health & Social Security
Health and Safety Commission & Executive	Promoting and regulating industrial safety	Employment
Herring Industry Board	Promoting and regulating the Scottish herring industry	Scottish
Horserace Betting Levy Board	Supervising horserace betting	Home Office
Independent Broadcasting Authority	Regulating independent broadcasting	Home Office
Manpower Services Commission	Operating a range of training and job promotion schemes	Employment
Meat and Livestock Commission	Promoting and regulating livestock production	Agriculture
Medical Research Council	Promoting medical research	Health & Social Security
Milk Marketing Board	Promoting milk sales	Agriculture
Monopolies and Mergers Commission	Regulating monopolies and company mergers	Trade & Industry
National Consumer Council	Promoting and protecting consumers' interests	Trade & Industry
National Economic Development Office	Advising the government on economic development	Treasury
National Film Finance Corporation	Assisting British film production	Trade & Industry
National Marriage Guidance Council	Co-ordinating marriage guidance work	Home Office
National Research Development Corporation	Promoting research and development	Trade & Industry

Name of Quango	Functions	Sponsoring Department
National Savings Committee	Promoting and advising on national savings	Treasury
National Water Council	Advising on the conservation and use of water	Environment
Post Office Users' National Council	Acting as consumer watchdog on postal services	Trade & Industry
Potato Marketing Board	Promoting and regulating the sale of potatoes	Agriculture
Race Relations Board	Supervising race relations legislation	Home Office
Royal Fine Arts Commission	Advising on fine arts	Education & Science
Schools Council	Advising the government on schools	Education & Science
Science Research Council	Encouraging and promoting science research	Education & Science
Sports Council	Promoting and assisting sport	Environment
United Kingdom Atomic Energy Authority	Controlling research and development of atomic energy	Energy
University Grants Committee	Supervising the distribution of grants to universities	Education & Science
White Fish Authority	Promoting the production and sale of white fish	Agriculture

The ministers in charge of the sponsoring departments usually appoint quango members and chairmen but for key organisations, such as the BBC and IBA, the Prime Minister may wish to become involved. They are nearly always part time appointments but the supporting administrative staff will be full time.

15.4   The Nationalised Industries

Another part of the fringe of government includes the nationalised industries, responsible for some of Britain's key sources of energy, production and communications. Although there were some examples of state enterprise prior to the Second World War, the major nationalisation programme took place during the Labour government of Clement Attlee, between 1945 and 1950. The form of control and ownership was devised by a leading Labour minister, Herbert Morrison, or Lord Morrison of Lambeth as he later became. It was the **public corporation**.

Morrison's aim was to combine freedom for commercial enterprise with public accountability. He therefore provided for the appointment of chairmen and other members of the governing board of a Corporation to be by a minister, to whom they were ultimately responsible.

Each Corporation was then established by an Act of Parliament, which set out its objectives, including any public service obligations it might be given. For example, the National Coal Board, as it was then called, was required to ensure adequate supplies of coal at reasonable prices. What was meant by 'adequate supplies' and 'reasonable prices' was left to be agreed between the Board and the minister. Similarly, the British Railways Board was required to provide an adequate transport system.

Figure 15.2 lists the major nationalised industries in Britain, with an indication of their origins.

Fig. 15.2

Britain's Major Nationalised Industries

Name	Origins
British Airports Authority	Set up to own and manage Heathrow, Gatwick, Stansted, Glasgow, Prestwick, Edinburgh and Aberdeen Airports.
British Airways	British Overseas Airways Corporation (BOAC) was established just before the outbreak of the Second World War. After the war there were three corporations, British European (BEA), British South American (BSAAC), and BOAC. BSAAC was merged with BOAC and in the 1970s BEA merged with BOAC to become British Airways.
British Coal	The coal industry was nationalised immediately after the Second World War and placed under the National Coal Board (NCB). Previously, few of the privately owned companies had been profitable. The NCB changed its name to British Coal in 1986.

Name	*Origins*
British Gas	Before the Second World War gas had been manufactured and distributed by private companies and local authorities. The industry was nationalised in 1948, and Area Boards, co-ordinated by the Gas Council, were set up. The name British Gas was adopted in the 1970s.
British Leyland	British Leyland was the product of a long series of mergers starting in the 1960s. Austin joined Morris cars and then they acquired Wolsey, Riley, MG, Standard, Triumph and Jaguar cars and later merged with Leyland trucks and buses. The group was rescued from bankruptcy in 1974 by the Labour government of Harold Wilson.
British Railways Board	Before the Second World War the railway system in Britain was in the hands of privately owned companies, operating on a regional basis, such as the Great Western, London Midland and Scottish, Southern, and London and North Eastern Railways. The industry was nationalised in 1948 and originally managed by the British Transport Commission. The British Railways Board was established in 1963.
British Steel Corporation	The British iron and steel industry was first nationalised in 1949, in the face of stiff opposition from the privately owned companies and the Conservative Party. In 1953 the Conservative government started a process of returning the industry to private hands. The process was never fully completed and in 1967 Harold Wilson's Labour government re-nationalised about 90% of the companies.
Electricity Boards	Like gas, before the Second World War electricity was generated and supplied by a mixture of privately owned companies and local authorities. The industry was nationalised in 1947 and given a structure of regional boards co-ordinated by a central body, the Electricity Council.

Post Office

The Post Office was originally a government department. It was released from tight Treasury control in 1960 and subsequently became a public corporation.

Rolls Royce

The privately owned company of Rolls Royce Ltd was rescued from bankruptcy in 1971 by the Conservative government of Edward Heath.

15.5 Government and the Nationalised Industries

Although the idea behind the public corporation was to free the boards from Whitehall control, and particularly control by the Treasury, their history has been one of government interference and fluctuations in policy. The corporations were, in any case, faced with the dilemma of operating on sound commercial lines and, at the same time, providing a public service.

In the 1950s the public service aspect took precedence, with a former army general running the railways and an ex-miner as head of the National Coal Board. But by the early 1960s the Conservative Party was arguing that the nationalised industries should not become a social service. As governments changed so attitudes towards the public corporations changed with them. The Labour Party tended to pick engineers as chairmen while the Conservatives, for a time at least, chose people from banking institutions.

The chairmen felt themselves becoming increasingly the scapegoats for mistakes made by ministers and, at the instigation of Lord Robens when he was head of the National Coal Board, took to holding monthly luncheon meetings to discuss their problems and to try to work out a concerted strategy. This developed into the **Nationalised Industries Chairmen's Group** (NICG), which now has a small staff and, among other things, arranges annual lectures on industrial topics.

The arrival of Margaret Thatcher's government, in 1979, saw the most abrupt change in approach. She was philosophically opposed to public ownership and determined to make the existing industries profitable and, eventually, return them to private ownership, even though many of them had come into the public sector because they had been unable to survive on their own.

One of her first steps was to bring in, as chairmen, people who shared her unquestioning conviction about the virtues of free enterprise and whose career records showed that they could be relied upon to force through new attitudes in the industries they were to lead.

Her government had, of course, inherited a number of chairmen and all could not be removed overnight but they were becoming quickly aware that a wind of change was blowing through the public sector. In any case, some chairmen, such as Michael Edwardes at British Leyland, were beginning to push their industries into just the attitudes Mrs Thatcher wanted.

In June 1980 Sir Keith Joseph, who was then Secretary of State for Industry, appointed Ian McGregor, a tough 67-year-old Scottish-American, who had made a reputation in the United States as a hard, decisive manager, to the chairmanship of the British Steel Board, at a reputed fee of £2m. Within three years McGregor had turned the nation's biggest loss maker into a largely self-supporting undertaking, but at an enormous cost in lost jobs. He then went on to tackle similar problems as Chairman of the National Coal Board and, by the time he left office in August 1986, had moved the industry towards profitability, but, again, at considerable cost: a long and bitter national strike and great cutbacks in the labour force.

Another important appointment, in 1981, was that of Sir John King, now Lord King, to chair British Airways. King was a self-made businessman who had started his own engineering company after the Second World War and went on to become chairman and director of a wide range of companies. He was given a clear target, to prepare British Airways for sale to the private sector. By 1986 he was able to claim that he was well on the way to doing this.

15.6   Public Ownership and Party Politics

The nationalised industries have always been a 'political football', kicked from one end of the political field to the other, and suffering, not only changes of referee, but changes of rules, and even movement of the goal posts.

Clause 4 of the Constitution of the Labour Party makes public ownership of the 'means of production' a firm commitment, but Labour Leaders have chosen to interpret this commitment in different ways.

Clement Attlee was clear about the need for state ownership of the key industries and services but believed that they should, while safeguarding the national interest, operate on efficient, commercial lines. His successor, Hugh Gaitskell, took an even more moderate line and, before his untimely death in 1963, vigorously fought the left wing of his Party over the issue of Clause 4.

Harold Wilson, although seeming to be on the left wing, was moderate in most of his views and during his long leadership, from 1963 to 1976, managed to steer his Party between its left and right extremes. James Callaghan took a broadly similar line. Michael Foot was more clearly to the left but the present Leader, Neil Kinnock, although from the same wing of the Party, has proved to be very much more a realist.

He has sensed that the public in general do not feel strongly, one way or the other, about nationalisation. They are more concerned about getting a good service and value for money. He is, therefore, moving his Party into the sort of moderate line Harold Wilson might have taken. He and his colleagues have even judged that the word 'nationalisation', or 'public ownership', has an outdated ring, which could be electorally unpopular. The new term they prefer is **social ownership**.

15.7 Privatisation

Under Margaret Thatcher, the Conservative Party would seem to have no doubts. It believes public ownership to be bad for industry and bad for the nation and the sooner state enterprises are returned to private hands the better. Since coming into office in 1979, her government has embarked on an ambitious programme of **privatisation**.

Privatisation, in Mrs Thatcher's eyes, means more than just returning the nationalised industries to the private sector. It includes reducing people's dependence on government in all areas of life and exposing industry to the forces of the market and to every kind of competition. In fact the whole approach of her government has become centred around her own personal beliefs and attitudes. It can be summed up in one word, **Thatcherism**. We will look more closely at this unique development in a later chapter.

Between 1979 and 1983 the government introduced the necessary legislation to make its privatisation programme possible and, although the process started gradually. it soon accelerated, as Figure 15.3 shows.

Fig. 15.3

Britain's Privatisation Programme 1979–1987

Year	Undertaking Privatised
1979	British Petroleum (BP)
	International Computers (ICL)
1980	Ferranti Electronics
	Fairey Aviation
1981	British Aerospace
	British Sugar Corporation
	Cable and Wireless Ltd
1982	Amersham International
	National Freight Corporation
	Britoil
1983	Associated British Ports
1984	Enterprise Oil
	British Telecom
	Jaguar Cars
	Sealink Ferries
	Yarrow Naval Shipbuilding Yard
1985	Unipart
1986	British Gas
1987	British Airways

The pros and cons of privatisation are strongly argued on both economic and political grounds.

Arguments For Privatisation	*Arguments Against Privatisation*
1 Private ownership and management are more efficient than public.	1 Many of the privatised undertakings are vital national assets and should be kept under public control.
2 Greater efficiency will lead to lower prices.	2 Long term income is being sacrificed for short term gain.
3 Proceeds from the sales can reduce government borrowing and provide money for tax cuts.	3 There is a danger that the public will be exploited in the interests of private profit.
4 Greater competition will help to curb trade union power.	4 Privatisation just puts more wealth into the hands of the already wealthy.
5 The small saver is given a chance to invest.	5 It is dangerous to put strategic resources into private hands.

The debate will clearly continue for many years to come.

Questions and Assignments

1 What is the public sector?
2 What is a quango?
3 Why have so many quangos been set up?
4 Why was the public corporation chosen as the best form of organisation for a nationalised industry?
5 Why have chairmen of nationalised industries been suspicious of governments?
6 Why is Margaret Thatcher so opposed to public ownership?
7 Carry out a survey among your friends and relatives to find out how many have bought shares in privatised firms. Ask them whether they are happy with their decision and whether, if another opportunity comes along, they would do the same again.

   Present your conclusions in the form of a brief report.
8 Using the list of quangos in Figure 15.1, single out six which you consider could be wound up, saying why you think they are unnecessary.

PART IV

GOVERNMENT AND THE ECONOMY

Chapter 16

Managing the Economy

One of the functions of modern governments is to manage the economy and to do this they can follow a range of policies. In post-war Britain two broad approaches have been adopted: one based on Keynesian and the other on monetarist economic theories. The Keynesian approach tries to influence consumption and production, mainly through changes in taxation, whereas the monetarist strategy puts emphasis on controlling the money supply. British economic management has generally followed a mixture of both approaches.

Despite all the efforts of government, Britain's economic performance since 1945 has not been good, particularly when compared with most of her overseas competitors. The exact reasons for this relatively poor showing are not easy to pinpoint, but there are some deficiencies in government which have certainly contributed. First, no government has been really successful in establishing a good working relationship with business. Second, no government has been able to develop and operate a long term strategy for industrial development. Third, the Treasury, as the government's major economic department, has tended to think short term, rather than long, and has been more concerned about controlling public spending than promoting economic growth.

The government's getting and spending process starts in early autumn, with the preparation of estimates, and ends in spring, when the Chancellor of the Exchequer presents his budget to the House of Commons. In his budget speech he will propose, among other things, certain taxes. Some, such as income tax, will be paid directly by the individual taxpayer. Others, such as VAT, will be added to the price of goods and services and so paid indirectly. The taxes which take account of a person's ability to pay are called progressive and those which ignore the ability to pay, regressive.

In trying to compare how a government manages the economy with how a successful business operates, it must be admitted that the need for political accountability makes it impossible to apply competitive commercial standards in the public sector.

16.1   Some Basic Economic Terms

Economists use various words and terms as a shorthand way of describing economic conditions and activities. To avoid confusion, and to make sure we are all 'speaking the same language', we shall quickly look at some of these basic terms. They are grouped in what seems to be a logical order. The index at the back of the book can be used for an alphabetical search.

The economy means the sum total of all the activities of production, distribution and consumption of goods and services within a particular country. It is often used in comparative terms, such as 'the Japanese economy is stronger than the British'.

The **national income** of a country is the nation's total income or total production for a year. It is usually shown as the **gross domestic product** (GDP), which, in money terms, is the annual output of goods and services. The **gross national product** (GNP) is the GDP plus investments from abroad.

A **market economy** describes a situation in which there are no restrictions by government on the production or consumption of goods and services, so that the balance between what is produced and consumed is decided by supply and demand, or what are called market forces. A true market economy is purely theoretical because all governments interfere in some way or other with economic activity. A **managed economy** is one in which the state deliberately intervenes to make market forces operate in the way it wants.

A **capitalist economy** is one in which all wealth is privately owned, whereas a **collectivist economy** is one in which the state owns all wealth. Both terms are more theoretical than real. A **mixed economy** is one in which there is a mixture of state and private ownership. Most countries, including Britain, have mixed economies.

Perfect competition is another theoretical situation in which there are no restrictions on the production and consumption of goods and services, so that price is determined wholly by the market. **Monopoly** is the opposite state of affairs, in which there is only one supplier of goods or services. **Imperfect competition** is a position between these two extremes and represents most practical circumstances.

Unemployment occurs when there are people able and willing to work who cannot find it. Sometimes a distinction is made between **frictional unemployment**, caused by blockages in the free movement of labour from one job to another, and **structural unemployment** which is seen when an industry is declining. Frictional unemployment is usually temporary and structural longer term. Structural unemployment occurs when a country, or a region, is going through a stage of **deindustrialisation**, with an industrial economy becoming a service one. To some degree this is happening in Britain today, as some of the old manufacturing industries die.

A **recession** occurs when demand falls below the level of production and there is an under-use of resources, resulting in unemployment. When demand starts rising, stimulating production, a **recovery** is said to be taking place. Because recessions tend to come in cycles the unemployment linked to them is called **cyclical**.

Full employment was a term introduced during and after the Second World War to describe a situation in which there was no unwanted unemploymemnt. It was recognised that there would always be some temporary, frictional unemployment but even this would be small, no more than 3% of the total labour force. A report by Sir William Beveridge, 'Full Employment in a Free Society', was accepted by all British political parties as a basis for post-war economic and social policies. Unemployment in Britain stayed at under 3% until the 1970s.

Investment means the production of goods for future, rather than immediate, use. Investment is concerned with the production of **capital** goods, such as machinery and factories, which will make the future production of consumer goods easier and cheaper. For example, millions of pounds were invested in North Sea exploration before a single barrel of oil could be produced. There had to be more investment in refineries, transport and filling stations before the motorist eventually bought his petrol for use in his car.

The **standard of living** is normally measured as the GNP per head of the population. Some European countries, such as Switzerland and Sweden, have the highest standards of living in the world. The standard of living in Britain is now one of the lowest of the members of the European Community, below that of

Germany, France, Holland, Belgium, Luxembourg, Denmark or Italy.

The **cost of living** is an indication of the price level in a country at any one time. It is normally shown as an **index of retail prices**, constructed by recording the prices of a representative 'basket' of goods and services in one month and comparing them with the prices of the same 'basket' in another month.

Inflation is a tendency to spend on consumption and investment at a faster rate than consumption and investment goods are being produced. The main symptom of inflation is rising prices, reflected in an increase in the cost of living. It is possible for a country to live with a high level inflation by linking incomes and pensions to an index of prices. Israel, for example, has had very high inflation rates for many years. If, however, a country is a major exporter there is a danger that inflation will push up costs of production and so make exports uncompetitive. Economists sometimes distinguish between **demand pull inflation**, caused by excessive demand pulling up prices, and **cost push inflation**, caused by rising production costs pushing up prices.

Deflation is a means of trying to reduce inflation by dampening demand. The problem with deflation is that it can create unemployment. **Disinflation** is a milder form of deflation, practised in an attempt to avoid unemployment. **Reflation** means stimulating demand to increase economic activity and so reduce unemployment. The difficulty with reflation is that it is difficult to control and prices may start rising too rapidly.

The **opportunity cost** of something is the cost in real terms of doing this rather than doing that. Thus, the opportunity cost of an evening spent watching television could be a visit to the cinema, or reading a book, or going out for a meal. Time is an important element in opportunity cost because the present is lost for ever once it has becomes the past.

The **real cost or value** of something is usually compared with its **money cost or value**. Thus, in money terms a salary might be £15000 per year, but in real terms it would be the material things which could be bought with it.

Unit cost is a measure of the cost of producing a single unit of something. Electricity or gas can be expressed in terms of the cost of a unit, or, considering a motor car as a unit of production, the cost of producing it in one country can be compared with the cost of producing it in another. For example, although the unit costs of many goods manufactured in Britain have fallen in recent years they are still much higher than in Japan, because productivity is higher there. The **balance of payments** is the difference between the value of goods and services exported during a given period of time and the value of goods and services imported. The balance of payments on capital account is the difference between investments in overseas countries and investments from abroad. The **balance of trade** is the difference between goods exported and goods imported. Countries which sell more abroad than they import have favourable balances, while those which import more than they export have adverse balances. It is possible to have an adverse trade balance which is offset by the export of services, such as banking and insurance, normally called **invisible earnings**. Thus the balance of trade consists of visible items and the balance of payments, visible and invisible items.

The **exchange rate** is the price of one unit of currency in terms of another. Thus, the dollar exchange rate for the £ might be 1.5. In other words, you can exchange £1 for 1 dollar and 50 cents. If the £ becomes stronger it will buy more dollars, if it is weaker it will buy less. In exporting and importing terms the level of the exchange rate is important. If the exchange rate of the £ goes up British goods will cost more abroad, but imports into Britain will cost less. If the exchange rate goes down the reverse will happen.

Governments may wish to stop money being exported so they use **exchange control**, which puts restrictions on dealings in foreign currency.

For a long time after the Second World War many countries, including Britain, had **fixed exchange rates**, controlled by the government. This gave stability to exporters and importers. Since exchange rates are decided by the amount of one currency being exchanged for another, fixed rates often had to be maintained by buying or selling foreign currency or by adjusting interest rates. Therefore, a **floating exchange rate** was adopted, the currency being allowed to 'float' to its natural level, determined by supply and demand. Floating rates, however, bring uncertainty for exporters and importers.

The **European Monetary System** (EMS), is an arrangement by members of the European Community to keep exchange rates fixed within an agreed band. Britain has so far declined to join the EMS, although many people have advocated membership. The initial difficulty would be that of deciding the right time to join. That time would be influenced by the level of the £ in relation to the currencies of the other European countries.

The **rate of interest** is the price paid for borrowing money. Interest rates can be influenced by decisions of the central bank and the commercial banks and other lenders, such as building societies.

The **central bank** of a country is the government's banker. In Britain the central bank is the Bank of England. The government can give directions to the Bank of England, which, in turn, can instruct the commercial, 'high street' banks.

The **exchange reserves** are the stocks of gold and currency held, on behalf of the government, by the central bank.

Economic management is a term used to describe a government's attempts to make the economy behave in the way it wants. To do this, it can choose from a range of policies. In the post-war years two distinctive, and contrasting, policies have been used: Keynesianism and monetarism.

Keynesianism takes its name from John Maynard Keynes (1883–1946), the internationally famous Cambridge economist. He argued that unemployment could be reduced by stimulating demand through lower taxes and interest rates and increased government spending. Inflation would not necessarily result because idle resources would be put to use and more would be produced to satisfy the increased demand.

Monetarism is a theory which argues that inflation can be tackled by controlling the supply of money. The best known exponent of the theory was Professor Milton Friedman, of Chicago University. **Monetary policy** has been developed from monetarism. It is operated by controlling the money supply through changes in interest rates and reductions in government spending and borrowing.

The **quantity theory of money** puts the influence of the money supply on the price level in simple terms.

$$P \text{ (price level)} = \frac{M \text{ (quantity of money)} \times V \text{ (velocity of circulation)}}{T \text{ (total volume of goods and services available)}}$$

The **velocity of circulation** is the average number of times a unit of currency changes hands during a given period of time, e.g. a year. If M or V or both, increase more rapidly than T, prices will rise. If T equals MV, prices will remain steady. The equation, sometimes called the **Fisher Equation**, is little more than a truism. All it really says is that the money spent must be equal to the value of the goods and services bought. It does, however, show clearly why inflation occurs.

Measuring the amount of money is, in any case, a problem. The Bank of England calls the total amount of coin, notes and money deposited in current accounts in banks **M1**. A more widely used measure is **M3**, which is M1 plus deposit accounts in banks and building societies, plus public sector deposits, plus foreign currency in the country. With the widespread use of credit cards, the measurement of the velocity of circulation of money is even more difficult.

From 1980 monetary policy in Britain operated through what was called the **medium term financial strategy (MTFS)**. This involved a progressive reduction of the money supply, taxes, and public sector spending and borrowing.

Fiscal policy means controlling demand through taxation. Higher taxes will reduce demand and lower taxes stimulate it. Fiscal policy is the main weapon in a Keynesian approach to economic management.

An **incomes policy** is an attempt to control demand by restricting pay rises. It can operate by agreement or be imposed by law. Without an incomes policy there is **free collective bargaining**, which means that unions and employers are able to negotiate without government interference.

An **industrial policy** operates when the government has worked out a strategy for maintaining, or expanding a country's manufacturing base, usually by encouraging investment and training. The **National Economic Development Council** (NEDC), sometimes called Neddy, was originally set up in 1961 by the Conservative government of Harold Macmillan. It is a forum for discussion between the government and representatives from both sides of industry, employers and unions. The idea was to achieve 'planning by consent'. The NEDC has an office (NEDO) which produces useful reports on various aspects of the economy It also has sector working parties (little Neddies), whose reports are also well thought of.

The **International Monetary Fund** (IMF) was set up in 1944, in the closing years of the Second World War, to promote international monetary co-operation and the expansion of world trade. It can help a country which is in balance of payments difficulties by making short term loans. The **International Bank for Reconstruction and Development**, popularly called the World Bank, was set up at the same time to make longer term loans, particularly to help Third World countries.

16.2 The Aims of Economic Management

Although policies change as governments change, the overall aims of economic management remain constant. They are to achieve:

1 A stable price level
2 Full employment
3 A favourable balance of payments
4 Economic growth

No British government has, since 1945, succeeded in achieving all four aims simultaneously, so each has chosen one or more as a major priority. During the past 10 years the concept of full employment has been reconsidered by all political parties and the original idea of a maximum unemployment rate of 3% is now seen as a long term, rather than immediate, aim.

16.3 Economic Management in Britain 1945–1979

For some 20 years after 1945 all governments in Britain managed to preserve full employment, in Beveridge terms, to such an extent that people began to believe that national unemployment was conquered for ever. Regional unemployment, of the structural kind, persisted however in Northern England, Wales, Scotland and particularly in Northern Ireland, where it was twice the national average.

Throughout the period there were, however, recurring problems with inflation and the balance of payments, while economic growth continued to lag behind that of Britain's main overseas competitors.

Inflation was tackled mainly by fiscal policies and the balance of payments was protected by exchange controls. So, despite poor economic growth, people's real incomes rose substantially in the 1960s and, with a generally strong world economy, the British people began to feel that they 'had never had it so good'.

The methods of economic management by Labour and Conservative governments, based on moderate Keynesian lines, were so similar that they became popularly known as **Butskellism**, linking the names of the two prominent Chancellors of the Exchequer, R A Butler, Conservative and Hugh Gaitskell, Labour.

Unemployment started to rise in the early 1970s, to about 4%, but, despite the sudden jump in world oil prices in 1973, and the miners' strike which accompanied it, Keynesian policies were still followed, helped by a statutory incomes policy. When that was withdrawn problems began to accumulate.

Because of Britain's low economic growth rate, it became obvious that the £ was over-valued. It had been successfully devalued by Roy Jenkins in 1967, when he was Chancellor in Harold Wilson's government, but by 1976 its over-valuation was again apparent. James Callaghan was now Prime Minister and Denis Healey his Chancellor. They decided to allow the £ to fall gradually but international confidence suddenly slipped and the slow fall became a rapid slide. There was a risk of using up most of Britain's gold and foreign currency reserves to support the £.

Eventually Callaghan and Healey felt obliged to apply for a loan from the IMF. As part of the agreed package, the representatives of the IMF insisted that Britain should reduce public spending and curb the money supply. A monetary policy had been more or less forced on them.

Meanwhile, the Conservatives in opposition under the influence of Sir Keith Joseph and their new Leader, Margaret Thatcher, were making plans for a full blown monetary policy if returned to power. They saw inflation as the prime enemy and argued that by controlling it they would, automatically, cut unemployment.

In the two years before the 1979 general election there was, however, a marked recovery in the health of the British economy. After having risen to 20%, inflation was below 10% and still falling. The balance of payments had moved into surplus, industrial output was improving and the IMF loan had been repaid. All this had been done through an easing of monetary restrictions, a mildly expansionist fiscal policy and a voluntary incomes agreement with the unions. The fact that North Sea oil was beginning to come on stream made the future look rosy. James Callaghan was being affectionately called 'Sunny Jim', the worker of an 'economic miracle'.

Callaghan decided to hold back the general election date until the last possible moment, to allow the economic recovery to make itself really felt, but, in retrospect, he miscalculated. The agreement on pay restraint collapsed, resulting in a wave of strikes, mostly in the public sector: the so-called 'winter of discontent'.

The Conservatives, with Margaret Thatcher, won the 1979 general election and the scene was set for Britain's first major monetarist experiment.

16.4   Economic Management Since 1979

Looking from across the Atlantic, the renowned Keynesian economist, J K Galbraith, commented in 1980 on what was happening in Britain.

> 'Britain has, in effect, volunteered to be the Friedmanite guinea pig. There could be no better choice. Britain's political and social institutions are solid, and neither Englishmen, Scots nor even the Welsh take readily to the streets . . . There are other advantages in a British experiment. British social services and social insurance soften what elsewhere might be intolerable hardship. British phlegm is a good antidote for anger; and so is an adequate system of unemployment insurance'

The practical application of monetarism proved to be more difficult than had been thought. The first budget of Sir Geoffrey Howe, the new Chancellor, with income tax cuts, as an incentive to higher earners, and an increase in value added tax (VAT), proved to be inflationary. This was fuelled by a number of generous public sector pay awards which the government had inherited. Howe and his political colleagues at the Treasury, John Biffen and Nigel Lawson, decided to set themselves tight spending budgets and strict targets for cuts in the money supply. As a result, they got the worst of all worlds: higher inflation and higher unemployment.

Under Chancellor Howe and, from 1983, Nigel Lawson, tight monetary controls were attempted within the medium term financial strategy but, as the figures in Figure 16.1 show, the only areas of real success were in reducing inflation and the size of the PSBR.

Fig. 16.1

UK Economic Performance 1978–1985

	1978	1979	1980	1981	1982	1983	1984	1985
Industrial growth (%)	+ 4.0	+ 2.5	– 7.0	– 3.5	+ 2.1	+ 3.3	+ 0.9	+ 5.4
Unemployment (%)	5.8	5.1	6.4	10.0	11.7	12.4	12.7	13.1
Inflation (%)	11.0	13.0	19.0	11.0	6.6	5.8	5.4	5.5
Wages (%)	+ 14.0	+ 18.0	+ 21.0	+ 13.0	+ 9.4	+ 8.4	+ 6.1	+ 7.0
Public spending (% of GNP)	41.0	43.0	44.0	46.0	46.0	47.0	46.0	46.0
PSBR (% of GNP)	5.8	7.3	6.2	5.0	5.5	3.5	3.2	3.2
Exchange rate (US dollars)	1.9	2.0	2.3	2.4	1.9	1.6	1.4	1.1

Using international comparisons, the economic performance of the United Kingdom in 1986 was still unimpressive as Figure 16.2 shows. Of the 13 countries listed, the UK was in eighth position in the fight against inflation; in twelth position as far as the levels of pay increases were concerned; in ninth position in the levels of unemployment; in eleventh position on the scale of increases in industrial output; and in eleventh position as far as improvements in the size of the GDP were concerned. If Figure 16.2 represented positions in the First Division of the Football League, the United Kingdom would be in the relegation zone and possibly heading for the Second Division.

Fig. 16.2

International Comparisons of Economic Performance: 1986

Country	Inflation %	Earnings %	Unemployment %	Industrial output %	GNP %
Australia	8.4	+ 7.1	8.3	+ 3.8	+ 4.7
Belgium	0.8	+ 3.0	11.7	+ 3.5	na
Canada	4.2	+ 2.6	9.9	+ 3.0	+ 3.6
France	2.0	+ 4.8	9.7	+ 1.5	+ 2.6
W Germany	− 0.5	+ 4.0	8.9	+ 1.8	+ 3.5
Holland	− 0.7	+ 2.1	14.7	− 1.9	− 2.1
Italy	5.9	+ 5.0	14.0	− 0.1	+ 2.2
Japan	0.8	+ 2.2	2.7	+ 0.2	+ 3.2
Spain	9.3	+ 10.0	20.4	− 0.9	+ 3.2
Sweden	4.1	+ 4.5	2.3	− 0.9	+ 3.2
Switzerland	0.5	+ 3.8	0.7	+ 1.0	+ 2.2
UK	2.4	+ 7.5	11.7	− 1.3	+ 1.5
USA	1.6	+ 2.4	6.9	nc	+ 2.6

na = figures not available   nc = no change from previous year

So what can be said about Britain's economic performance? Has the monetarist experiment been worthwhile?

It is difficult to speculate on what might have happened had other policies been followed, because like is never being compared with like. Equally, it is difficult to make international comparisons with complete reliability because the circumstances of each country are different. It should be noted that, of all the European countries listed, only Britain had the benefits of North Sea oil and in 1986 this accounted for about 6% of GNP. Whether the absence of this income would have been ruinous to the UK economy or whether other forms of production would have taken its place, is a matter for conjecture. What can be said, objectively, is that the British government's economic management after 1979 was no more successful than that of any of its predecessors.

16.5   Government and Business

The relationship between British governments and business has seldom been good. It contrasts sharply with similar relationships in other countries.

In the United States, for example, presidents regularly include leading businessmen in their teams of advisers. In France civil servants move in and out of business frequently and easily. In Japan the government's association with business is strong and co-operative.

In Britain, however, few ministers and virtually no civil servants have had business experience. There have been examples of businessmen being brought into government but the experiments have not always been happy. John Davis, who had been a successful businessman before becoming Director-General of the CBI, was made a Cabinet minister by Edward Heath, in 1970. He left a few years later, apparently disillusioned. Margaret Thatcher has had rather more success, with people such as Lord Young, but only a very small proportion of her Cabinet ministers have had strong business experience, and even fewer have been in manufacturing industry.

We have already noted some of the views of Sir John Hoskyns, a former head of Mrs Thatcher's Policy Unit. He argued, in a lecture given to the Institute of Directors in 1982, that Prime Ministers should form governments from a wider range of people than the small pool of career politicians which was usually available, and that top-quality outsiders should be brought into the civil service.

Others would argue that the problem is deeper and a solution would have to be even more radical, including a complete shake-up of the civil service machine, including the Treasury.

16.6   Government and Planning

Planning involves three elements: anticipating future events; preparing alternative courses of action for dealing with these events; and anticipating the likely consequences of any actions taken.

We all plan in some way or another. It is an essential part of our lives. We plan holidays, journeys, how we will spend our money. Nowadays, most married couples practise family planning.

Yet governments in Britain often seem suspicious of planning and civil servants are very good at making arrangements for the current year, and even one or two beyond that, but long, or even medium, range planning is seldom tried. There have, however, been some attempts.

When he was Prime Minister, Harold Macmillan was impressed by the success of national planning in France. For years after the Second World War the economic performance of France had not been good, whereas that of her neighbours, including defeated West Germany, had often been spectacular. The return to power ￢f Charles de Gaulle, as president, breathed new life and direction nto the country and the economy showed a dramatic improvement. Then change was spearheaded by a planning system, the 'Commissariat au Plan', which involved ministers, civil servants, ˜ usinesmen and industrialists in consultative planning.

The setting up of NEDC in 1981 was an attempt to follow the French example but it has had very limited success.

16.7   The Role of the Treasury

Harold Wilson once said 'Whichever party is in office, the Treasury is in power'. Although it is one of the smallest Whitehall departments, its status and influence are considerable. This is partly because of its political hierarchy but more because of its position within the civil service machine.

The Prime Minister's official title is First Lord of the Treasury and the government Whips are junior Treasury Lords. The Chancellor of the Exchequer is arguably the next senior Cabinet member to the Prime Minister, at least as powerful as the Foreign Secretary, and he has a stronger ministerial team than any of his colleagues. The political power of the Treasury is physically concentrated in Downing Street, London, with the Prime Minister at No 10, the Chancellor at No 11 and the Chief Whip at No 12.

The permanent staff of the Treasury are respected within the civil service, and sometimes feared. The Permanent Secretary used to be head of the civil service and, although this post was surrendered in recent years to the Secretary of the Cabinet, it is unlikely that this will be a permanent arrangement. The Treasury's traditional dominance will surely return.

Despite, or possibly because of, the Treasury's power, it is subjected to frequent criticism. Over the years attempts have been made to demote it but it has succeeded in resisting them and has always come out on top.

In 1964 the Department of Economic Affairs (DEA) was set up by Harold Wilson to take over part of the Treasury's role as economic manager. Five years later it was disbanded. In 1968 the

Civil Service Department (CSD) was created to take over the Treasury's personnel management role. It was dissolved in 1981.

Over the years the Treasury has developed, and to some extent refined, a still rather crude approach to economic management. It sees its main job as that of ensuring that the central departments stay within whatever spending limits the Cabinet has determined. Even though five year spending targets are agreed, annual **cash limits** have come to dominate Treasury thinking, to the irritation and frustration of non-Treasury ministers as well as people outside the central government machine.

This emphasis on annual budgeting sometimes has strange, and expensive, consequences. For example, if the Foreign Office wants a new embassy for its staff in some foreign country it might decide that, in the long run, it would be cheaper to purchase a building than to pay rent. But, if a purchase pushed expenditure beyond the annual limit, the Treasury might insist on renting, regardless of the higher long term cost.

There have been other cases of the Treasury apparently taking the short term view and missing out on long term savings. The Treasury reply to these criticisms would be that if it did not hold the spending line, who would?

16.8   Getting and Spending

Virtually everyone has to work within some kind of budget, whether it is on a weekly, monthly or annual basis. A budget represents the relationship between what is available to spend and what there is to spend it on. If a person's annual income is £10000 he must spend within that limit, or borrow and go into debt.

Public spending is a little different. A government can decide how much it wants to spend and then work out where it is going to get its money from. This does not mean that it can spend as much as it likes, because the effects of its spending and revenue collection on the nation's economy will be significant. That is why the Treasury sees cash limits as so important.

In the 19th century Chancellors of the Exchequer took the view that public expenditure should be kept to a minimum and that the government should collect in taxes just enough to cover it, and no more. The acceptance of Keynesian economics has persuaded modern Chancellors that getting and spending need not necessarily balance, and that they could budget for a surplus if they wanted to deflate the economy, or for a deficit, if they wished to expand it. For example, the Reagan administration successfully stimulated the United States economy in the 1980s by allowing substantial budget deficits to accumulate.

Monetarist policies, as we have seen, have tended to revert to the 19th century view, but even the most anti-Keynesian Chancellor realises that government spending and tax collection have important economic, as well as financial, implications.

The Treasury line is that whatever the Cabinet decides it will try to make it happen, but this is a rather simplistic account of what really takes place. Since the Chancellor is, in economic and financial matters, head and shoulders above his Cabinet colleagues, with only the Prime Minister able to challenge his authority, the Cabinet's view of economic policy is really his. Thus, the annual getting and spending routine is ultimately determined by the Treasury.

16.9 The Budgetary Process

Although the government's financial year dates from 6 April, the budgetary process begins in early autumn, when the departments start preparing their spending estimates. At about this time the Treasury will be telling the Principal Finance Officer in each department how it views the state of the economy and, consequently, how much money is likely to be available.

By February the departments will have submitted their estimates for consideration by Treasury officials and a certain amount of 'horse trading' will have been done.

Once the estimates have been agreed they are presented to the House of Commons as **Civil Estimates** by the Financial Secretary to the Treasury, and as **Defence Estimates** by the Secretary of State for Defence.

Meanwhile, the Chancellor, with the help of his senior civil servants, will have been working out how he is going to obtain his revenue and his final proposals will be put before the House of Commons, usually in or around March, in the form of his **Budget Statement**.

The House will initially approve the Budget for a short period of ten days, during which time the proposals will be debated. Eventually, the Finance Bill will be passed and the government will have the authority to collect the revenue it needs, which will be paid into the **Consolidated Fund**, which is, in effect, the government's current account.

16.10   The UK Taxation System

A **tax** is a charge made by the government on people, property or businesses. It can be **specific**, such as a tax on cars, or it can be **general**, such as **value added tax** (VAT), which is levied on a wide range of goods and services.

A tax can be **direct**, in that it is paid directly by the tax payer to the collecting authority, or it can be **indirect**, meaning that it is added to the price of goods or services and paid to the government by the person selling the goods or supplying the service. **Income tax** is an example of a direct tax and VAT an indirect one. Economists also make a distinction between **progressive** and **regressive** taxes. A progressive tax is one which takes into account a person's ability to pay, whereas a regressive tax does not.

The United Kingdom income tax system, for example, includes an initial personal allowance, more for a married person than someone who is single, before the tax is calculated. Furthermore, the rates of tax increase in income bands, so the more you earn the more you pay. VAT, on the other hand, is payable at the same rate by everyone, regardless of income.

Figure 16.3 illustrates how a tax can be progressive or regressive in its effects. In the examples given two taxpayers are used. Both are married, taxpayer A earning £8000 per year and tax payer B £24000, or three times as much. The examples have been deliberately simplified. In reality, it is likely that both taxpayers would receive other allowances, such as mortgage interest relief, in addition to their basic personal allowances, and if taxpayer B had a bigger mortgage than A, as he would be likely to, then his total of allowances would be greater.

Fig. 16.3

Progressive and Regressive Taxation
(Based on the 1986–87 UK Tax System)
INCOME TAX – PROGRESSIVE

	Taxpayer A	Taxpayer B
Gross annual income	£8000	£24000
Married person's allowance	£3655	£3655
Taxable income	£4345	£20345
Tax on first £17200 at 29%	£1260	£4988
Tax on next £3000 at 40%	—	£1200
Tax on next £4800 at 45%	—	£65
Total tax payable	£1260	£6253
Tax payable as proportion of gross income	15.75%	26.05%

VALUE ADDED TAX – REGRESSIVE

15% VAT charged on a video recorder priced at £450 = £67.50
VAT as proportion of Taxpayer A's gross monthly income 10.1%
VAT as proportion of Taxpayer B's gross monthly income 3.4%

In addition to income tax, the other main forms of direct taxation are **capital gains** and **capital transfer** taxes. Capital gains tax is payable on the profits you make from selling a property you have bought as an investment, rather than a residence for yourself. Capital transfer tax is payable on money or property which is passed as a gift to dependants or left to them on death. Both of these taxes are progressive.

VAT, as we have seen, is a tax added to the price of goods and services. Some goods, such as food, are either zero rated or exempt entirely from the tax.

Prior to 1966 UK companies had to pay both income tax and profits tax on their earnings. These were replaced by a **corporation tax**, which is levied on profits earmarked for distribution to the shareholders. Profits which are not distributed, but ploughed back into the business, are exempt, as an encouragement to invest.

The various parts of the tax revenue of central government are shown in Figure 16.4.

Fig. 16.4

UK Central Government Revenue 1984

		Amount £ million	% of Total
Taxes on income:	Income tax	32817	27.70
	Petroleum revenue tax	6883	5.81
	Corporation tax	6886	5.81
	IBA levy	48	0.04
Taxes on expenditure:	VAT	17960	15.16
	Hydrocarbon oils	5944	5.01
	Tobacco	4039	3.41
	Beer	1794	1.52
	Wines and spirits	2073	1.75
	Customs duties	1288	1.09
	Car tax	743	0.63
	Betting and gaming	651	0.54
	EC agricultural levies	154	0.13
	Motor vehicle duties	2096	1.77
	National Insurance surcharge	1077	0.91
	Gas levy	496	0.42

	Amount £ million	% of Total
Sugar levy	58	0.05
Stamp duties	961	0.81
Northern Ireland rates	124	0.11
Other taxes on expenditure	46	0.04
National Insurance contributions	22484	18.98
Royalties and licence fees on oil and gas production	2447	2.07
Dividends and interest from local authorities	2364	2.00
Dividends and interest from public corporations	2458	2.08
Other income	2565	2.16
TOTAL	118456	100

16.11   Government and Business Compared

If the government really was running a business, as UK Ltd, how successful would it be? How well is the country being managed compared with a large company in the private sector?

It is difficult to make a truly objective and accurate comparison because, again, like is not being compared with like. The big difference between the public and private sectors is, of course, the need for political accountability, and this alone can be time consuming and costly. Nevertheless, some comparisons can usefully be made, and lessons drawn.

Apart from the sheer scale of the operation, a major difficulty facing any government is getting a coherent and concerted policy agreed and implemented right across all the central departments. Despite the Cabinet and its committees, central government in Britain still operates in a largely unco-ordinated fashion, with each department determining its own policies and setting its own priorities. The civil servants carry out their work conscientiously but mainly from the standpoints of their own departments.

The **span of control** of a minister is, like that of everyone else, limited. In other words, it is impossible for one person to oversee successfully more than a limited number of operations by a limited number of people. He must delegate if he is to survive. But even the largest departments have only a relatively small number of ministers and junior ministers so, in the end, most delegation will be to the permanent civil servants. But, conscious of the need to be politically accountable, they will, inevitably, err on the side of caution so as to protect their ministers. Furthermore, as we have already said, very few civil servants have had experience outside the public sector and their training does not equip them particularly well for the task of corporate management.

A business could not be run on the lines of central government in Britain and survive in a competitive world. But it is equally certain that the general public would soon complain if all the restraints and controls which a businessman would find intolerable, were removed from the political system. So the best we can probably hope for is some improvement in government policy and decision making to make it more relevant to the nation's commercial and industrial needs. To ask for more would be unrealistic.

Questions and Assignments

1 What are the main differences between Keynesian and monetarist economics?
2 What was meant by Butskellism?
3 Why did J K Galbraith say that Britain was the ideal country in which to practise monetarism?
4 What are the main reasons for Britain's relatively poor economic performance?
5 What is the difference between a progressive and a regressive tax?
6 Why cannot a country be run as if it were a business?
7 Using the information in Figure 16.2, draw up an international economic league table for 1986, giving 1–13 points to each country for its position in each of the five performance columns.
8 Are rates a progressive or regressive form of taxation? Explain carefully the reasoning behind your answer.

Chapter 17

The State as an Employer

More than 12% of the working population of the United Kingdom are in the public sector. Just over 600 000 people are in the civil service and the rest in local government, the National Health Service, the armed forces and the nationalised industries.

Although they perform a wide variety of tasks, they have certain things in common. One common factor is that they all have their pay and working conditions determined by national collective bargaining, through Joint Councils consisting of employer and worker representatives. Most are members of a trade union or staff association which speaks for them on one of the Joint Councils.

Since civil servants have no measurable end product by which to judge their worth, their pay, since 1955, has been based on a 'fair comparison' of what equivalent workers are paid in the private sector. In addition to the collective bargaining machinery, occasionally an 'ad hoc' inquiry is set to advise on whether or not pay has fallen behind the going rate.

Industrial relations in the public sector have not always been good and disputes have mostly arisen over pay and working conditions. It is regrettable that in recent years some politicians have denigrated public servants unfairly.

17.1 The Scale of Public Employment

The state is Britain's largest employer, with a total of more than 3 million people engaged in some form of public sector work activity, or about 12% of the national labour force. By any standards this is a very large number and it includes virtually every kind of occupation from people with low skills to highly qualified specialists.

In one way or another they are all in what can be called the public service but the conditions of their employment vary so much that it is misleading to think of them as part of one big national business. Nevertheless, there are some common features which characterise employment by the state.

17.2 National Collective Bargaining

Collective bargaining is a process of reaching agreement on pay and working conditions through discussions between employers, on the one side, and trade unions, representing employees, on the other. It is a widespread practice in British industry in both the private and public sectors. Sometimes collective bargaining is carried on at local level, and is then called **plant bargaining**. In the public sector it is invariably conducted at national level and the accepted machinery is the **National Joint Council** (NJC), containing employer and employee representatives.

In the civil service, the National Health Service and local government the NJC is called a **Whitley Council**. In the nationalised industries it is usually a **Joint Industrial Council**. The principles behind each and their origins are the same.

In 1916, during the First World War, the government set up a committee, under the chairmanship of an MP, J M Whitley, to look at methods of pay bargaining throughout the country, with a view to improving them and the relationships between employers and employees. In their five reports, Whitley and his colleagues recommended the setting up of joint industrial councils throughout industry and in the public sector. The idea did not prove as popular as had been hoped in privately owned industry but it became the standard mechanism in the public sector.

Whitley Council machinery was adopted for the civil service and local authority manual workers in 1919 and, over a period of time, it spread to all local government employees. When the major nationalisation programme was drawn up, between 1945 and 1950, Whitley Councils were built into the structures of the new public corporations.

Whether called a Whitley Council or a Joint Industrial Council, the membership and methods of working are the same. Each Council consists of two corresponding groups, one from the employers and one from the employees' representatives. In the civil service the chairman is always drawn from the employers', or official, side. Elsewhere the chairman is chosen by the Council itself.

Agreement within a Council is not reached by a vote. Either there is unanimous agreement, usually on the basis of compromise, or there is a breakdown of negotiations and perhaps a resort to the judgement of an outside person or body. This process of looking for a solution outside the Council is called **arbitration**.

A weakness of national collective bargaining is that it makes little allowance for local variations in circumstances. For example, a teacher in a bleak inner city school will be paid on the same scale as one working in a pleasant rural environment. It is not surprising, therefore, that local authorities have difficulty in recruiting good quality staff where they are most needed.

17.3   Trade Unions in the Public Sector

Trade union membership is widespread throughout the civil service. A civil servant is free to join a trade union or staff association, although the banning from union membership of staff employed at the government security headquarters in Cheltenham **(GCHQ)** cast some doubts over the government's attitude towards its employees. Trade union membership is generally encouraged in local government and other parts of the public sector.

The main unions representing non-industrial civil servants are:

Civil and Public Services Association (CPSA) – mainly clerical workers

Institution of Professional Civil Servants (IPCS) – professional and technical people

Society of Civil and Public Servants (SCPS) – executive and administrative staff

Inland Revenue Staff Federation (RSF) – Inland Revenue staff

Civil Service Union (CSU) – mostly manual, non-industrial workers

Association of First Division Civil Servants (FDA) – the top administrators

Industrial civil servants are mainly members of one of the big industrial unions, such as the **Transport and General Workers' Union (TGWU)**, the **General, Municipal, Boilermakers and Allied Workers' Union (GMBWU)** or the **Amalgamated Union of Engineering Workers (AUEW)**.

In local government, non-manual staff are mostly members of the **National and Local Government Officers' Association**

(NALGO), although there are also some smaller, more specialist bodies. The main unions for local authority manual workers are the **National Union of Public Employees (NUPE)**, the GMBWU and the TGWU.

Teachers and health service employees have their own specialist unions, such as the **National Union of Teachers (NUT)** and the **Confederation of Health Service Employees (COHSE)**, and their own negotiating machinery, based on Whitley Council principles.

In the nationalised industries workers are either represented by one of the general or craft unions or by one peculiar to their particular industry. They include the **National Union of Mineworkers (NUM)**, the **National Union of Railwaymen (NUR)** and the **Union of Communication Workers (UCW)**. These are only a few: there are many others.

17.4   The Government as the Paymaster

Determining the correct level of pay for workers in the public sector presents some problems. Profitability cannot be used in the civil service or local government as there is no end product that can be easily measured.

It was because of this that the Priestley Royal Commission on the Civil Service, which reported in 1955, recommended the principle of **'fair comparison'** with staff outside the service doing 'broadly comparable work'. 'Fair comparison' was accepted the following year by the civil service National Whitley Council and it became the basis for determining pay. A **Civil Service Pay Research Unit** was set up to study job comparability and equivalent pay settlements in the private sector.

Following a major dispute, the government instituted, in 1981, another inquiry into civil service pay, this time under Sir John Megaw, a former High Court judge. His report, presented in 1982, recommended that the 'fair comparion' principle should be retained but that other factors, such as the ability to recruit and retain staff, should also be taken into account.

Pay in the local government and teaching services is normally agreed through the Whitley Council machinery or by arbitration but occasionally the government has been persuaded to set up an 'ad hoc' committee to look objectively at a particular problem, particularly when a dispute has occurred or is likely. For example, in 1974, there was a wholesale review of teachers' pay by the Houghton Committee.

Pay negotiations in the nationalised industries usually operate on broadly similar lines to those in the private sector, but the public sector unions have often been able to force higher awards because of their 'industrial muscle'. It will be remembered that a miners' strike forced Edward Heath to call a general election in 1974. Ten years later Margaret Thatcher was better prepared and the long and bitter strike of 1984–85 ended in defeat for the NUM.

Chairmen and board members of the nationalised industries, judges, top civil servants, MPs and senior officers in the armed forces have their pay determined by a **Top Salaries Review Body**, originally established in 1971, which reports every two years directly to the Prime Minister.

Not only is the state the ultimate paymaster as far as the public sector is concerned, settlements there have often set the standard for pay in the private sector and governments have therefore seen the need to keep them as low as possible. Also, of course, tight public spending limits mean tight public pay limits too.

Even governments which have professed to favour free collective bargaining and have claimed to be opposed to incomes policies, have usually tried to apply one in the public sector in an indirect way.

17.5   Industrial Relations in the Public Sector

The term **industrial relations** is used to describe the attitudes of workers to their bosses and vice versa. When attitudes on both sides are good industrial relations are said to be good. Some of the most successful firms in the world claim that they owe their success in great measure to good industrial relations. The Japanese, for example, go to considerable pains to establish and maintain a good relationship between management and workers, even though the methods they use might not necessarily be acceptable in countries outside Japan.

The presence of good industrial relations can be recognised in a number of ways: a willingness to accept change; a willingness to negotiate and to strike only as a very last resort; an open system of communication within the organisation. Poor industrial relations are evidenced by opposition to change; the presence of an 'us and them' mentality; and a tendency to strike at the least provocation.

As the nation's biggest employer, the state ought to set a good example in its industrial relations. Unfortunately, this is often not the case.

The nationalised industries have not enjoyed particularly good industrial relations, as demonstrated by a poor strike record, and yet they were set up with great expectations of a new approach to industrial ownership and management. It must be said that an opportunity has been missed and, instead of the publicly owned industries giving a lead to the private sector, it has often been the other way around. Although strikes have been relatively few in the civil and local government services, relations there have often been soured because of the government attempts to restrict pay settlements. There has also been a tendency in recent years, mainly because of the Conservative government's strenuous commitment to private enterprise, for politicians to denigrate the work of public servants and imply that only employment in the private sector makes a genuine contribution to the nation's wellbeing. This is an unfortunate development which ought to be resisted.

There is a comment in the Northcote-Trevelyan Report on the Civil Service, of 1854, which bears repetition, because it applies to all parts of the public sector.

> '. . . as matters now stand, the Government of the country could not be carried on without the aid of an efficient body of permanent officers, occupying a position duly subordinate to that of the Ministers who are directly responsible to the Crown and to Parliament, yet possessing sufficient independence, character, ability and experience to be able to advise, assist, and to some extent, influence those who are from time to time set over them.'

Questions and Assignments

1 What is meant by collective bargaining?
2 What is a Whitley Council?
3 What is arbitration?
4 What is meant by the principle of 'fair comparison'?
5 How can you recognise the presence of good industrial relations?
6 Why have industrial relations in the public sector often been unsatisfactory?
7 There are several trade unions representing teachers. Would it be to their advantage to have just one?

Think carefully about this and consider asking teachers for their opinions. The final view, however, must be yours and you should give reasons for your answer.

This topic can also be used as the basis for a group debate on the motion 'This House believes a single union would be beneficial to the teaching profession'.

8 Using the salary bands below, carry out a survey among people you know to discover into which bands different occupations fit. Do not ask people for exact salaries and assure them that the information they supply will be treated in confidence. Take at least 20 samples and set out the results of your survey in the following form.

Salary	*Occupation*
Up to £10000	—
£10000–£15000	—
£15000–£20000	—
Over £20000	—

Chapter 18

The World Beyond

In 1945 Britain headed an empire, called the Commonwealth, which included a quarter of the world's population. From 1947 onwards this empire was progressively dismembered, most countries within it gaining independence. With the end of empire, Britain turned towards Europe. Its commitment to Europe was, however, belated so that by the time it became a member of the Community, in 1972, it was well established.

The European Community now consists of 12 countries but its institutions and decision taking processes are dominated by the leading four: France, West Germany, Italy and the United Kingdom.

The biggest effects of Community membership on Britain have been in trade and economic matters. Europe is now Britain's biggest export market and is growing. With a population larger than that of either the USSR or the United States, Europe's potential as a major force in world affairs is immense.

Britain has other important international commitments. Some result from its membership of the United Nations Organisation and some from its defence responsiblities, particularly within the North Atlantic Treaty Organisation.

Although no longer a leading world power, Britain still has an important voice in world affairs. Its relationship with the United States remains strong but it is within Europe that its future lies.

18.1 From Empire to Commonwealth

At the end of the Second World War London was still the hub of the greatest empire history has ever recorded. It covered a quarter of the world's surface, included a quarter of its population and had spread over every continent to every race.

From Whitehall three departments of state ruled this vast complex of independent countries and dependent colonies and protectorates. The Dominions Office was responsible for the white-governed dominions of Australia, Canada, Newfoundland, South Africa and New Zealand. The India Office administered the sub-continent of India, still one country of 400 million people. The Colonial Office was responsible for the rest of the Commonwealth, as it was now called, and this included large parts of Africa, Malaysia, Burma and territories in the Far East and South America.

The potential wealth and influence of this huge international conglomerate were incalculable and yet Britain, as the mother country, had emerged from the war virtually insolvent and, like most of the other European countries, heavily dependent on the United States for economic support.

Surveying the scene in 1945, the newly elected Labour government, led by Clement Attlee, saw an enormous task ahead in rebuilding the British economy. It did not have the time or resources to spend on overseeing its still growing overseas empire. In any event, the war had changed attitudes and relationships and there was an increasing call for greater independence in virtually all the countries concerned.

Australia, Canada, Newfoundland, South Africa and New Zealand had been awarded independence before the First World War and the Statute of Westminster of 1931 formally restated their rights to be separate and sovereign under the King, as the formal symbol of the free association of the British Commonwealth of Nations.

The strongest immediate post-war pressure for independence came from India and in 1947 it was granted, but the sub-continent was divided into the predominantly Hindu state of India and the Muslim state of Pakistan.

Although rule from London was progressively ended, the concept of allegiance to a single Crown remained until 1949 when India decided to declare itself a republic. The other members of the Commonwealth agreed to this, provided the King was still accepted as the symbolic head. When Elizabeth II acceded to the throne she was recognised as the new Head of the Commonwealth, but in a personal capacity, and not in the name of the British Crown. This is the position that exists today.

From 1947 onwards the process of decolonisation continued, with some countries leaving the Commonwealth completely. Burma withdrew in 1948 and Ireland in 1949. British Somalia joined the independent Italian Somalia and left the Commonwealth in 1960.

South Africa, following objections to its policy of apartheid, withdrew in 1961. In the same year the British Cameroons split, one part joining Nigeria and the other the independent French Cameroons. Qatar ceased to be a British protectorate in 1971 and in the same year East Pakistan became the new state of Bangladesh, Pakistan itself leaving the Commonwealth.

18.2 The Modern Commonwealth

Of the 49 independent sovereign states, including the United Kingdom, now in the Commonwealth, 18 accept the Queen as head of state, 26 are republics and 5 have their own local monarchs. The full list is given in Figure 18.1.

Fig. 18.1

The Commonwealth, 1986

State	Region of the World	Population	Date of Independence	Status
Antigua & Barbuda	Caribbean	80 000	1981	British monarchy
Australia	Pacific	15 265 000	1901	British monarchy
The Bahamas	Caribbean	223 000	1973	British monarchy
Bangladesh	S E Asia	96 535 000	1971	Republic
Barbados	Caribbean	251 000	1966	British monarchy
Belize	Central America	154 000	1981	British monarchy
Botswana	Africa	1 001 000	1966	Republic
Brunei	S E Asia	209 000	1984	Local monarchy
Canada	N America	24 882 000	1967	British monarchy
Cyprus	Mediterranean	653 000	1960	Republic
Dominica	Caribbean	74 000	1978	Republic
Fiji	Pacific	676 000	1970	British monarchy
The Gambia	Africa	700 000	1965	Republic
Ghana	Africa	13 367 000	1957	Republic
Grenada	S America	111 000	1974	British monarchy
Guyana	S America	833 000	1966	Republic
India	S Asia	730 572 000	1947	Republic
Jamaica	Caribbean	2 347 000	1962	British monarchy
Kenya	Africa	18 580 000	1963	Republic
Kiribati	Pacific	60 000	1979	Republic
Lesotho	Africa	1 438 000	1966	Local monarchy
Malawi	Africa	6 612 000	1964	Republic
Malaysia	S E Asia	14 995 000	1957	Local monarchy
The Maldives	Indian Ocean	168 000	1965	Republic
Malta	Mediterranean	358 000	1964	Republic
Mauritius	Indian Ocean	1 002 000	1968	British monarchy
Nauru	Pacific	8 000	1968	Republic
New Zealand	Pacific	3 203 000	1907	British monarchy
Nigeria	Africa	85 219 000	1960	Republic
Papua New Guinea	Pacific	3 259 000	1975	British monarchy
Saint Kitts-Nevis	Caribbean	44 500	1983	British monarchy
Saint Lucia	Caribbean	119 000	1979	British monarchy
Saint Vincent and the Grenadines	Caribbean	134 000	1979	British monarchy

State	Region of the World	Population	Date of Independence	Status
The Seychelles	Indian Ocean	65000	1976	Republic
Sierra Leone	Africa	3705000	1961	Republic
Singapore	Malaysia	2501000	1963	Republic
Solomon Islands	Pacific	254000	1978	British monarchy
Sri Lanka	Indian Ocean	15300000	1948	Republic
Swaziland	Africa	632000	1968	Local monarchy
Tanzania	Africa	20524000	1961	Republic
Tonga	Pacific	104000	1970	Local monarchy
Trinidad & Tobago	S America	1149000	1962	Republic
Tuvalu	Pacific	8000	1978	British monarchy
Uganda	Africa	13819000	1962	Republic
United Kingdom	Europe	56009000		British monarchy
Vanuatu	Pacific	127000	1980	Republic
Western Samoa	Pacific	160000	1962	Republic
Zambia	Africa	6346000	1964	Republic
Zimbabwe	Africa	8077000	1980	Republic

In addition, Britain has a number of colonial dependencies, which include:

Europe: Gibraltar

West Indies: Some of the Leeward Islands, the Virgin Islands, Anguilla, the Cayman Islands and the Turks and Caicos Islands

North Atlantic: Bermuda

South Atlantic: The Falkland Islands and Dependencies, British Antarctic Territory, St Helena and Dependencies, Ascension Island

Asia: Hong Kong

Indian Ocean: British Indian Ocean Territory

Pacific: Pitcairn Island

The United Kingdom itself consists of England, Scotland, Wales and Northern Ireland. The British Isles includes the United Kingdom plus the Channel Islands of Jersey and Guernsey, with its dependencies, Alderney, Brechou, Great Sark, Little Sark, Herm, Jethou and Lihou, and the Isle of Man. The Channel Islands exist separately from the UK and have Lieutenant Governors appointed by the Crown. The Isle of Man also has its own Lieutenant Governor and separate laws, and a two chamber parliament, the Tynwald.

18.3   Britain's Commonwealth Role

Commonwealth heads of government meet every two years to discuss international affairs and areas of co-operation. Finance ministers meet annually and other ministers as and when the need arises. The Commonwealth is not a mutual defence organisation and some member countries are committed to international treaties, such as the North Atlantic Treaty Organisation (NATO).

The **Commonwealth Secretariat** was established in 1965 and is the main agency for communication between member states. It is based in Marlborough House, London, which was given by the Queen in 1959 for Commonwealth meetings.

During the half century which has passed since the British Empire became the Commonwealth there have been many changes. The original 'white man's club' of the United Kingdom and the old dominions has become an association of equal, but very diverse, partners. In recent years this partnership has been put under some severe strains, particularly on the issue of South Africa and concerted Commonwealth action to end apartheid.

Indeed, the strains have been so great that Britain's natural right to leadership has been questioned. Although the Queen is still accepted as Head of the Commonwealth, it is in a personal capacity and not as the British Crown. Other countries, such as India, have emerged as possible leaders, particularly among the group of 'non-aligned' states who shun the camps of both the super powers.

Britain's clear and legally binding commitment to Europe is in stark contrast to its loose, and mainly emotional, links with the Commonwealth. It does not have the economic significance of the old Empire so its value now rests on cultural and political foundations. Some people have doubted its continuing value but they are as yet in a minority compared with the many who see it as a force for stability in the world.

18.4   Commonwealth to Europe

As Europe began to reassemble in the aftermath of the Second World War it soon became clear that the economies of all the countries which had been involved were virtually shattered and would need a huge injection of capital if they were to recover. The United States again came to Europe's rescue with a plan which was set out in a speech at Harvard University, on 5 June 1947, by Secretary of State George Marshall, who had himself been a US general during the war.

His proposals, which soon became known as the **Marshall Plan** could be seen in two lights. They were another example of typical American generosity, but, at the same time, an act of enlightened self-interest, because the United States knew that, as an international trader, it would eventually benefit when Europe became prosperous again and able to buy American goods.

The original plan was intended to include the USSR but the Russians disliked the idea of a link with capitalist countries so declined the offer. In July 1947 a **Committee for European Economic Cooperation** was set up, its members being Britain, France, Austria, Belgium, Denmark, Greece, Iceland, Ireland, Italy, Luxembourg, the Netherlands, Norway, Portugal, Sweden, Switzerland and Turkey. Although Italy was admitted into membership, Germany was not, and Britain and France acted on its behalf.

The permanent committee for distributing Marshall Aid funds, which started pouring into Europe, was the **Organisation for European Economic Cooperation (OEEC)**. At the same time, in Eastern Europe, the USSR was setting up its own equivalent organisation, the **Cominform**. The post-war pattern for Europe was now established, with, in Winston Churchill's famous phrase, 'an iron curtain' dividing the capitalist west from the communist east.

While Leader of the Opposition, between 1945 and 1951, Winston Churchill was advocating closer links between West European countries and even speaking about a possible United States of Europe. The Labour government, however, and particularly Foreign Secretary Ernest Bevin, was wary of a close European connection when Britain, with a large part of its old Empire still intact, had a world role to play. The opportunity to lead Europe was therefore lost and even Churchill, when he returned to power in 1951, had become less enthusiastic.

Churchill's successor, Sir Anthony Eden, had even stronger dreams of empire when, in 1956, he embarked on the ill advised Suez adventure. Its failure marked the end of any imperialist ambitions Britain might have had and forced it to look towards Europe for its future.

But by this time Europe had changed. The Marshall Plan had worked. Industrial output in many countries was now higher than pre-war and, with this renewed prosperity, they were beginning to plan for a future in which there would be such close political an' economic cooperation that a Third World War would b impossible.

In 1948 the Netherlands, Belgium and Luxembourg had set up a **Benelux Customs Union**, to encourage trade between them, and in 1951 France, West Germany, Italy, the Netherlands, Belgium and Luxembourg formed the **European Coal and Steel Community (ESC)**, so as to share coal and steel resources. This was followed, in 1955, by the setting up of a **European Investment Fund** and, in 1957, by the momentous decision to sign the **Treaty of Rome**.

The Treaty of Rome established the **European Economic Community (EEC)**, which was to become popularly known as the Common Market, and the **European Atomic Energy Community (Euratom)**. The preamble to the Treaty of Rome declared its objectives as being: the establishment of the foundations of an ever closer union among European peoples; the improvement of their working and living conditions; the progressive abolition of restrictions on trade between them; and the development of the prosperity of overseas countries. The practical aims were to abolish internal tariffs and barriers to trade, to develop a common agricultural policy, and to ensure the free movement of labour, capital and services throughout the Community.

Initially, Britain tried to maintain its economic links with the Commonwealth and, without committing itself to the EEC, expand its trade in Europe. It therefore set up, with Austria, Norway, Portugal, Sweden and Switzerland, and later Finland and Iceland, a **European Free Trade Area (EFTA)**, which proved to be a pale shadow of the Common Market. In the end EFTA collapsed and the British government decided to apply for EEC membership only to meet opposition from France, led by President de Gaulle. He was not convinced that 'France's old enemy' was sufficiently committed to European integration to make a wholehearted contribution.

Attempts to join by Harold Macmillan, in 1961, and Harold Wilson, in 1967, were blocked by de Gaulle and it not until after his retirement, in 1969, that the path was clear for Britain's entry. On 22 January 1972 Edward Heath signed the **Treaty of Accession** and the European Community of Six, with Ireland and Denmark, became the Community of Nine. In 1981 Greece was admitted into membership and, in 1985, the addition of Spain and Portugal made it a European Community of Twelve. It now had a total population of more than 320 million, nearly 100 million more than the United States and 50 million more than the USSR.

18.5   How the European Community Works

Of the 320 million people who live in the European Community, about 70% are in the four largest countries, France, West Germany, Italy and the United Kingdom. The Community's institutions and decision taking machinery reflect this population distribution. The Community structure is shown in Figure 18.2.

Fig. 18.2

*Main Institutions
of the European Community*

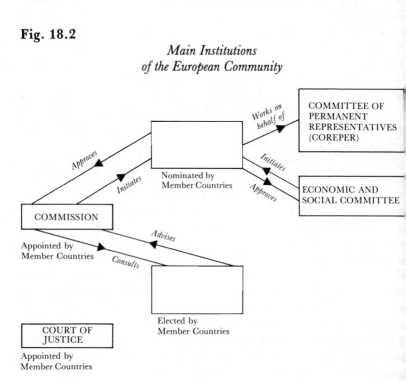

The **Commission** is at the heart of the decision taking process in the Community. It consists of 16 members: 2 each from France, West Germany, Italy and the United Kingdom, and 1 each from Belgium Denmark, Greece, Ireland, Luxembourg, the Netherlands, Portugal and Spain. The members are nominated by each state for a four year, renewable, term of office. One member is chosen as President for a two year, renewable, term. The post of President is a mixture of prime minister and head of the European civil service, and a highly respected appointment.

Although the commissioners are drawn proportionately from member states, each takes an oath on appointment not to promote national interests. They head a large bureaucracy, with 20 directorates-general, each in charge of a particular department, and corresponding to a permanent secretary in the British system.

The **Council of Ministers** is the supreme decision taking body and consists of one minister from each of the 12 member countries. The actual representatives vary according to the subject under discussion. If it is economic policy it will be the finance ministers, if agricultural policy, the agriculture ministers. It is the foreign ministers, however, who tend to be the most active and it is the Foreign Office which has the biggest British involvement.

The Presidency of the Council changes hands at six monthly intervals, each member state taking its turn.

The **Committee of Permanent Representatives (COREPER)** is a subsidiary body of officials, often called **ambassadors**, who work on behalf of the Council. The members of COREPER are senior civil servants who have been temporarily released by member states to live and work in Brussels.

The **Economic and Social Committee** is a consultative body consisting of representatives from member countries and covering a wide range of interests. For example, they may include employers, trade unionists, people from the professions, farmers and so on. The Committee advises the Council of Ministers and the Commission.

Members of the **European Parliament** are elected by the 12 states in proportion to populations. The United Kingdom has 81 members, representing 66 English, 8 Scottish, 4 Welsh and 3 Northern Ireland **Euro-constituencies**. Each is equivalent to about 8 UK parliamentary constituencies, with an electorate of about half a million.

Policy is made and carried out within the Community in the following way.

The Commission makes a particular proposal, which will have first been worked on by one of its 20 directorates. The proposal is sent to the Council of Ministers who will initially pass it to COREPER for further examination. At the same time it will be passed to the European Parliament for consideration. The Parliament's role is mainly consultative, although it does have power to reject the European Community budget and to dismiss the Commission if it chooses to do so.

After examination by COREPER, with the addition of any

views of the European Parliament, the proposal is formally considered by the Council of Ministers to decide whether or not action should be taken.

Voting in the Council is weighted in favour of the larger member states, but votes are hardly ever taken. Either there is a unanimous decision or, if one or more of the ministers argues that the policy would be against national interests, the proposal is shelved.

Once the Council of Ministers has agreed a policy proposal it is passed back to the Commission's permanent staff for implementation.

A policy decision can take one of two forms. It can be a **regulation** or a **directive**. Both are legally binding but a regulation applies to all member states whereas a directive only relates to one or more specific countries.

The **European Court of Justice** consists of judges and officials appointed by the member states. Its task is to ensure that the European Community Treaty is fairly observed and that the regulations and directives of the Council of Ministers are followed. The Court can make rulings but it has no powers of its own to enforce them. This is the responsibility of the individual member states in their own national courts.

The European Court of Justice, sited in Luxembourg, should not be confused with the **International Court of Justice**, based in The Hague, in Holland, or the **European Court of Human Rights**, which is located in Strasbourg, in France.

18.6   The Implications of European Community Membership

Britain has been a member of the European Community for more than 15 years. What effects has this membership had?

For the average person the most notable effect has been the comparative ease of travel within the Community, coupled with the ongoing movement towards a common tariff. Travellers in Europe will have noticed these changes.

Membership has had a considerable effect on the government and civil service. There is now a 'mini-Whitehall' established in Brussels and a constant movement of politicians and staff across the Channel.

The European Court of Justice is making its weight increasingly felt. On signing the Treaty of Rome, to become a Community member, Britain had to accept that Community law would take precedence over domestic law. Ordinary people in Britain are now applying to the European Court in increasing numbers, challenging laws made by the United Kingdom Parliament. The European Court has thus become the nearest equivalent to a Supreme Court for all member states of the Community.

The role of the European Parliament is also undergoing quiet but important changes. It now operates on a clear party basis, as Figure 18.3 shows, and is beginning to feel a genuine identity of its

Fig. 18.3

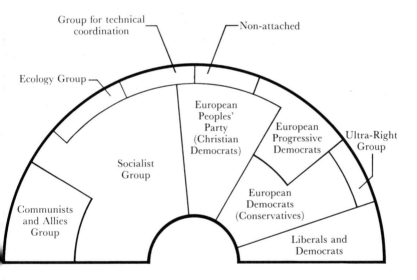

Party Composition
of the European Parliament

own. Whether this will mean a shift of power from the Council of Ministers and the Commission is too early to say. At the moment, however, the Community is run mainly by officials and this does not make for responsible and accountable government.

The biggest impact of Community membership has been in the field of trade and economic affairs. In 1975 trade between Britain and the other Community countries accounted for 32% of UK exports. In 1985 this had risen to 46%. Figure 18.4 shows the change in exports between 1977 and 1985.

Fig. 18.4

UK Exports to the European Community:
1977 and 1985

(Percentage Shares of Member States)

	1977	1985
Belgium & Luxembourg	11.0	8.8
Denmark	6.3	3.6
France	17.3	20.3
West Germany	19.7	23.5
Greece	1.6	0.9
Ireland	12.6	9.5
Italy	7.9	9.1
The Netherlands	17.3	19.2
Portugal	2.4	1.1
Spain	3.9	4.1

In some cases the export performance has worsened, particularly with Belgium, Luxembourg and Denmark, but in others, and notably West Germany, which is generally seen as a tough market to sell in, there has been a big improvement. Greece, Spain and Portugal are, of course, fairly new members of the Community and the pattern of exports to them may well change in the next few years.

18.7 Britain's Other International Commitments

Although without its Empire and no longer one of the 'super powers', Britain still has enormous international interests and commitments.

It was, of course, a founder of the **United Nations Organisation (UNO)**, which now has over 150 members and is one of the few international organisations which bridge the gulf between the Soviet dominated East and the United States dominated West. As well as its two main institutions, the **General Assembly** and the **Security Council**, there is a network of agencies and bodies operating under its umbrella.

The General Assembly meets in regular sessions and is composed of member countries' representatives, with each nation entitled to one vote. It is essentially a debating chamber, with few executive powers.

The Security Council consists of 15 members. Five are permanent: China, France, the USSR, the United Kingdom and the United States. Their right to seats is based on their having been allies, against Germany and Japan, in the Second World War. The other 10 members are elected for two year terms. The Council has the job of maintaining international peace and supervising the work of the many United Nations' peacekeeping forces. When decisions are taken they must be on the basis of a vote by at least 9 of the 10 members, and the 9 votes must include those of all permanent members or no decision is taken.

Rather like its predecessor, the League of Nations, the United Nations Organisation has always promised more than it has been able to deliver. When the vital interests of the super powers are involved, national considerations always seem to override those of international peace.

Among the main UNO bodies are the **International Labour Organisation (ILO)**, which sets standards for labour relations: the **Food and Agriculture Organisation (FAO)**, which sponsors farming efficiency; the **World Health Organisation (WHO)**, which assists health authorities throughout the world and tries to wipe out disease; the IMF and World Bank, which we looked at in an earlier chapter; the **International Civil Aviation Organisation (ICAO)**, which establishes technical aviation standards: the **Universal Postal Union (UPU)**, which encourages international cooperation in postal services; the **International Telecommunications Union (ITU)**, which allocates radio frequencies; the **World Meteorological Organisation (WMO)**, which develops international collaboration in weather forecasting; and the **General Agreement on Tariffs and Trade (GATT)**, which is an international treaty laying down ground rules for the conduct of trade between nations. These are some of the most significant organisations: there are many more.

Most of Britain's other international commitments are associated with its membership of the European Community or with its role as a world policeman.

Britain's major defence involvement is as a member of the **North Atlantic Treaty Organisation (NATO)**. It was created in 1949 with an initial membership of Belgium, Canada, Denmark, France, Iceland, Italy, Luxembourg, the Netherlands, Norway, Portugal, the United Kingdom and the United States of America. Turkey, West Germany and Spain joined later and France withdrew in 1966, preferring an independent defence policy. On joining, members of NATO pledge themselves to settle disputes by peaceful means and to pool their resources for common defence. They regard an attack on one as being an attack on all.

The communist bloc equivalent of NATO is the **Warsaw Pact**, which was signed in 1955, creating a mutual defence organisation for Bulgaria, Czechoslovakia, East Germany, Hungary, Poland, Rumania and the USSR. Albania had also been a member, but withdrew in 1968 following the Soviet invasion of Czechoslovakia.

As a world policeman, Britain has forces stationed in all parts of the world, as the map in Figure 18.5 shows.

Fig. 18.5

Britain's International Defence Commitments

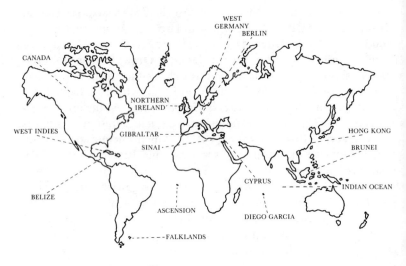

18.8   Britain's World Future

Britain's role in the world has changed fundamentally during the present century. Fifty years ago, as we have seen, it headed a mighty empire and only thirty years ago was a leading international power. Today its economic strength is less than that of most nations of similar size and, unless there is a dramatic improvement in the years to come, it will continue to fall in relative terms.

Nevertheless, its voice is still listened to and its values generally admired. In the fields of scientific and technical invention, and in the arts, it continues to be a world leader. London is still a major international finance centre, although increasingly challenged by New York and Tokyo.

One aspect of Britain's world role is the so-called 'special relationship' with the United States. This relationship is built on historical and cultural foundations. It was particularly strong when Winston Churchill was Prime Minister, and Margaret Thatcher has tried hard to extend and consolidate it. There is an obvious advantage in two nations sharing a common language but there are other areas of agreement. The approach to law and the legal systems of the two countries are similar and, although their constitutions are very different, there is a shared belief in the virtues of democratic government. However, the special relationship, if it does exist, should not be taken too much for granted. There have been occasions when the United States has adopted a very isolationist policy and there have been fundamental differences of attitude on world affairs.

Britain's long term future clearly lies in Europe. The Commonwealth may well continue for many years but it will never regain its former power and influence. And yet, although physically on the door step of continental Europe, Britain still seems reluctant to commit itself wholeheartedly to it. For some politicians a United States of Europe is the ultimate dream, but it is a dream which may well take several generations to achieve.

Questions and Assignments

1 Why was the British Empire disbanded?
2 Why did Britain take so long to join the European Community?
3 How is policy made within the European Community?
4 What is COREPER?
5 What are the two most powerful defence alliances in the world today?
6 Where does Britain's international future lie?
7 Make an alphabetical list of as many international bodies of which Britain is a member as you can find.

   There are a number of sources you can use. Your library will be able to advise you.

   This assignment can be used as the basis for a group competition, a prize going to the compiler of the longest list.
8 Using the information in Figure 18.1, draw a map showing Commonwealth membership throughout the world.

PART V

THE INDIVIDUAL AND THE STATE

Chapter 19

The Welfare State

The term Welfare State is used to describe the system of social service provision which has been built up in Britain since the Second World War. People have different attitudes towards it, some seeing it as an essential obligation of government and others as an unnecessary intrusion into personal and family life and a burden on the taxpayer.

The main features of Britain's Welfare State are support for the family, through allowances for children; unemployment and retirement benefits; and a National Health Service. Some people would include a public education system and public housing as part of it, but these existed before the post-1945 Welfare State was created. Whether or not the maintenance of full employment is another essential feature is open to debate.

Although most of the Welfare State was established by the Labour government, between 1945 and 1950, plans for it were made by the wartime coalition government and, since 1945, all parties have continued to suppport it. From the 1970s onwards however, the system has been under strain, partly because of competing demands for public expenditure and partly because of increased demands made upon it.

Since 1979 government policies have become increasingly associated with the views of the Leader of the Conservative Party, under the label, Thatcherism. Thatcherism is not so much opposed to the idea of a Welfare state as providing an alternative to it. The alternative is one of more private provision of social services and greater self-reliance by everyone.

The future of the Welfare State in Britain now depends on two factors: the level of prosperity which the country can achieve, and the willingness of governments to give priority to social provision in the face of other competing demands for resources, particularly in the areas of law and order and defence.

19.1   The Idea of a Welfare State

The term **Welfare State** means different things to different people. To the old, the poor and the sick it suggests a guarantee of a minimum standard of care and provision, regardless of income. To the political right winger it means an unnecessary interference by the state in the lives of individuals, and the 'feather bedding' of people who ought to be able to stand on their own feet and fend for themselves. To the average person, with moderate opinions, whether he is politically active or not, it suggests the fulfilment of a natural and essential duty of a democratically elected government to help the disadvantaged and to ensure that no human being suffers the degradation of poverty and all the problems associated with it.

The origins of the Welfare State in Britain can be traced back to the Poor Laws of the 17th century, but these were only minimal attempts to deal with the worst excesses of poverty. The 19th century saw the first real measures to help underprivileged groups, through legislation controlling the working conditions of women and children, and then everyone, who worked in factories and mines.

The general election of 1906 was a political watershed because not only was a Liberal government,committed to social reform, returned to power, but the first 27 Labour MPs were elected.

Just before the outbreak of the Second World War a limited national insurance scheme was introduced but it was not until the end of the war that the foundations of a genuine Welfare State were laid.

While Winston Churchill successfully led the nation through the war, his deputy, Clement Attlee, helped by Conservative, Labour and Liberal politicians in the coalition government, was preparing for peace. Two major documents published during the war years provided the bases for Attlee's post-war plans. One was the Report on Social Insurance and Allied Services, by Sir William Beveridge, popularly known as the **Beveridge Report**, which was published in 1942. The other was the **White Paper on Full Employment**, published in 1944, which showed how parts of the Beveridge Report could be put into effect.

The Beveridge Report proposed a comprehensive system of social security for everyone, which would provide pensions and health and community services. In other words, there would be care for all 'from the cradle to the grave'. The White Paper gave a firm pledge for 'the maintenance of a high and stable level of employment after the war'.

Another important piece of social legislation was also passed during the war years. It was the Education Act of 1944, pioneered by the Conservative politician, R A Butler.

Butler's Act provided for the division of education into three stages: primary, secondary and higher. Within secondary education there was to be selection between secondary modern and grammar schools. This Act formed the basis of education policy for at least a generation, although the division between secondary modern and grammar schools, linked to the 11+ examination, was to become a big political party debating point in the 1960s.

19.2 The Creation of the Welfare State in Britain

The Labour Party won an overwhelming victory in the 1945 general election and immediately set about implementing the programme of social and economic reform which had been developed during the war years. Although it fell to a Labour government to bring in the necessary legislation, most of the provisions had been agreed by all parties.

The main pieces of legislation which created the Welfare State were: the **Family Allowances Act, 1945**, which gave mothers, irrespective of circumstances, an allowance for the maintenance of their children; the **National Insurance Act, 1946**, which was the basis for funding the health, unemployment and pensions systems; the **National Assistance Act, 1948**, which, replacing the old Poor Laws, made provision for people who, in one way or another, did not have an entitlement for benefit under the National Insurance Act; and the **National Health Service Act, 1948**, which established a free National Health Service.

The National Health Service was to be the most ambitious part of the programme and the Health Minister, Aneurin Bevan, had the task of creating it. He would have preferred a fully salaried service, with clear career structures for all medical staff, but met considerable opposition from some sections of the profession. In the end he had to settle for a system where doctors and dentists were paid fees for their services, and for the retention of a private medical system, running alongside state provision.

His aim, however, was to create a free, national service which was so good that private medicine would become virtually irrelevant. To a large extent he succeeded, in spite of all the other demands made on the economy, and the British National Health Service became the envy of the world.

The unemployment benefits and pensions system was also firmly established and in the quarter of a century after the war Britain managed to maintain an acceptable minimum level of social and economic provision, as well as fulfilling all her other competing commitments. Changes in population distribution were, however, to be big problems in the future.

Whether or not the maintenance of full employment, in the sense Beveridge defined it, was really a firm part of the Welfare State is a matter for debate. In any event, it did not become a political issue. All governments, Labour and Conservative, pursuing mainly Keynesian economic policies, kept the level of unemployment well below the 3% target until the mid-1970s, as the graph in Figure 19.1 shows.

Fig. 19.1

Unemployment Trends in the UK: 1945–1986

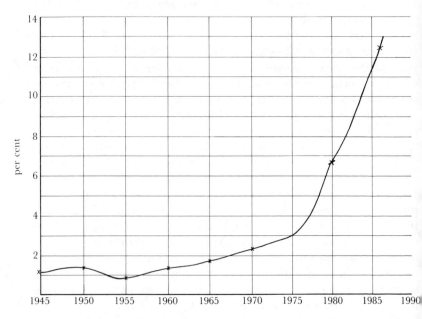

19.3   Strains on the Welfare State

The Conservatives returned to power in 1951 and, in most respects, continued the social policies of the Labour government.

World economic conditions improved, enabling the government to go even further. An ambitious programme of public sector house building was successfully carried through as well as improvements in roads and the general social infrastructure. The 1950s proved to be a period of affluence, summed up in Prime Minister Harold Macmillan's now famous phrase ' You've never had it so good'.

The 1960s saw the beginnings of change. Britain's economic performance fell in comparison with those of her competitors and, with less prosperity, the ability to maintain a Welfare State on the lines originally planned came to be questioned.

Gradually the original idea of free benefits for all began to be eroded. Varying contributions for graduated pensions were introduced in 1959 and in 1966 supplementary benefits for the unemployed were linked to earnings. The rising cost of health care eventually brought an end to free prescriptions, except for the old, the young and the very poor.

By the 1970s a Welfare State, providing services for everyone, regardless of income, had given way to means-related benefits, and yet the party consensus remained pretty well intact. The problem was how to provide on the generous scale originally intended while the numbers needing help were going up and the numbers producing the necessary wealth were fewer. For example, in 1974 the number of people in the United Kingdom aged 65 or over was under eight million, or less than 14% of the population. By 1984 it had risen to nearly eight and a half million, or just under 15% of the population.

19.4   The Phenomenon of Thatcherism

It is not often that a person gives his or her name to a whole philosophy. The writings of Karl Marx in the 19th century resulted in Marxism. This was developed in Russia in the early years of this century into Leninism, or Marxist-Leninism, and later Maoism appeared in China.

Whether Thatcherism can be put into this kind of category is difficult to say. What can be said, however, is that the attitude of Margaret Thatcher and the policies of her government have extended beyond economic matters into a whole, distinctive approach to the relationship between the state and the individual. She has proudly described herself as a 'conviction politician' and it is her own personal convictions about what is right for Britain that have been reproduced in the philosophy of Thatcherism.

Her attitudes and beliefs seem to have come less from any original thought as from the influences of particular men, notably her father, her husband and her political mentor, Sir Keith Joseph.

She was born at Grantham, Lincolnshire in 1925, the daughter of Alfred Roberts, who had a small but growing grocery business and was to become an Independent mayor of the town. Her father was undoubtedly very influential but her mother was a more shadowy figure.

As a girl, Margaret Roberts helped her parents in the corner shop over which the family lived, at the same time working hard at Grantham High School before going to study chemistry at Somerville College, Oxford. The significance of this upbringing was revealed in a speech she made at the Lord Mayor of London's banquet in November 1982, when she replied to criticisms that she approached the financial management of the nation as if she was looking after the family budget.

> 'Some say I preach merely the homilies of housekeeping or the parables of the parlour. But I do not repent. Those parables would have saved many a financier from failure and many a country from crisis'.

It was from Alfred Roberts, a strict teetotal Methodist and self-made man, that she inherited her belief in the virtues of thrift, enterprise and good housekeeping. This conviction was strengthened by her marriage to another businessman, Denis Thatcher, who, ten years her senior, had inherited a paints firm, run it successfully and made his wealth available for her to study for the Bar and start a political career, while producing and rearing two children.

The third important influence was Sir Keith Joseph who, with her, set up the Centre for Policy Studies, under Alfred Sherman, in 1974, to translate the monetarist theories of Milton Friedman into a set of policies for a future Conservative government.

Not only did Thatcherism become a political philosophy, but Margaret Thatcher herself had sufficient resolve and personal authority to put it into practice. At the same time she was able to tap an instinctive streak in lower-middle and working class voters which showed more concern about the size of their net pay packets, the evils of rising crime, the abuse of trade union power and the inefficiency of state bureaucracies than about unemployment or the welfare services.

This populist basis of Thatcherism explains the support that the Conservative Party, under her leadership, received from people who, according to their backgrounds and economic circumstances, ought to have voted Labour.

The impact of Thatcherism and popular support for it are shown in a number of ways:

1 The growth in home ownership, with half a million council houses and flats being sold between 1979 and 1983.
2 The growth of share ownership, with sales of British Telecom, the Trustee Savings Bank, British Gas and British Airways being widely supported.
3 The growth in private medicine, with the number of people taking out private health insurance rising from 2.5 million in 1979 to 4.2 millon in 1982.
4 The growth of small businesses, even though some may only enjoy a short life.
5 Support for legislation curbing trade union power.
6 The revival of a jingoistic patriotism during and after the Falklands Campaign.

Against these signs of support for Thatcherism must be placed:

1 A growing concern about unemployment.
2 An unease about Britain's increasing dependence on the United States, particularly in the field of nuclear defence.
3 Anxiety about Mrs Thatcher's opposition to sanctions against South Africa and the implications of this for the Commonwealth.
4 Disquiet about the rising crime rate and the deteriorating relations between the police and the less privileged sections of society.
5 Doubts about the increasing polarisation of British politics.
6 Concern about Britain's decaying infrastructure, particularly in the inner cities.

Thatcherism is not so much a philosophy as an instinctive attitude. As such, it is more likely to be a temporary phenomenon than a lasting addition to British politics. It would be surprising if Margaret Thatcher's successor as Leader of the Conservative Party was someone in the same mould.

But when she has left the political stage some effects of Thatcherism may well remain. She has not succeeded in creating the 'enterprise culture' she obviously admires but has tapped some enterprise instincts and these could be developed by other governments which show more compassion for ordinary human failings than she has been able to. On these foundations a more united nation might be built.

19.5   Thatcherism and the Welfare State

Thatcherism or the Thatcher Experiment must be judged by what it has and has not achieved. In the case of the Welfare State the record can be judged in five main areas: social security, employment, education, housing and the health and community services.

The social security record reflects a continuation of some slide in benefits which had started earlier in the 1970s before Mrs Thatcher's government took office. The lean years began before 1979. Since then they have become a little leaner. The most obvious development has been the widening gap between the haves and the have nots. Those in work have seen their incomes increase at a faster rate than inflation while those dependent on the state for pensions or unemployment benefit have been tied to the cost of living index.

The record for unemployment has not been good, as Figure 19.1 clearly shows. New jobs have been created, but many of them have been part time and in the service sector. The greatest losses have been in manufacturing.

The rise in home ownership has been matched by a dramatic fall in the rate of public sector house building. In the three years between 1979 and 1982 new public sector house completions fell from 104000 to 49200 a year, a drop of over 50%. In some areas council estates have become mixed estates and this has resulted in a voting shift from Labour to the Conservatives. In many cases privately owned houses are better maintained and this is to be welcomed, but the sudden drop in public housing for rent made life more difficult for those unable or unwilling to purchase.

The period since 1979 has seen a falling school-age population, from about 10 million in 1979 to just over 9 million in 1983, and the downward trend is continuing. The opportunity presented to reduce the pupil-teacher ratio has, however, only partially been seized, dropping by about 3% in the early 1980s. According to reports from the Education Inspectorate there has been a fall in provision of books and equipment in some schools and the gap between the best and the worst, particularly in inner cities, seems to have widened. Higher education expenditure has been substantially reduced so that the principle in the Robbins Report, of 1963, that higher education should be available to all who have the ability to benefit from it, has been under threat.

Speaking at the Conservative Party conference at Brighton in October 1982, Margaret Thatcher said:

'The National Health Service is safe with us. As I said in the House of Commons on December 1st last, "The principle that adequate health care should be provided for all regardless of ability to pay must be the function of any arrangements for financing the NHS". We stand by that'.

There is evidence to support this claim. Figures for England show that between 1978 and 1982 the number of doctors and dentists rose by 4000 to 40000 and the number of nurses and midwives increased by 45000 to 396000. These statistics show signs of continuity but, although expenditure in real terms rose, the number of people requiring care rose even more. The National Health Service has had to run faster just to stay still.

Thatcherism has been not so much a threat to the Welfare State as a challenge. Its main impact has been one of attitude, best summed up by the Social Services Secretary, Norman Fowler, in a lecture he gave to the Conservative Bow Group in January 1983.

He gave these as his broad considerations in formulating social policy : that the state of the economy should be the starting point for deciding social provision; that the government should aim to get the best possible value for money; and that not everything could, or should, be done by the state.

Questions and Assignments

1 What is meant by the Welfare State?
2 What were the origins of the Welfare State in Britain?
3 Why have there been strains on the Welfare State since the 1960s?
4 What is Thatcherism?
5 Why is Thatcherism supported by some and opposed by others?
6 How good is the government's record since 1979 as far as the Welfare State is concerned?
7 By questioning all the members of it, draw up a list of the benefits your family currently receives from the Welfare State. It will be imposible to calculate them all in money terms, so a series of headings will be enough.
8 Conduct a group debate on the motion 'This House believes that Britain can no longer afford the luxury of a Welfare State'.

Chapter 20

The State and the Individual

There seems to be an inevitable conflict between what the state sees as the public interest and the views of the ordinary citizen. In an attempt to resolve this conflict, various devices have been introduced to make governments more accountable.

The doctrine of *ultra vires* says that officials and public bodies must not exceed the powers given to them by Parliament. If they do the courts can declare their actions illegal and make orders to reverse or change them.

Tribunals and inquiries set up by government are also accountable for their actions and are expected to operate fairly. There is now a Council on Tribunals which oversees and reports on their activities.

Until recent years the ordinary citizen had little or no redress against maladministration by officials. Now there are national and local ombudsmen to whom he or she can take a grievance. Although the ombudsmen have been welcomed, they are still thought to be underused because access to them is not easy and they are not well enough known.

There has also been disquiet in recent years about the relationship between the police and the public and there is a growing body of opinion calling for a review of the role of the police within society.

Finally, there is widespread agreement that governments in Britain are too secretive, particularly when compared with other countries. The main source of complaint is the Official Secrets Act of 1911, which, it is argued, should be repealed and replaced by legislation which positively encourages access to official information.

20.1 Public versus Private Interest

Although democratically elected governments are, in theory, set up to carry out the wishes of the voters, in practice what is seen by

238

the state as in the public interest is often seen by individuals as against their private interests. There are many examples of this conflict of views to choose from.

Someone wants to erect a garage near his house and cannot see why, as it is intended for private use, the government should interfere. The planning authorities, on the other hand, are concerned about the effects of the new building on the existing environment, including the neighbours.

A proposal to dump nuclear waste is bound to be resisted by people who live near the site of the dump. Yet, from the government's point of view, the waste has to be put somewhere, so it can never be done without offending someone.

Most people will be in favour of an improved road system, provided the improvements do not adversely affect the area where they live.

These are all examples of what can be called the 'NIMY (Not In My Yard)' syndrome. Understandable when considered from the ordinary person's standpoint, but frustrating to those in power.

The problem in any democratic community is how to reconcile the public and private interests and, when they cannot be reconciled, how to ensure that the individual has a chance of putting his own case forward, knowing that he is going to get a fair hearing.

20.2   Public Accountability

The theory of parliamentary government in Britain is that the House of Commons is democratically elected and the government formed, mainly from its ranks, is accountable to it. As we have already seen, in practice this does not always work.

When it does work the people in the firing line are ministers who, as politicians, are accustomed to having high profiles and being in the public eye. Many of the actions of government are, however, taken by civil servants or local officials or bodies set up by the State.

Ministers are supposed to take responsibility for the actions of their civil servants and, as we have seen, sometimes they do and sometimes they do not. Much seems to depend on the political implications at the time.

There are also legal checks on administrative actions. They are centred on the doctrine of *ultra vires*. Ultra vires, translated from the Latin, means 'beyond the powers'. In other words, if someone can show that a minister, or a civil servant, or a local authority has exceeded the powers given by Parliament any action taken can be ruled by the courts as invalid.

There are three main ways in which an action can be said to be ultra vires:

1 Something has been done which was not authorised.
2 Something has not been done which should have been done.
3 Something which has been authorised has been done in the wrong way.

Some simple examples will help to explain.

A minister authorises the sale of a public asset without having obtained the approval of Parliament. This is an example of the first kind of infringement.

A local authority is required by Act of Parliament to prevent a public nuisance, such as the discharge of smoke from a factory, and fails to do so. This is an example of the second kind.

A local authority closes a stretch of road without giving notice of its intention to do so. This is an example of the third kind.

In all three cases the courts can take action. Anyone objecting to what has been done, or not been done, can apply for a High Court Order. There are four main types of Order which may be issued.

1 A **Prohibition Order** requires a minister or public body to refrain from doing something.
2 A **Declaration** is a formal statement of the law as far as the rights of the person complaining are concerned.
3 An **Order of Mandamus** commands the public body to carry out its duties.
4 An **Order of Certiorari** overrules a decision of a lower court in favour of the person complaining.

Local authorities, since everything they do has to be legally authorised, are particularly subject to the doctrine of ultra vires. If they spend beyond their authorised limits or if they spend on things outside their responsibilities, the expenditure may be declared invalid and the councillors concerned, and sometimes the officials as well, if they know the expenditure is unlawful, can be required to repay it. This does not happen often, but there have been recent cases.

20.3   The Accountability of Tribunals and Inquiries

During the present century, as governments have become more involved in economic, social and industrial affairs, they have found it necessary to set up procedures and bodies for dealing with disputes between them and members of the public.

For example, before planning permission by a local authority can be granted for a new development, notice to the public and an opportunity to object have to be given. If the local authority goes ahead, despite objections, members of the public can appeal to the Secretary of State for the Environment. He will then send one of his inspectors to the locality to conduct a **public inquiry**, at which objections from the public can be made and the local authority and the people asking for planning permission can reply.

The inquiry will be conducted on the lines of an informal court of law and, at the end, the inspector will give his recommendations to the Secretary of State, who can either accept or reject them. He can, in other words, support or overrule the local authority's decision.

Disputes between members of the public and officials also arise in other areas, such as claims for social security benefits. In these cases **tribunals** have been set up to hear complaints and to decide who is right, the minister or the individual. They, too, operate like informal courts.

In 1955 the government appointed a committee, under the chairmanship of Sir Oliver Franks, as he then was, to look at the way public inquiries and administrative tribunals operate. The Committee reported in 1957 and most of its recommendations were accepted and put into effect.

The Franks Committee decided to assess the working of tribunals and inquiries on the basis of 'openness, fairness and impartiality'. Its recommendations have resulted in a much more satisfactory system and there is now a permanent **Council on Tribunals** which keeps a close watch on their activities and publishes annual reports, which are treated with great respect.

20.4 The Redress of Grievances

Although the report of the Franks Committee did a lot to improve the way in which public inquiries and tribunals operated, there were still areas in which the relationship between the State and the individual seemed very one sided, with the balance in favour of the State.

Earlier we referred to the Crichel Down case, in 1954, which resulted in the resignation of the Minister of Agriculture. In this case farm land had been requisitioned for military use and, after the war, the ministry decided to pass it back into private hands. But instead of giving the first chance to purchase to the original owners, the civil servants concerned made a deal with someone else, without the minister's knowledge. It was only because of the persistence of Lieutentant-Commander Marten, whose family had owned the land on Crichel Down in Dorset, and who demanded to see the minister, that his grievance was listened to and eventually he was redressed.

There was no machinery available to investigate his complaint as there was, for example, in some other countries.

In Sweden, as long ago as the 18th century, an independent official had been appointed by the parliament to investigate complaints by citizens about the administration of the law and the actions of officials. He was called the **ombudsman**, which, roughly translated, means 'complaints commissioner'. The Swedish example was copied in most Scandinavian countries and later all over the world.

There are now ombudsmen, at national or local level, or both, in Australia, Canada, Denmark, Finland, Fiji, France, West Germany, Guyana, Hong Kong, India, Israel, Italy, Mauritius, New Zealand, Norway, Papua-New Guinea, Sweden, Switzerland, Tanzania, the United States and Zambia.

After considerable discussion and delay, the first British ombudsman was appointed, in 1967, with the title **Parliamentary Commissioner**. The White Paper which announced the establishment of the office had this to say:

> 'Under our proposals, the Parliamentary Commissioner will be an independent officer, whose status and powers will be conferred by statute. He will be appointed by the Crown; his salary and pension will be a charge on the Consolidated Fund; he will be secure from dismissal, except by parliamentary motion. He will report to Parliament each year and otherwise as occasion requires'.

The British ombudsman has been in office, although the actual holders have changed, for 20 years. What has been achieved?

Although there have been a number of successful interventions which have helped individuals, it must be confessed that the device has not lived up to the optimistic expectations of some of its supporters. A study of the work of the ombudsman, published in 1977, reported that he was not being used as much as he could be and that his terms of reference were too narrow.

The Widdicombe Report, taking its name from its chairman, David Widdicombe QC, made a number of recommendations:

1 Access to the Commissioner should be easier and more uniform. The Parliamentary Commissioner also acts as the Health

Service Commissioner and although the public can complain directly to the Health Service Commissioner, in the case of the Parliamentary Commissioner they have to go through an MP.

2 His powers of investigation should be extended from merely looking at cases of 'maladministration' to examining 'unreasonable, unjust or oppressive action'.

3 The Commissioner's staffing should be better and more generous. He is at present dependent on whatever the government supplies.

4 He should take more steps to publicise his activities.

It is sad to report that little progress, of any significance, has been made since the publication of the Widdicombe Report.

Under the Local Government Act 1974, local ombudsmen and women, called **Commissioners for Local Administration** were appointed. There are separate commissioners for Scotland and Wales and England is divided into three areas, London and the South East, the North and East, and the West and Midlands. Complaints to them have to be made through councillors, although if a councillor refuses to pass on a complaint, an individual may go directly to a commisioner.

Regrettably, the defects noted by the Widdicombe Committee apply more or less equally to the local ombudsmen.

20.5 The Police and the Public

Britain has always been justifiably proud of its police service. Features which have made it the envy of the world are: the fact that policemen do not normally carry firearms; the fact that there is not a national police force, controlled directly by the government; the fact that there are no separate, para-military, police forces; and the fact that the ordinary policeman is subject, like everybody, to the rule of law. In recent years, however, there has developed what has been called a ' crisis of confidence in the police force'.

There are in Britain 43 police forces, including one for Metropolitan London. That is under the control of a Commissioner, while the others are directed by Chief Constables. There is also a small, separate police force for the square mile of the City of London. There are now just over 130000 police officers, or about 1 for every 430 or so citizens, which is roughly the same ratio as in the United States of America. The current annual cost of running these police forces is over £3 billion. In other words, each police officer costs about £23000 per year.

There are several reasons for the 'crisis in confidence'. The policeman is now more remote from the public because the average size of a force is bigger than it used to be. He spends more time out of the public eye, driving or working inside his office, rather than being seen walking his beat. Some chief constables, such as Kenneth Oxford of Merseyside and James Anderton of Manchester, have become powerful, and sometimes controversial, figures, seeming at times almost contemptuous of their police authorities.

The Home Secretary is responsible for the London Metropolitan police force. Elsewhere it is the job of **police committees**. These consist of two thirds councillors and one third magistrates. Their powers are restricted to maintaining a police force and appointing a chief constable, but even this appointment, as well as those of his deputy and assistants, are subject to the Home Secretary's approval.

Although the police service itself is non-political, in its representation in Parliament it seems to have moved to the right. The Police Federation, representing the majority of policemen, used to have the Labour MP, James Callaghan, as their spokesman. They now have the Conservative Member, Eldon Griffiths. The Superintendents' Association, representing senior police officers, chose another Conservative, Sir Bernard Braine.

Without any wish on their part, the police forces have, in recent years, become involved in politically sensitive issues, such as the riots in Toxteth on Merseyside, in Mosside, Manchester, and in Brixton, Birmingham and Bristol. The Brixton riots resulted in the inquiry by Lord Scarman. In his subsequent Report, while praising the police for certain things, Lord Scarman criticised 'hard policing', lack of consultation, inadequate complaints procedures and the racist attitudes of some policeman. The current Metropolitan Commissioner, Sir Kenneth Newman, subsequently announced steps to improve the situation.

Concern has also been expressed about the increased carrying and use of firearms and by what seemed to be the national co-ordination of police activity during the miners' strike of 1984–85.

Complaints against the police are initially considered by the Chief Constables themselves but since 1976 there has been an independent **Police Complaints Board** to review any actions which have been taken or not taken. This has brought some improvement, but disquiet remains.

The last time there was a major inquiry into the police service was by the Willink Royal Commission, which reported in 1962. There is now perhaps a case for a new independent study, supported by all political parties, to enable the police forces to regain their former public esteem.

20.6   The Right to Know

The British system of government is probably the most secretive in the western world, and in recent years the position has deteriorated rather than improved. At the centre of the problem lies the Official Secrets Acts.

The most significant of these Acts is that of 1911. Section 1 deals with spying and Section 2 with wider matters. It is Section 2 which has come in for most criticism. It is an 'all catching' Section which says, in effect, that if anyone reveals official information in an 'unauthorised' way he or she is guilty of a criminal offence. Every civil servant, whatever his grade, at the start of his working life has to sign a declaration that his attention has been drawn to the Act, and, on retirement, he is still bound by its provisions. In theory, he should not discuss any part of his work with someone outside the service, however trivial it might be. In practice, it puts him in an impossible dilemma.

In 1984 Sarah Tisdall, who was a junior civil service clerk, was convicted and imprisoned for six months under Section 2, for providing 'The Guardian' newspaper with a copy of a minute from the Secretary of State for Defence to the Prime Minister about the arrival of cruise missiles at the Greenham Common air base in Berkshire. The publication of the document was politically embarrassing but not a threat to national security.

In 1985 Clive Ponting, who held a senior post in the Ministry of Defence, was prosecuted under Section 2 for releasing papers dealing with the sinking of the Argentinian warship, the 'General Belgrano', during the Falklands campaign. In this case the jury decided that Ponting had acted in the interests of the State by passing the papers to the Labour MP, Tam Dalyell, and he was acquitted.

The criticisms of the Official Secrets Act of 1911 are not based just on how it has been used but also on the way in which it was originally passed by Parliament.

It replaced an earlier Act of 1889 and was introduced at a time when there were fears about German spies in Britain, three years before the start of the First World War. The Bill was introduced in the House of Lords just before Parliament adjourned for its summer recess. It went through the Lords very quickly and was immediately passed to the Commons. There it passed through all its stages in one day, 2 August 1911, and Section 2 was not debated at all. The explanation given was that the Act was needed to meet a national emergency, but it seems just as likely that MPs were anxious to get away to start their summer holidays.

Since the 1960s there have been moves in Britain to create more open government, by introducing a Freedom of Information Act, similar to those which operate in other countries, particularly Sweden and the United States. In Sweden the public has general right of access to all official documents, under the Freedom of the Press Act, 1949. In the United States a guarantee of open access is given in the Freedom of Information Act, 1967, which was amended in 1974.

In 1978, following much discussion and an inquiry into the working of Section 2 of the 1911 Act, by Lord Franks, as he now was, the government of James Callaghan announced a firm intention to amend the Act, as the Franks Committee had recommended, and to introduce an Official Information Bill. Before the Bill was produced the general election of 1979 was held and the Conservative government of Margaret Thatcher came into power. Since then she has shown no signs of wishing to follow Callaghan's lead.

There is now considerable all-party support for a more open system of government and the next Parliament might well see a Freedom of Information Bill, or something like it, introduced.

20.7   The Press and the Public

Not only are the media handicapped by the operation of Section 2 of the Official Secrets Act, the government, through its Press Secretaries, is not averse to manipulating news stories itself. 'Leaking', as it is generally called, has now become commonplace in government circles.

During the Falklands campaign the Ministry of Defence obviously 'managed' the news and this was resented by the press as well as the general public. In October 1983 new rules were introduced for reporting military operations. 'The Times' defence correspondent said of them that if they had existed at the time of the Crimean War his distinguished predecessor would not have been allowed to report the Charge of the Light Brigade.

Lobby correspondents, as they are called, are the journalists who write columns in the newspapers based on conversations with politicians and information provided by government Press Secretaries. They attend regular 'briefings' at No 10 Downing Street and other places and even have an annual Lobby Lunch. They are expected to abide by Lobby Rules, which set out how they are permitted to report information. For example, sometimes it can be attributed to a particular department or minister but at other times it must be presented as the journalist's own view. Some newspapers, such as 'The Observer' and 'The Guardian', have strongly criticised the use of 'the Lobby', and the new publication, 'The Independent', decided from the start not to use it.

Over all of them, however, hangs the 'Sword of Damocles', represented by Section 2 of the Official Secrets Act, and until this is repealed, and replaced by a system of genuinely open government, the ordinary citizen will continue to be at a disadvantage in his dealings with the state.

Questions and Assignments

1 Why is there often a conflict between public and private interests?
2 What is meant by the doctrine of ultra vires?
3 What remedies are available if the rule of ultra vires has been broken?
4 Why has the practice of using public inquiries and administrative tribunals grown?
5 Why were ombudsmen appointed?
6 Why does Britain need more open government?
7 Carry out a survey among your family and friends to discover how many:
  1 Know that an ombudsman is available
  2 Know how to make use of him
  3 Know of anyone who has made use of the ombudsman system, and with what results.
  Present your conclusions in the form of a brief report.
8 By reading as many newspapers as you can obtain for the past week, compare the articles by the various Lobby Correspondents to discover the extent to which their stories agree or disagree with each other.
  Again, present your conclusions in the form of a brief report.

Chapter 21
Improving the Quality of Government

Cynics often say that people get the governments they deserve. To a great extent this is true.

If we view government as a business then, like any business, the service it provides will only be as good as its customers demand. Rolls Royce did not achieve an international reputation for quality by producing inferior goods. The most successful manufacturers and sellers of consumer goods are those who have done their market research thoroughly and, in consequence, are able to give the public what they want.

The difference between government and a normal business, however, is that if you do not like what is provided you cannot choose an alternative, unless you are prepared to leave home and emigrate as, of course, some people do. You can, however, through the political system, demand a better service and show your satisfaction or dissatisfaction by the way you vote.

Unfortunately, as we have already noted, the great majority of people are politically apathetic. They show their apathy by the newspapers they read, the way they turn out at elections and by the cynicism they show towards politics and politicians.

Political education in Britain is generally not good. People are likely to begin their adult lives with either an imperfect knowledge of government or a distrust of it, bred from ignorance.

For many people politics, instead of being something vital and exciting, is dull and uninteresting. The popular press is more concerned with gossip and scandal while people who are active politically are often given misleading labels or regarded as cranks.

What can be done to reverse the process?

Politics should be taught more vigorously and interestingly in schools. Of course there is a danger of political indoctrination but it is a danger which should be faced and handled courageously.

Politicians should be invited to play a bigger part in the educational process. A balance can be maintained by ensuring that all views are given a fair hearing.

There should be more school visits to Parliament, local authorities and other public bodies, but they should not be directed only towards the forms and structures of government. The emphasis should be on substance and activity. 'Question Time' in the House of Commons can be exciting. A council debate can bring local issues vividly to life.

Representatives of interest groups can be invited to give their views on current social and economic problems. An objective balance can be preserved by providing a broad range of opinions.

These suggestions for improving the quality of political education are not just the opinions of an author with a hobby horse to ride. They should be of interest and importance to everyone. The quality of political coverage in the media will only improve if we insist that it does.

This book has not just attempted to give a picture of what the business of government is and how it is conducted. It has also tried to stimulate an interest in the political process. If it has gone at least part of the way towards realising these aims it will have achieved some success.

Index